THE GREENWOOD ENCYCLOPEDIA OF

ROCK HISTORY

The Greenwood Encyclopedia of Rock History

Volume 1
The Early Years, 1951–1959
Lisa Scrivani-Tidd

Volume 2
Folk, Pop, Mods, and Rockers, 1960–1966
Rhonda Markowitz

Volume 3
The Rise of Album Rock, 1967–1973
Chris Smith

Volume 4
From Arenas to the Underground, 1974–1980
Chris Smith with John Borgmeyer, Richard Skanse, and Rob Patterson

Volume 5
The Video Generation, 1981–1990
MaryAnn Janosik

Volume 6
The Grunge and Post-Grunge Years, 1991–2005
Bob Gulla

THE GREENWOOD ENCYCLOPEDIA OF

ROCK HISTORY

The Video Generation,
1981–1990

MARYANN JANOSIK

GREENWOOD PRESS
Westport, Connecticut • London

Library of Congress Cataloging-in-Publication Data

The Greenwood encyclopedia of rock history.
      p.   cm.
   Includes bibliographical references and index.
   ISBN 0–313–32937–0 ((set) : alk. paper)—ISBN 0–313–32938–9 ((vol. 1) : alk. paper)—ISBN
0–313–32960–5 ((vol. 2) : alk. paper)—ISBN 0–313–32966–4 ((vol. 3) : alk. paper)—ISBN
0–313–33611–3 ((vol. 4) : alk. paper)—ISBN 0–313–32943–5 ((vol. 5) : alk. paper)—ISBN
0–313–32981–8 ((vol. 6): alk. paper) 1. Rock music—History and criticism.
   ML3534.G754   2006
   781.66'09—dc22   2005023475

British Library Cataloguing in Publication Data is available.

This book is included in the *African American Experience* database from Greenwood Electronic Media.
For more information, visit www.africanamericanexperience.com.

Library of Congress Catalog Card Number: 2005023475

ISBN 0–313–32937–0 (set)
     0–313–32938–9 (vol. 1)
     0–313–32960–5 (vol. 2)
     0–313–32966–4 (vol. 3)
     0–313–33611–3 (vol. 4)
     0–313–32943–5 (vol. 5)
     0–313–32981–8 (vol. 6)

First published in 2006

Greenwood Press, 88 Post Road West, Westport, CT 06881
An imprint of Greenwood Publishing Group, Inc.
www.greenwood.com

Printed in the United States of America

The paper used in this book complies with the
Permanent Paper Standard issued by the National
Information Standards Organization (Z39.48–1984).

10 9 8 7 6 5 4 3 2 1

To
R.E.M.

For gifts of peace, friendship, and love

CONTENTS

# SET FOREWORD

Rock 'n' roll, man, it changed my life. It was like the Voice of America, the real America, coming to your home.

—Bruce Springsteen[1]

The term *rock 'n' roll* has a mysterious origin. Many have credited legendary disc jockey Alan Freed for coining the term. Some claim that it was actually a blues euphemism for sexual intercourse, while others even see the term rock as having gospel origin, with worshippers "rocking" with the Lord. In 1947, DeLuxe Records released "Good Rocking Tonight," a blues-inspired romp by Roy Brown, which touched off a number of R&B artists in the late-1940s providing their own take on "rocking." But many music historians point to the 1951 Chess single "Rocket 88" as the first rock record. Produced by Sam Phillips and performed by Jackie Brenston and Ike Turner's Kings of Rhythm (though released under the name Jackie Brenston & His Delta Cats), the record established the archetype of early rock and roll: "practically indecipherable lyrics about cars, booze, and women; [a] booting tenor sax, and a churning, beat-heavy rhythmic bottom."[2]

Although its true origins are debatable, what is certain is that rock 'n' roll grew into a musical form that, in many ways, defined American culture in the second half of the twentieth century. Today, however, "rock 'n' roll" is used with less and less frequency in reference to the musical genre. The phrase seems to linger as a quaint cliché co-opted by mass media—something that a *Top Gun* pilot once said in voicing high-speed, mid-air glee. Watching MTV these days, one would be hard-pressed to find a reference to "rock 'n' roll," but the term *rock* survives, though often modified by prefixes used to denote the growing hybridization of the genre: There is alternative rock, blues rock, chick rock, classic rock, folk rock, funk rock, garage rock, glam rock, grunge rock, hard rock, psychedelic rock, punk rock, roots rock, and countless other sub-genres of rock music. It seems that musicians found more and more ways to rock but, for some reason, stopped rolling—or to paraphrase Led Zeppelin's "Stairway to Heaven," the music world opted to rock, but not to roll.

Call it what you will, rock music has never existed within a vacuum; it has always reflected aspects of our society, whether it be the statement of youth culture or rebellion against adult society; an expression of love found, lost, or never had; the portrayal of gritty street life or the affirmation of traditional American values; the heady pondering of space-age metaphysics or the giddy nonsense of a one-hit wonder, rock music has been an enduring voice of the people for over five decades. *The Greenwood Encyclopedia of Rock History* records not only the countless manifestations of rock music in our society, but also the many ways in which rock music has shaped, and been shaped by, American culture.

Testifying to the enduring popularity of rock music are the many publications devoted to covering rock music. These range from countless single-volume record guides providing critics' subjective ratings to the multi-volume sets that lump all forms of popular music together, discussing the jazz-rock duo Steely Dan in the same breath as Stravinsky, or indie-rock group Pavement with Pavarotti. To be sure, such references have their value, but we felt that there was no authoritative work that gives rock music history the thorough, detailed examination that it merits. For this reason, our six-volume encyclopedia focuses closely on the rock music genre. While many different forms of rock music are examined, including the *influences* of related genres such as folk, jazz, soul, or hip-hop, we do not try to squeeze in discussions of other genres of music. For example, a volume includes the influences of country music on rock—such as folk rock or "alt.country"—but it does not examine country music itself. Thus, *rock music* is not treated here as synonymous with *popular music*, as our parents (or our parents' parents) might have done, equating whatever forms of music were on the charts, whatever the "young kids" were listening to, as basically all the same, with only a few differences, an outsiders' view of rock, one that viewed the genre fearfully and from a distance. Instead, we present a six-volume set—one that is both "meaty" and methodical—from the perspective of the rock music historians who provide narrative chapters on the many different stories during more than five decades of rock music history.

The Greenwood Encyclopedia of Rock History comprises six information-packed volumes covering the dizzying evolution of this exciting form of music. The volumes are divided by historical era: *Volume 1: The Early Years, 1951–1959*, spans from the year "Rocket 88" (arguably the first rock single) was released to the year of the infamous "Day the Music Died," the fatal airplane crash that took the lives of Buddy Holly, Ritchie Valens, and J. P. Richardson (a.k.a. The Big Bopper). *Volume 2: Folk, Pop, Mods, and Rockers, 1960–1966,* covers the period when the British Invasion irrevocably changed the world, while such American rock scenes as Motown and surf rock held their own. In *Volume 3: The Rise of Album Rock, 1967–1973*, Chris Smith chronicles the growing experimentation during the psychedelic era of rock, from *Sgt. Pepper* to *Dark Side of the Moon* and everything in between. In *Volume 4: From Arenas to the Underground, 1974–1980*, Smith et al., record how rock became big business while also spawning hybrid forms and underground movements. *Volume 5: The Video Generation, 1981–1990* starts with the year of MTV's debut and captures the era when video threatened to kill the radio star. Finally, in *Volume 6: The Grunge and Post-Grunge Years, 1991–2005*, Bob Gulla captures the many innovations of millennial rock music and culture. Within each volume, the narrative chapters are supplemented by a timeline, discography, bibliography, and a glossary of encyclopedia entries for quick reference.

We hope that librarians, researchers, and fans alike will find endless nuggets of information within this reference. And because we are talking about rock, we hope you will find that reading *The Greenwood Encyclopedia of Rock History* will be a whole lot of fun, too.

Rock on.

Rob Kirkpatrick
Greenwood Publishing Group

NOTES

1. Rock and Roll Hall of Fame and Museum home page, http://www.rockhall.com.
2. All Music Guide entry for Jackie Brenston, http://www.allmusic.com.

 **PREFACE**

When I first told friends and colleagues that I was writing a book about rock music in America between 1981 and 1990, I received as many condolences as congratulations. "Did you actually *choose* the 1980s, or did someone *assign* you that decade?" one well-meaning friend queried. "Will you really have to write about Flock of Seagulls and Tiffany?" "The '80s were a real low point in rock 'n' roll." Such questions and observations made me think about our perceptions of rock 'n' roll: not only how our ages and life experiences shape the music we listen to but how certain artists and world events forever connect our notions about which artists and styles of rock music are cutting edge and which ones are not.

Like many late boomers who were children during the 1960s and thus unable to experience that decade's social and political revolution as active members of the counterculture, I used to bemoan the fact that I was born too late to participate in what seemed like rock's greatest generation. I have since learned why it is easy to see how so many of our notions about what is important in rock music stem from that time. It is also easy to see how the early baby boomers hold on to the memories of Elvis, Chuck Berry, Buddy Holly, and many of rock's seminal artists, or why Kurt Cobain remains a viable force in the music culture of Generation Xers. Each generation is shaped by the artists whose music dominated their passage from teenage to adulthood.

So what is left for those of us who came of age in the post-disco, new wave punk era of the late 1970s and early 1980s? Plenty. The pages that follow will identify, explore, and interpret some of the major rock artists and musical trends of the 1980s.

SCOPE

When MTV (originally formally called "Music Televison") began broadcasting in August 1981, no one could have predicted the impact music video would have on rock 'n' roll. In an industry that had already become fragmented by various rock genres during the 1970s (heavy metal, art rock, soft rock, and folk rock), specialized via the advent of FM radio and commercialized with the promotion of mega-albums like *Frampton Comes Alive* and *Saturday Night Fever*, MTV threatened to take rock 'n' roll one step further in what many considered to be an already downward spiral.

In that way, the implications of music video underscored ongoing issues already facing rock 'n' roll and the recording industry. The question of whether MTV would use its media base to promote important, influential, and upcoming artists or whether artists who chose to use the video format would be given airplay regardless of musical quality related as much to the role MTV would play in the industry as it did to industry equity as a whole. In addition, other areas involving racism and sexism—already staple criticisms against rock 'n' roll—were exacerbated when early MTV videos heavily promoted sexy, cover-girl babes, while at the same time almost completely excluded African American artists from airplay rotation.

On the other hand, artists like Madonna, Cyndi Lauper, and Michael Jackson used MTV as a way, subtly or not, of commenting on images of women and African Americans by employing satire or irony as a way of selling their music and making their point. Lauper's classically campy hit "Girls Just Want to Have Fun" is a good example of an artist using video to turn the song's superficially sexist concept about party girls around and making it a strong, and amusing, feminist statement. Likewise, Madonna's "Like a Virgin" forces the viewer to look past her coyly suggestive attire and listen to the lyrics and message of the song, which is clearly more innocent and benign than some early criticisms might have suggested. Jackson similarly used an air of urban cool to add mystery and intrigue to already publicized problems with street gangs and ghetto violence with videos of "Beat It" and "Billie Jean." As MTV grew and expanded, in terms of both artist selection and programming, its role as an assertive force in shaping pop culture embraced more rock genres and expressed other, larger societal patterns and trends.

The overarching link to the chapters in *The Video Generation* is MTV. While not all the artists included in these pages used MTV to the fullest (i.e., the Dead Kennedys were clearly anti-MTV), their image, commercial viability, and ultimate success were often connected to the music video medium. The other link that binds chapters together is the focus on rock musicians, rather than pop or other crossover artists. For that reason, there is no discussion of Whitney Houston, one of the most successful commercial artists of the decade—but clearly not a rock 'n' roll artist. Ditto artists like Janet Jackson, M. C. Hammer, and INXS.

Some pop-inspired artists, like Madonna and Michael Jackson, are included because of their influence on the rock industry as a whole. For example, Madonna's music emanated from a post-punk disco environment, but her own recording choices, along with her image and ability to control her career, served as models for artists as diverse as Alanis Morissette and Courtney Love. Like her or not, the "Material Girl" has always been slightly ahead of any American rock music trend and has consistently (not perfectly) made good choices in terms of her own music career path. Michael Jackson, while reigning as the "King of Pop," integrated rock riffs and arrangements into what might have otherwise been simple pop pablum. For example, "Beat It" might never have packed the edgy, emotional wallop it did without Eddie Van Halen's tough but funky guitar riff. It is Van Halen who gave Jackson's arrangement the touch of cool needed to push it beyond mere pop fluff. And Jackson's arrival on the MTV scene opened the door for other black artists, notably the hip-hop culture that would dominate MTV after 1985.

Another focal point in this volume is the concentration on artists who arrived or were reborn during the 1980s. While acts like Aerosmith, the Rolling Stones, and Elvis Costello continued to record and to enjoy commercial success during the 1980s (some of their work may be found on the various "best" lists included in the appendices), their respective stars ascended during another time. The exception to that might be Bruce Springsteen, analyzed a bit more closely in Chapter 3, who recorded extensively in the 1970s but who did not achieve rock superstar status until the release of *Born in the U.S.A.* in 1984.

The reader will find that many of the artists discussed here began their professional music journeys in the late 1970s, recording and/or releasing their debut efforts early in the 1980s. Their connection to the 1970s post-disco new wave scene is often phantomlike, while their role in foreshadowing musical trends in the 1990s becomes clearer with some comparative analysis. Chapter 8 on teen idols, for instance, is one that presents 1980s pinup boys like Rick Springfield and George Michael in a transitional context: integrally tied to earlier teen idol stars of the 1960s and 1970s but also artists who moved the music and images often associated with teen idols to a new level.

Another point to emphasize regarding this volume is that it focuses on the artists' music. While some personal information may be found, content has been limited to situations, events, or behavior that can be linked directly to the artist's music. The section on Ozzy Osbourne is one example where information relating to several personal events is presented as catalysts for his subsequent reinvention and reemergence as a solo artist during the 1980s.

Finally, the inclusion of some foreign acts in a series about rock music in America merits some explanation. Most of the artists here are homegrown, but it would be inappropriate and incomplete to examine the years 1981–1990 in American rock without mentioning artists like U2 or The Police. Their impact on American rock 'n' roll as well as on American culture is as important as the rise of Bruce Springsteen or the arrival of Run-D.M.C. and Public Enemy.

Their significance relates to a concept in a book by historian Bernard Bailyn titled *Education in the Forming of American Society* (1960). One of Bailyn's secondary arguments is that education, often seen as a passive reflector of cultural and political trends, sometimes acts as a proactive agent for social change by turning those issues back around onto society, forcing a kind of reciprocal relationship between institution and society. In the same way, artists like U2, who initially observed American culture, eventually turned some of our societal issues back at us through their music and their political activism. The same might be said of hip-hop artists, whose sometimes controversial lyrics, as conveyed through the songs, begin responses to societal concerns, then become anthems for social and political change. Whenever an artistic expression of ongoing or controversial issues is turned back on society and provokes a reaction, the venue—in this case, rock 'n' roll—takes on a more active role as stimulant for discussion and possibly changes within our culture. Ultimately, the relationship between artist and audience, between music and society, creates an exciting dynamic that pushes the bounds of popular culture into the deeper realm of examining social and cultural mores and folkways.

The Video Generation represents the breadth of rock music and various rock genres between 1981 and 1990; however, this volume does not attempt to review every rock artist, album, or video. Instead, the chapters and individuals surveyed here should, I hope, identify and define key musical trends, significant artistic innovation, and important contributions to the rock 'n' roll recording industry, as well as to American culture. There will, no doubt, be exclusions that some readers feel passionately about and some different perspectives on how artists and their music are represented. I welcome and encourage comments from readers as part of the ongoing dialogue between historian and audience. Only then can we continue to create a sharper, more definitive truth about rock music and America.

ACKNOWLEDGMENTS

Compiling such a volume as this was both energizing and, at times, daunting, and I could not have completed this project without the support and encouragement of friends, colleagues, and family—even those who initially offered condolences.

Thanks first to those who generously offered to read and comment on various draft chapters, especially Greenwood editors Anne Thompson and Rob Kirkpatrick. You always kept me on track and did not let me drift too far afloat from my focus. Thanks also to Bill Paige, for lending me some of his vintage MTV tapes; to David Cole, for our many conversations on metal bands; and to Oakton Community College's librarians for their generous assistance in finding bibliographic references. As an educator who loves learning new things from my students, I am deeply indebted to one of them—the best rock 'n' roll student a professor could hope to work with, Charlie Short, whose encyclopedic knowledge of the recording industry proved invaluable as he helped me compile some of the "best-selling" lists. Thanks, Charlie.

I would not have been considered for this project if it were not for my fifteen-month stint as Education Director at the Rock and Roll Hall of Fame and Museum in Cleveland, Ohio. I will not forget the importance of that experience in my life and career or its role in writing this book. Thanks and love to my colleagues at Oakton Community College and Ohio University for their interest in and support of this research endeavor. Special nods go to Oakton's social sciences and business division office staff, especially Rosann Scalise, who helped immensely with the final preparation of this manuscript, and student employee Sameksha (Simi) Khurana, who generously (and enthusiastically) downloaded and printed important documentation when my computer refused to cooperate.

During the final editing phase of this project, I returned to my native Ohio and began a new phase in my professional life. I am most appreciative of the generous support and enthusiasm for the completion of this book from the Ohio University Lancaster Campus faculty and staff and grateful to my administrative coordinator, Carolyn Bateson, for securing and protecting various copies of my revisions.

Finally, thanks to my doctoral adviser, Michael Grossberg, for years of constant encouragement and friendship and for telling a once-nervous graduate student that he did not want disciples, only creative, independent scholars. I hope this effort meets some of the high standards set for me then. Most of all, to my mother Mary, thanks and love for being there as only a mom can. My parents, including (and especially) my late father George, impressed upon me that dreams do come true through hard work, determination, and desire. This volume is proof of that.

TIMELINE: 1981–1990

1981

Paul McCartney and Wings disband after over twenty hit singles.

March 28: Rick Springfield's "Jessie's Girl" was released and set new standards for pop/rock music. The hit single stayed on the charts for thirty-two weeks, peaking at No. 1 in August.

May 19: The Who returned to the Top 20 when "You Better You Bet" scored at No. 18.

June 17: Pink Floyd gave its twenty-fourth and final performance of *The Wall* in Dortmund, Germany.

July: R.E.M. records its first single, "Radio Free Europe."

August: *Tattoo You* continues to interest Rolling Stones' fans.

August 1: MTV launches its music video channel at midnight. The first video shown was a song that barely scraped the Top 40, "Video Killed the Radio Star," by the Buggles.

1982

January–December: Blue-eyed soul duo Darryl Hall and John Oates, better known simply as Hall and Oates, bookend the year with No. 1 hits "I Can't Go for That" and "Maneater," and, in doing so, were on their way to becoming the most successful duo of all time.

January 20:	Ozzy Osbourne reportedly bit off the head of a bat during a concert in Des Moines, Iowa.
	The Eagles disband "until hell freezes over."
February 24:	John Lennon and Yoko Ono's *Double Fantasy* won "Album of the Year" at the twenty-fourth Annual Grammy Awards.
April:	Madonna is signed to her first recording contract with Warner Bros./Sire Records.
May:	Paul McCartney's *Tug of War* is released to enthusiastic critical acclaim. A duet with Stevie Wonder, "Ebony and Ivory," hits No. 1 and stays there for seven weeks. The album reunited McCartney with former Beatles' producer George Martin.
June 21:	Crosby, Stills, and Nash released the album *Daylight Again*, with Top 10 hit "Wasted on the Way."
July 14:	MTV covered the premiere of film *The Wall*, with members of Pink Floyd in attendance.
October 4:	Bruce Springsteen's *Nebraska*, originally intended as a demo tape for E-Street Band members, is released as a solo acoustic album, the singer's most raw and critically acclaimed effort to date.
November:	*American Fool* turns John (Cougar) Mellencamp into a rock superstar.
November 20:	U2 plays its first American concert at New York City's Ritz.
December 2:	Michael Jackson's mega-album, *Thriller*, is released. The album's first video single, "Billie Jean," made Jackson the first African American artist to appear on MTV. By December 25, the album reached No. 1 and held its spot for thirty-seven weeks.

1983

CDs begin appearing on store shelves, a new format developed jointly by Phillips and Sony.

April:	David Bowie's "Let's Dance" hits No. 1, with Stevie Ray Vaughn on guitar.
May:	Madonna performs "Holiday" at Studio 54 in New York City.
May 16:	Michael Jackson performs his famous "moonwalk" on the *Motown 25: Yesterday, Today, Forever* television special.
May 23:	First "Heavy Metal Day" at the U.S. Festival in San Bernadino, California featured performances by Quiet Riot, Mötley Crüe, Ozzy Osbourne, Judas Priest, Triumph, Scorpions, and Van Halen.

July 27:	Madonona's self-titled first album is released.
August:	Michael Jackson's fourteen-minute video for *Thriller* set new standards for music videos as art when it aired on MTV.
September:	*Sports* gives the heart of rock 'n' roll to Huey Lewis & the News.
October:	*Hearts and Bones*, an intended comeback reunion album for Simon and Garfunkel, instead is released as a solo album for Paul Simon, with Art Garfunkel's vocals erased.
November:	Tina Turner launches a comeback, releasing a cover of Al Green's "Let's Stay Together."

1984

January:	Van Halen kicks off the year with the release of *1984*.
March 24:	An opening ceremony for "Strawberry Fields" is dedicated in Central Park, New York, in memory of John Lennon.
	Def Jam Records was founded by Russell Simmons and Rick Rubin.
June 17:	*Born in the U.S.A.*, culled from over 100 songs, is released to the delight of Springsteen fans and critics alike.
July:	Prince's *Purple Rain* soundtrack climbs the charts, while the film captivates fans and filmgoers.
September:	First MTV Video Awards broadcast from Los Angeles' Universal Amphitheatre.
November 12:	*Like a Virgin* is released. The next day, MTV airs the video for the title song. On December 22, the single hits No. 1 in the United States and stays there for six weeks.
December 31:	Rock 'n' roll pioneer teen idol Rick Nelson was killed in a plane crash following a concert performance in Guntersville, Alabama. His final song that night was an encore version of Buddy Holly's "Rave On."

1985

January 28:	USA for Africa's founding fathers, Quincy Jones, and Lionel Richie, lead a group of politically-interested artists, including Bob Dylan, Michael Jackson, and Bruce Springsteen, in a recording of "We Are the World," bringing global awareness to world famine.
February:	John Fogerty took center stage with the release of *Centerfield*.
March 2:	Former Van Halen lead singer David Lee Roth hit No. 2 with

	a cover (and playfully sexy video) of the Beach Boys' surfer hit "California Girls."
July 13:	Live Aid concert televised simultaneously from venues in London and Philadelphia.
August:	Run-D.M.C. releases a new version of "Walk This Way," featuring the song's original recording artists Aerosmith. It becomes the first rap-rock crossover.
October:	"We Built This City," by Starship (formerly Jefferson Starship and before that, Jefferson Airplane), shoots to No. 1. It is the first of three Starship chart-toppers, with "Sara" (1986) and "Nothing's Gonna Stop Us Now" (1987) following suit.
November 21:	Dire Straits hits No. 1 with "Money for Nothing," an achievement strengthened by an original video, a digital recording, and the background vocals of Sting.
December:	MTV was bought by Viacom, and the company was renamed MTV Networks. One of Viacom's creations was an MTV spin-off network called Video Hits 1 (VH1), which became *the* premiere music station.

1986

Headbangers' Ball premiered on MTV, expanding heavy metal's primarily adolescent male audience to include women and adults.

February 25:	Rolling Stones awarded Grammy for Lifetime Achievement.
March:	Metallica's brilliant album *Master of Puppets* was released.
August:	*Graceland*, the signature album of Paul Simon's career, was released. The album, recorded in South Africa, included many native singers and musicians.
August 9:	Queen performed its 658th and final concert at Knebworth Stadium in Britain.
September:	Bon Jovi's breakthrough album *Slippery When Wet* was released, establishing the band are more than mere glam metal.
	The Bangles' "Walk Like An Egyptian" became a monster hit, peaking (and holding for several weeks) at No. 1.
October 16:	Run-D.M.C.'s "Walk This Way," featuring Aerosmith, enters the Top 40, peaking at No. 4.

1987

Club MTV premiered on the music network, making it one of the first successful reality-based shows.

March:	U2's *The Joshua Tree* became an instant classic that would later rank as the 80s top album.
May 16:	"With or Without You" becomes the first No. 1 hit from U2's *The Joshua Tree.*
July 25:	*Touch of Grey*, by the Grateful Dead, entered the Top 40. It would go on to peak at No. 9, putting the Dead in the Top 10 for the first (and last) time.
August 1:	MTV Europe, the continent's only twenty-four-hour music network, is launched at 12:01 a.m. The first video shown was Dire Straits' 1985 hit, "Money for Nothing."
August:	Guns N' Roses' *Appetite for Destruction* and Def Leppard's *Hysteria* thrilled metal fans and critics alike.
	Aerosmith makes a comeback with the release of the album *Permanent Vacation.*
October:	*Faith*'s release signaled George Michael's arrival as a solo artist.
October 31:	American born Adam Curry, named "Best European Radio and TV Personality" for three consecutive years, signed on as an MTV VJ.
December:	CDs were outselling vinyl records.

1988

Comebacks dominated the recording industry, with George Harrison ("Got My Mind Set On You"), Chicago ("Look Away"), and the Beach Boys ("Kokomo"), scoring No. 1 hits.

March 2:	Frank Zappa won a Grammy for "Best Rock Instrumental Performance" for his album, *Jazz From Hell.* On June 9, Zappa performed what would be his final concert tour performance at the Palasport in Genoa, Italy. Zappa died of cancer in December 1993.
	Yo! MTV Raps arrived as the first rap series on television.
July:	*It Takes a Nation of Millions to Hold Us Back* emerged as both rap anthem and political statement for Public Enemy.
September 23:	Elton John concludes a sold out, five-night gig at New York City's Madison Square Garden, his twenty-sixth consecutive sell out at that venue, which broke the record held by the Grateful Dead.
October:	*Rattle and Hum*, a documentary about U2, created strong buzz as both documentary and soundtrack.
November 3:	*American Dream*, the second studio album by Crosby, Stills, Nash and Young (and recorded at Young's California ranch), is

	released after an eighteen-year time gap from their first studio effort, *Déjà vu*.

December 6:   Rock 'n' roll legend Roy Orbison died of a heart attack.

1989

January 28:   The Traveling Wilbury's first album, *Vol. 1* moved to No. 3 on the charts. The Wilburys, a faux-named supergroup, included Jeff Lynne, George Harrison, Roy Orbison, Bob Dylan, and Tom Petty.

February 14:   Original MTV VJ Martha Quinn returned to the network to host *Classic MTV*, a half-hour series spotlighting the early days of MTV music videos.

February 22:   Carlos Santana won a Grammy Award for "Best Rock Instrumental Performance" for his album *Blues for Salvador*.

March 3:   Madonna's controversial video, *Like a Prayer*, aired on MTV. The following day, Famiglia Domani, a Roman Catholic family group, threatened to file a lawsuit against MTV, claiming the video contained blasphemous symbolism. A subsequent threat by the American Family Association to boycott all Pepsi products, for which Madonna had been named spokesperson, resulted in Pepsi canceling all commercials featuring the singer. On April 22, both album and single (named like the video) reached No. 1.

June: Tom Petty's solo effort, *Full Moon Fever*, was released to critical and commercial success that peaked at No. 3, producing hits that included "I Won't Back Down," "Runnin' Down a Dream."

September: Neil Young released what was considered his best album in over a decade, *Freedom*. Young's performance of the album's first single, "Rockin' in the Free World," on *Saturday Night Live* that same month is still held as one of the best performances ever on the late night series.

December: By the end of the year, *House of Style*, hosted by supermodel Cindy Crawford, had moved MTV programming into the broader realm of popular culture.

1990

Rock the Vote is founded in response to attacks against freedom of speech and artistic expression in the recording industry.

"Censorship is UnAmerican" became the first campaign led by artists including Iggy Pop and Red Hot Chili Peppers.

February 22: Metallica won the Grammy Award for "Best Metal Performance."

Milli Vanilli won the Grammy as "Best New Artist," only to have their award revoked when it was discovered the duo lip-synced on the recordings.

September: The Righteous Brothers re-entered the charts with two different recordings of their originally recorded hit, "Unchained Melody," from the movie *Ghost*.

November: Chris Isaak's video for *Wicked Game* was hailed as the most erotic yet on MTV. Originally recorded as a track on his 1989 *Heart Shaped World* album, "Wicked Game" caught the ear of film director Jonathan Demme, who included it in his 1990 film *Wild at Heart*. The single and album both went on to crack their respective Top 10s and, in 1991, Isaak received MTV's Video Music Award for "Best Male Video."

MTV: DEFINING A NEW ERA IN ROCK 'N' ROLL

Some rock 'n' roll historians would point to Elvis Presley's choreographed production number with prison inmates in the film *Jailhouse Rock* (1957) as the first example of music video. Others would identify Richard Lester's 1964 Beatles film romp *A Hard Day's Night* as capturing the spirit of what would later be referred to as MTV. A few diehard Monkees fans might even consider their television show a forerunner of music television. But whether we look back to the late 1950s or mid-1960s for its conception, music video was undeniably christened on August 1, 1981, at 12:01 a.m. (ET) on a cable television network called MTV. Rock 'n' roll music would never be the same.

Appropriately, the very first video shown on MTV was *Video Killed the Radio Star* by the British group the Buggles. (Similarly tongue-in-cheek was the first video shown on British MTV: Dire Straits' "Money for Nothing," which begins with the line, "I want my MTV.") MTV's first hour featured videos by Pat Benatar, Rod Stewart, The Who, the Pretenders, Styx, and others. Viewers were also introduced to MTV's hosts, selected from over 1,500 applicants who auditioned in New York, Chicago, and San Francisco: Video jockeys (VJs) Nina Blackwood, Alan Hunter, J. J. Jackson, Mark Goodman, and Martha Quinn (a last-minute replacement for Meg Griffin). Pairing veteran radio DJ (disc jockey) Jackson with a quartet of young, hip television-friendly personalities turned out to be a stroke of programming genius. The *Welcome Back, Kotter*-esque foursome (with Jackson as their unofficial Mr. Kotter) ran the gamut of viewer accessibility and became celebrities in their own right: ethnic goofball Mark Goodman, coolly handsome heartthrob Alan Hunter, gorgeously smart sexpot Nina Blackwood, and innocently cute geek Martha Quinn. Within six months of its debut, MTV boasted over 2 million subscribers and was on its way

**VIDEO KILLED THE RADIO STAR—
THE BUGGLES (1981)**

If MTV could be captured in one classic video, fans, historians, and critics need look no further than the video that started it all in August 1981. Unfortunately, fans remember the song's title more easily than the group that performed it. The Buggles seemed to slip into the one-hit video wonder obscurity after setting a kind of video standard that would define a generation. Filled with exploding radios, geeks, and freaks, *Video Killed the Radio Star* raised subliminal issues about the state of the music industry while, at the same time, reflecting the fast, visual sound-bite era epitomized through music video. Its controversial, often profane lyrics alluded to the technology of the day: VCRs and cassettes in cars. The video is perhaps best immortalized in a similarly titled exhibit at the Rock and Roll Hall of Fame and Museum, which surveys a history of cutting-edge videos played on multiple television screens.

to becoming a major influence on popular culture.

MTV: HISTORY

The idea of visualizing what audiences had only imagined for the three decades since rock 'n' roll began clearly impacted the way audiences hear music, visualize artists, and interpret melodic themes. (Interestingly, Blackwood's pre-MTV work included a collaborative project with musician-manager Danny Sheridan and controversial underground director "@Mic" that found Blackwood conducting artist interviews at an imaginary television station. The interviews were interspersed between short "music-films" and original advertisement parodies.)[1] MTV opened up new venues for some artists and signaled the decline of others. In this way, the fragmentation—or perhaps *democratization*—of rock music that occurred during the 1970s (splintering off of specific rock genres like art rock, jazz rock, and heavy metal, along with the popularity of disco and the emergence of rap and punk) offered new and creative ways for artists to express their political, as well as their musical, ideas. Just as films of the late 1970s (i.e., *Rocky* [1976], *Saturday Night Fever* [1977], *Norma Rae* [1979]) began to examine the social, political, and economic plight of the working class, MTV allowed rock 'n' and roll and popular artists a new venue with which to explore similar social and political issues while, at the same time, expanding and reaching a whole new audience.

MTV's roots can be traced to 1977 when the merger of Warner Communications and American Express resulted in the creation of the Warner Amex Satellite Entertainment Company (WASEC). WASEC launched the first two-way interactive cable television system called QUBE. The Columbus, Ohio–based system offered many specialized channels, including a children's channel called "Pinwheel," which would later become Nickelodeon. Another of the specialized channels was Sight and Sound, a music channel that featured concert footage and music-focused programs. With the QUBE service, viewers could vote for their favorite songs and artists, and the channel would use their responses to plan programming. The popularity of QUBE encouraged Warner Amex to consider marketing the channel nationally to other cable services. And given its success with two other cable ventures, The Movie Channel and

Nickelodeon, WASEC's inclination toward music video seemed both auspicious and appropriate. However, WASEC's executives were slow initially in moving forward with a third cable channel.

Enter Mike Nesmith, formerly of the American pop/rock band of the 1960s, the Monkees. Nesmith had been producing promotional videos for his own songs and saw a promising future for such marketing. Unfortunately, he had no forum to air these videos. In 1978, he experimented with *Popclips*, a thirty-minute music show that featured video versions of pop songs, and tried selling it to several major television networks without success. Then Jack Holtzman, an executive at Warner Records, suggested Nesmith meet with John Lack, No. 2 man at WASEC who favored adding a music-oriented theme show to its cable network offerings. Lack liked Nesmith's music video concept and asked him to produce another pilot episode, which, if it worked, would air on Nickelodeon. The pilot, tested at QUBE's Columbus, Ohio, station, was overwhelmingly well received, and in March 1980, Nesmith's *Popclips* series, complete with VJ introducing the pop/rock videos, debuted on Nickelodeon.

Popclips' success caught the attention of WASEC's executives, who subsequently anted up $20,000 in start-up costs for a new all-music-themed cable channel called MTV (Other name choices included TV-1 and TV-M). At that point, Mike Nesmith decided to opt out of the project. When the vision of MTV was formally presented to WASEC executives in January 1981, their approval of the new music channel was given with some reluctance, as the music video concept had never been tested or tried nationally.[2] With a tight, six-month project initiative deadline, there was not much time or energy to spare.

MTV, or Music Television, aired its debut program on August 1, 1981, from New York City (transmission emanated from Long Island) and, with the national expansion of cable television, became available to most of the United States by the middle of the decade. The importance of that August night in 1981 cannot be overestimated. Before MTV, the recording industry was integrally tied to radio. Television had generally not been a major influence in the development and popularity of rock 'n' roll. For sure, variety vehicles from the 1940s through the 1950s and 1960s, like the *Ed Sullivan Show* (1948) and *Smothers Brothers* (1967)—and later, 1970s hits starring Sonny and Cher (1971) and Donny and Marie Osmond (1976)—featured and promoted numerous artists ranging from Elvis Presley to the Beatles, from the Doors to the Who. Other pop/rock series like *American Bandstand* (1957) and *Hullabaloo* (1965) centered on showcasing new and upcoming pop/rock talent. Still, these crossovers between music and television were more incidental than consistent in the United States (unlike England, where rock-oriented television shows were more common). In spite of such occasional pairings between music and television, radio remained the primary venue for record sales and promotion. During the 1970s, the advent of FM radio, with its ability to allow

MTV's video jockeys (VJs) added the term to American popular culture as well as new opportunities in media careers. Courtesy of Photofest.

longer music programming, used the simultaneous splintering of the record industry to produce newer, narrower musical formats for progressive rock, classic rock, and so on. By the 1980s, radio stations offered programs catering to the specific interests of their listeners, from all-news and talk stations to those that focused only on single musical genres like classical, jazz, or rock.

Initially, MTV behaved much like its radio counterparts. VJs offered the pleasant between-songs banter that viewers could associate with radio DJs. Videos were interspersed with commercials; interviews with artists augmented the video-chatter format, and news of tours and upcoming artist releases promoted the recording industry as a whole. Just as they had provided promotional discs to radio stations for airplay, record companies submitted rock videos to MTV at no cost. The promotional value of MTV to both artist and industry is incalculable, as artists and companies vied to create imaginative and innovative videos to complement new releases. Whether or not the video had anything to do with a song's music or lyrics was of little consequence to the possibility of greater record sales, as "video added a new weapon to the arsenal of the record companies in their continuing battle to promote artists and records."[3]

MTV played mostly mainstream album–oriented rock, with diversions toward punk and new wave. The channel featured continuous programming, rather than individual "shows," and cultivated a rule-breaking in-your-face attitude, perhaps best represented in its assertive "big M" logo, which was created by Manhattan Design. VJ segments were prerecorded, and a set, inspired by *Saturday Night Live*'s brick and wood loft, was constructed. Planning seemed to be moving along, but there remained a number of obstacles to overcome before the channel was ready to air its programming.

First, selling the mostly untested music service to cable providers and advertisers proved to be very difficult. Next, persuading the major record labels to provide videos for free was not any easier. To keep costs down, WASEC decided to use free public-domain footage for MTV's early promos whenever possible. Finally, cleaning up the videos once they were obtained, converting them to stereo, and superimposing credits at the beginning and end of each song proved time-consuming.

With thirteen advertisers in hand and a modest audience of 800,000 homes, John Lack became the first voice of MTV with his August 1 pronoucement: "Ladies and gentlemen . . . rock and roll!" Tom Freston, chair and chief executive officer (CEO) of MTV Networks who was then head of marketing, was concerned that when MTV went on the air, the network had a mere 168 clips. And thirty of them were Rod Stewart. Though Freston's comments suggest a lack of diversity and interest among artists and record companies, that shortage of material would soon change. Within six months, MTV not only had more artists contributing videos; it had started to develop programs and contests that offered cool prizes and attracted more viewers. Even so, MTV's success did not escape criticism in terms of its content, artistic selection, or impact on the rock 'n' roll industry.

Criticism and Controversy

During its first two years, MTV's playlist consisted almost exclusively of white artists. Four of its five VJs were white, and its commercial spots seemed to be aimed at a white, suburban audience. When criticized as racist, MTV executives countered by claiming there were few, if any, promotional videos available from or submitted by black and other minority acts. Still, an undercurrent of MTV's credibility by allegedly pandering to a white audience threatened to fuel an old flame about racism within the recording industry.

On March 31, 1983, MTV offered what might be its greatest counterattack to charges of racism when it began airing videos from Michael Jackson's album *Thriller*. In particular, the songs "Billie Jean" and "Beat It" became two of the most popular videos of all time. Later in the year, Jackson's fourteen-minute mini-film *Thriller* premiered, raising the bar for all music videos to follow and demonstrating that music video could be a viable art form. It is difficult to discern if MTV helped *Thriller*'s record sales or if Jackson's heavily promoted videos solicited more subscribers for MTV. Either way, it is safe to say that MTV helped Jackson achieve record-breaking album sales, and Jackson helped MTV almost double its subscriber list from 9.3 million in 1982 to 16.2 million at the end of 1983.[4] Art and commercialism clearly merged when Jackson's videos debuted on MTV, giving rise to more criticism about the fall of rock 'n' roll to crass consumerism. At the same time, Jackson's frequent appearances on MTV's playlist squelched earlier attacks of racism directed at the cable channel, reaching out to a more diverse audience and paving the way for subsequent spin-off channels like BET.

Michael Jackson's 1983 *Thriller* video broke new ground in video standards, and today it remains a landmark in the history of MTV. Courtesy of Photofest.

 CENTERFOLD—J. GEILS BAND (1981)

Playing to the concerns of feminists that MTV could, in fact, reduce the image of women in rock 'n' roll to cardboard Barbie-doll proportions, *Centerfold* seemed like a second-rate *Playboy* magazine come to life. As J. Geils Band lead singer Peter Wolf romped around a high school classroom while a group of lingerie-clad women performed pseudo-lap dances on top of the desks, the song's superficial lyrics and simplistic melody played over and over again. Despite harsh reviews from critics, fans seemed to love the soft-porn suggestion of the video's images played almost incessantly on MTV. Together with the band's follow-up video for *Freeze Frame*, *Centerfold* proved to be J. Geils' last hit song and album.

MTV continued to mirror attacks already associated with rock 'n' roll. Besides racism, MTV was derided for being sexist toward women. Early videos like the one for J. Geils Band's "Centerfold," which featured Victoria's Secret–clad women dancing suggestively to lead singer Peter Wolf 's high school fantasy memory, outraged some feminists and women rock artists who feared that MTV would set women's issues back to the pre–rock 'n' roll era. Others feared that the failure—or refusal—of women artists to create an appropriately sexy but feminine image would hurt record sales and thus potentially ruin careers. How could the punk tomboy in Patti Smith or the cool androgyny of Chrissie Hynde[5] compete with Whitney Houston's coyly seductive look or Madonna's raw sexuality?

The answers to these questions would come over time—and without resolution. For some fans, Madonna's image as sexual provocateur moved the postfeminist age forward to a place where women are in charge (as she has been in terms of her career). For others, the ongoing need for women to shock, astound, and capture audience attention using their sex seems to fly in the face of real empowerment. Whatever the conclusion to gender and music video might be, MTV opened another venue for women as rock artists to pursue, one that continues to spark debate and discussion parallel to other cultural issues surrounding the role of women in American society.

A third criticism of MTV centered on the process by which it selected videos for airplay and how its choices affected the recording industry. In selecting the videos, some critics wondered if MTV executives were looking for the best artists to spotlight (that is, musical value), or if they were more focused on using an interesting visual regardless of the musical quality. An extension of that concern suggests that MTV has been overly commercial, denigrating the importance of music in the recording industry by replacing it with a purely visual aesthetic. Some of this criticism came directly from musicians, perhaps most brutally by the Dead Kennedys in their song "MTV—Get Off the Air." If bands sell well because they get lots of exposure on MTV, is MTV responsible for picking the best bands, and if so, how much influence has MTV had on the music industry? These kinds of rhetorical questions may never have a definitive answer, but they have raised ongoing questions that speak to MTV's power and influence in deciding what music we hear and how we hear and see it.

New and Extended Projects

In the midst of—and, to some extent, because of—early criticism leveled against it and the music video format, MTV grew by developing new projects that not only responded to some of its detractors but also spoke to ongoing issues, ideas, and interests in rock 'n' roll and American culture. The aforementioned Michael Jackson video blitz that began in the spring of 1983 followed a series of other creative promotional events designed by MTV staff and executives to garner much-needed publicity for the fledgling channel.

Within the first six months of airing, MTV broadcast its first concert with REO Speedwagon. By fall 1981, MTV had ventured into what would become an audience favorite: celebrity-prized contests. The first of its kind was launched in October 1981 and promised one lucky winner a "one-night stand" with Journey. A second one-nighter, this one with the Rolling Stones, aired in November. MTV rang in 1982 with its first *New Years Eve Rock and Roll Ball*, a competitive entry for Dick Clark's perennial *New Years Rockin' Eve*. Going head to head with Clark's long-held niche as a pioneer in rock 'n' roll broadcasting was no easy task, but MTV's younger, more hip VJs and of-the-moment lineup of artists gave viewers a fresh alternative.

In February 1982, MTV added the popular House Party to its stable of fan-based contests. Winners received a dream party (with guest rock 'n' roll artist) and stereo equipment. The following month, MTV embarked on its "I Want My MTV" advertising campaign, with Pete Townshend, Mick Jagger, David Bowie, The Police, and Pat Benatar among the celebrity participants. Later that year, MTV began selling its own merchandise, adding its own logo to the "corporate branding" phenomenon that was surfacing among yuppies and teens alike, and giving the often-denounced label-conscious consumerism another shot of cool. The music channel celebrated a year of progressively successful programming—and 9.3 million subscribers—by airing a Go-Go's concert in August 1982.

After a whirlwind 1983, a year that was dominated by Michael Jackson's *Thriller*, MTV upped its own ante in terms of elaborate contests and increasingly extravagant prizes. Just as Jackson had pushed the artistic envelope in terms of what music videos could be, so did MTV embrace the opportunity to keep itself on the cutting edge of interactive music and television. In 1984, fans could win a weekend (not just one night) with Van Halen. The contest drew 1 million entries. Another concert offered a pink house in Indiana and a personal concert by John Mellencamp as its prize. In September 1984, *Saturday Night Live* alum and Blues Brother Dan Aykroyd and singer Bette Midler hosted the first MTV Video Music Awards. Seen by some as a bit of self-indulgence by the young network to honor itself, the VMAs developed into an important music-industry showcase and, more ironically, a hip antidote to often-tiresome and stodgy Grammy Awards. At year's end, another 5.2 million subscribers were added to the camp, for a total of 21.3 million.

As MTV's programming changed to include more heavy metal and rap, MTV networks created a second network, Video Hits 1 (VH1), in 1985. Featuring more pop music than MTV, VH1 eventually established its own musical image and by the late 1990s had become the cable's rock 'n' roll network historian by developing documentary series like the much-praised *Behind the Music* (1998), and examining the social impact of musical eras with *I Love the 70s* and *I Love the 80s*.

In July 1985, MTV's own social conscience emerged with its seventeen-hour live telecast of the Live Aid concert. Transmitting from two continents in an age when immediate imagery from such distances was almost unheard of, MTV made its own statement about the importance of global awareness in general and the plight of famine victims in Ethiopia in particular. Live Aid's broadcast was a true world event, gathering artists from around the world together to help secure famine relief, and a shining moment for MTV, given its involvement in bringing the project home to millions of Americans. MTV ended the year with 25.8 million subscribers.

The spring of 1986 brought many changes to MTV, beginning with its first broadcast from Florida during spring break in March. In May, "Downtown" Julie Brown became the first new VJ since the network's inception. Her arrival was followed quickly by the departure of VJ originals J. J. Jackson and Nina

Blackwood. The year 1986 also marked MTV's unofficial entry into pop culture vernacular—and celebrated it—when Dire Straits' video *Money for Nothing* was named Video of the Year at the annual MTV Video Awards. The song's lyrics, which echoed the "I Want My MTV" mantra, became synonymous with Music Television. The year ended with 29.3 million subscribers.

In 1987, MTV expanded beyond the music video/contest/concert format with a series of regularly scheduled shows: *Club MTV* (the first daily show) and reruns of *Monty Python's Flying Circus*, both entering the lineup in August; the audacious TV-trivia quiz show *Remote Control* and *The Week in Rock* news update, these two debuting in September. MTV also went global in 1987, moving into European and Australian markets, with a Spanish-language version the following year. Also debuting in August 1988 was *Yo! MTV Raps*, signaling that MTV's programming was once again changing, this time to focus more on rap and hip-hop, though, again, targeting a white, suburban audience with this venture. Viewers must have approved of these additions, as subscribers increased by over 10 million during 1987–1988, totaling 40.2 million as the network entered its eighth year.

MTV's Influence on Popular Culture

The year 1989 saw MTV move further into the broader realm of pop culture with a spin-off of *Club MTV* titled *Club MTV Live: The Tour.* In June of that year, supermodel Cindy Crawford hosted a new series called *House of Style*, a show that aspired to define the lifestyles of its viewers as well as capture youth couture in the process. The network appeared ready to close out the decade having scored with an impressive record of subscribers; innovative, interactive programming; and a place in the heart of postmodern popular culture. But there was still more to come.

On January 21, 1990, MTV rolled out what would become one of its—and rock 'n' roll's—musical landmarks: *MTV Unplugged.* The first show debuted with acoustic performances by Squeeze, Syd Straw, and Elliot Easton of the Cars. The show, whose concept was reportedly encouraged by Jon Bon Jovi and Richie Sambora's acoustic version of their hit "Wanted: Dead or Alive" (from the movie *Young Guns* [1988]), at a VMA show a few years earlier, *MTV Unplugged* hosted rock

R.E.M., performing here on *Unplugged* in 1991, became the first independent group to break through to a large, mainstream audience. Courtesy of Photofest.

'n' roll artists in a stripped-down, nonelectric concert, one that focused on the music, not on recording's sophisticated technology. The series became a hit, later boasting performances by artists such as Eric Clapton, whose appearance in 1993 inspired a Grammy-winning album. Today, an "unplugged" album is considered a necessary component to any worthy artist's repetoire. MTV closed out 1990 with 47.2 million subscribers.

Since its birth in 1981, MTV has moved away from the music video format, leaving VH1 to handle much of the hardcore music shows and itself moving more into the larger pop culture sphere. While not the first outlet for music videos, MTV took the concept of music television as an art form and ran with it, increasing the network's popularity and making music video a legitimate expression of popular music. Not to be overlooked is MTV's contribution to music television in general, as several other music-based shows emerged during the 1980s, including *Friday Night Videos* (NBC, 1983), *Night Tracks* (TBS Superstation, 1983), *Hot Tracks* (ABC, 1983), *Night Flight* (USA, 1983), *Video Jukebox* (HBO, 1981), *Radio 1990* (USA, 1983), and *Much Music* (Canadian cable, 1984).

Music videos created a whole new kind of star, and suddenly video image became just as important as musical quality. Some historians argue that artists like Madonna would never have gained the immediate or lasting success, had it not been for MTV. Of course, less enduring artists like Duran Duran are examples of those for whom stylist image and fan popularity were almost as fleeting as the length of one of their videos. MTV had a huge impact on popular culture during the 1980s, influencing everything from clothing and hairstyles to commercial television programming. *Miami Vice* (whose working title was *MTV Cops*) borrowed the music video format—and stylishly sexy actors Don Johnson and Phillip Michael Thomas—to breathe new life into the stale cop show formula. Even daytime dramas like *Days of our Lives* and *General Hospital* integrated music videos into their respective plotlines, encouraging fans to associate memorable characters with popular songs.

In 2001 as MTV celebrated its twentieth anniversary, *Cincinnati Enquirer* contributor John Kiesewetter tried to count all the ways the world would be different without MTV. He likened his task to trying to remember all the images flashing on a television screen during a commercial: nearly impossible to tally. Some of Kiesewetter's memories are silly, but a few merit mentioning because they underscore the historical and cultural significance of the music video phenomenon. Specifically, MTV introduced many new artists who might have otherwise gone unnoticed solely through record releases. MTV also changed our cultural vocabulary, adding new names and terms to a growingly important pop vernacular while, at the same time, changing the way in which we talked about and experienced music:

> Without MTV, we wouldn't have Madonna, Cyndi Lauper, David Lee
>   Roth, Paula Abdul, M.C. Hammer, the Spice Girls, Devo, Duran Duran
>   or Men without Hats. . . .

Without MTV, Eric Clapton and dozens of other artists would never have been *Unplugged*. . . .

Without MTV, "VJ" would mean the end of World War II—not Martha Quinn, "Downtown" Julie Brown or Funkmaster Flex. . . .

Without MTV, a boy toy would be something made by Kenner. . . .

Without MTV, we wouldn't have Michael Jackson's 14-minute *Thriller*, which elevated music video to an art form. . . .

Without MTV, we wouldn't have seen the Live Aid concert live from two continents for 17 hours in 1985, a day we could truly say, "We Are the World." . . .

Without MTV, a Flock of Seagulls would be just a flock of seagulls.[6]

In a decade that saw consumers move from vinyl to cassette-friendly Walkmans to the compact disc, MTV went with both the commercial and artistic flow, holding up to its viewers a music-infused mirror that changed to represent rock 'n' roll's (and society's) ever fluctuating moods and trends. Beyond that, MTV became a proactive agent that inspired and encouraged cultural change, that challenged its viewers to consider new musical and television programming and hear rock 'n' roll through new ears and eyes.

NOTES

1. See, for example, the following Web site: http://www.ninablackwood.com/fbiomain.asp.

2. Web sites like this one contain a variety of information including timelines and VJ bios: http://eu.wikipedia.org.

3. Joe Stuessy and Scott Lipscomb, *Rock and Roll: Its History and Stylistic Development*, 4th ed. (Upper Saddle River, NJ: Prentice Hall, 2003), 367–369.

4. David Kronke, "MTV through the Years," *Milwaukee Journal Sentinel*, July 25, 2001, and included at http://www.jsonline.com/enter/tvradio/jul01/mtvtime26072501 .asp.

5. Simon Reynolds and Joy Press, *The Sex Revolts: Gender, Rebellion and Rock 'n' Roll* (Cambridge, MA: Harvard University Press, 1995), 236–238.

6. John Kiesewetter, "How 20 Years of MTV Changed So Much," *Cincinnati Enquirer*, August 1, 2001; the entire article is included and can be found at the following Web site: http://www.enquirer.com/editions/2001/08/01/tem_how_20_years_of_mtv .html.

EARLY VIDEO STARS: MICHAEL JACKSON, MADONNA, AND PRINCE

If video did indeed kill the radio star, MTV definitely gave birth to a host of new artists, many of whom utilized the medium to market their music. Arguably, artists with minimal range, talent, or staying power (e.g., Flock of Seagulls, the Thompson Twins, Jack Wagner) added new meaning to the definition of a "one-hit wonder."[1] Some pre-MTV recording artists, like Steve Winwood, Peter Gabriel, and Tom Petty, used the medium to enhance their already lucrative/popular careers. And new artists found that success in the music industry would henceforth be integrally tied to TV exposure and music video marketability.

The 1970s failed to produce another Elvis or the Beatles, but it was not for lack of trying, as record producers hailed virtually every new artist as the next rock icon. However, even the likes of Elton John, Peter Frampton, the Bee Gees, or Led Zeppelin could not solidify an already fragmented music market that was really only one manifestation of a society that was divided as a whole. Contrasting this cultural schism, the record industry had, by the end of the 1970s, consolidated its power into just six major companies. Historians Joe Stuessy and Scott Lipscomb assert:

> Music was [no longer] an art; it was a *product*, like a pencil sharpener or electric toothbrush. The formula was simple: identify a viable (monied) submarket through sophisticated market research; determine what that submarket was willing to buy; design a product that met those criteria; create the product; and mass-produce it and mass-market it.[2]

Inheriting the practice of selling some hard rock, some soft rock, some art rock, some disco, jazz, punk, heavy metal, country, and folk, music moguls entered the 1980s challenged with how to unify an increasingly fragmented music market. That the decade produced any viable, creative, and marketable artists at all, given its growing diversity, is testament to the talent and business savvy of record executives, music video directors, and the artists themselves.

Stuessy and Lipscomb and others[3] have suggested that the 1980s did not produce a significant number of identifiable artists. In an admittedly "unscientific" survey conducted among their sixty rock history students in 1992, Stuessy and Lipscomb reported that fifty-six different names emerged from the prompt to name as many important pop music acts of the 1980s as they could.[4] Of those fifty-six, only two names received more than four votes: Michael Jackson and Madonna, both of whom are more often tied to pop music than to rock. Unfortunately, Stuessy and Lipscomb concluded that even such unscientific research should be evidence enough to support their narrow view of 1980s

Michael Jackson performs at the *25th Anniversary of Motown* show in 1983, where he introduced his now-famous "moonwalk." Courtesy of Photofest.

pop/rock, citing only five musical acts and two styles (rap and heavy metal) they claim have significance in rock history. In truth, the 1980s produced a variety of recording industry megastars, while MTV's visuals offered new, sometimes controversial notions about sexuality and gender-bending. As the musical fragmentation of the 1970s continued—and even grew—during the 1980s, videos became another medium by which artists' images were defined or enhanced, and the "Me" generation gave way to a generation that began pushing the boundaries of masculine and feminine style, dress, and behavior.

MICHAEL JACKSON: THE KING OF '80s POP

The MTV-driven decade produced a significant number of important musical artists and styles and, unlike the decade before, gave audiences the pop/rock icon they had been waiting for: Michael Jackson. Born Michael Joseph Jackson on August 29, 1958, the seventh of nine children to Joseph Walter and Katherine Esther (née Scrouse) Jackson, this Gary, Indiana, native had already achieved teen idol status as part of the Jackson 5 during the late 1960s and early 1970s. He had already taken a turn as a solo artist with his eerily sensitive hit rendition of "Ben," the title song from the 1972 horror film (the sequel to 1971's *Willard*) about a boy and his pet rat. Perhaps the irony of Jackson singing sweetly about vermin seems appropriate today, given his erratic personal history and record of odd, even perverse, private behavior. Nonetheless, Jackson's emergence in the early 1980s as the hottest pop/rock star since the Beatles deserves some discussion, not only for his music but also for the ensuing celebrity and pubic scrutiny that became synonymous with his image.

Jackson's first solo album of note was released in 1979. *Off the Wall* sold over 7 million copies and produced four Top 10 hits, including the two No. 1 singles "Rock With You" and "Don't Stop 'Til You Get Enough." Peaking at No. 3, *Off the Wall* marked a shift in Jackson's musical style, replacing his trademark dance-oriented songs with softer ballads and establishing him as a solo artist. From 1980 to 1981 *Off the Wall* and Jackson were honored with numerous awards, including five American Music Awards (three in 1980 for Favorite Male Soul Artist, Soul Album, and Single; two in 1981, again for Favorite Male Soul Artist and Album); two 1980 *Billboard* Awards for "Best Soul Artist" and "Soul Album"; Cashbox's "Best Soul Album," in 1980 and 1981; and a 1980 Grammy Award for best rhythm and blues (R&B) performance for "Don't Stop 'Til You Get Enough." The album also serves as an important transition for Jackson, who continued to tour and record with his brothers (1980's *Triumph* album and tour).

By the time the "Triumph Tour" had ended, Michael Jackson (MJ) and Quincy Jones had already reconnected for what would be their second, and perhaps, most important project, the making of *Thriller*. Released in November 1982, *Thriller* initially produced a No. 2 hit duet with Paul McCartney, "The Girl Is Mine." From here, the album's continued, unparalleled success makes an easy comparison to sales records from earlier icons Presley and the Beatles and also gives a rationale for Jackson's quick ascension to rock royalty: over 40 million copies sold (to date); remained in the No. 1 position for thirty-seven weeks, second only to the sound-track album from *West Side Story* (1961; curiously, the film that is paid an updated rumble-scene homage in "Beat It"); yielded seven Top 10 hits, including two No. 1s ("Billie

 THRILLER—MICHAEL JACKSON (1983)

The video that changed MTV forever, *Thriller* (directed by John Badham) raised music videos to a genuine art form. Inspired by the 1950s horror film *Night of the Living Dead*, *Thriller* ran an impressive fourteen minutes and boasted a story within a story. Jackson's already famous moonwalk melded with funky, urban black choreography and sleek Fred Astaire–like grace to catch the attention of both *Star Wars* and *Saturday Night Fever* fans (Note: Badham directed the latter). *Thriller*'s hip dance sequences became popular among high school and college fans, who often tried to mimic the intricately staged movements. Proof of the video's enduring popularity can be found in the 2004 film *14 Going on 30*, in which a grown-up corporate shark (played by Jennifer Garner) livens up a dull cocktail party by getting all the thirty-something guests to participate in an impromptu reprise of *Thriller*'s ghoulish dance.

Jean" and "Beat It," respectively); and so on. On May 16, 1983, with *Thriller*'s success rising, Jackson performed his now-famous "moonwalk" during NBC's two-hour salute to Motown's twenty-fifth anniversary. Dressed in a black mock-military-styled suit, white socks and black loafers, and the single white-sequined glove that would became another MJ trademark, Jackson, like Elvis and the Beatles before him, used his music to cut across regional, racial, age, and gender lines.

The phenomenal success of *Thriller* as a landmark pop/rock album was enhanced further by Jackson's innovative dance-based music videos. The aforementioned "Beat It," which captures hip, urban tension fueled by male gang–related rumblings is given an even harder edge with Eddie Van Halen's hip guitar solo. In truth, most critics would agree that it is Van Halen's solo that actually gives Jackson's hit a crossover link to real rock 'n' roll. Without Eddie's memorable riff, "Beat It" is another pop trifle, but with it (and the video's funky *West Side Story*–ish urban gang choreography), Jackson scores as an innovative influence on the blending of pop/rock music.

Choreography in both "Beat It" and the more ethereally eclectic "Billie Jean" highlighted Jackson's own versatility and drew unexpected praise from two other dance icons, Hollywood greats Fred Astaire and Gene Kelley. Jackson's ability to transcend and synthesize the music and video media peaked with the mini-movie version of *Thriller*'s title single. Using the "movie within a movie" format and the talents of feature film director John Landis, 1983's *Thriller* brilliantly fused all the necessary components of a hit song (a unique and recognizable bass riff, seamless hooks, catchy melody and beat, strong lead and backup vocals) and raised the standard for music videos to a new level. The video itself boasted state-of-the art makeup and special effects, sophisticated Jackson-esque dancing, and a funky closing rap by 1950s horror film star Vincent Price.

Jackson's arrival as a solo artist was further confirmed with more awards for his—and Quincy Jones'—thrilling album concept. Between 1983 and 1985, Jackson won over fifty awards internationally for *Thriller*, including major citations from *Billboard* and *Rolling Stone* and *Cashbox* magazines, as well as music and video awards from MTV, American Music, and Black Image. Noteworthy among these nominations is Jackson's movement between the R&B/soul category and the broader, more mainstream pop category. At the 1984 Grammy Awards, Jackson broke the record literally and figuratively with an unprecedented twelve nominations and a record eight wins, including "Record of the Year," and "Album of the Year" (co-produced with Quincy Jones). That same year, Jackson was honored for artist or record of the year in seven foreign countries and received both the NAACP (National Association for the Advancement of Colored People) Image Award, which brought him the H. Claude Hodson Medal of Freedom, and the Presidential Special Achievement Award, which he received from President Ronald Reagan at the White House. By the mid-1980s, Jackson claimed victory as "The King of Pop." Nonetheless, there remained many critics who continued to discount his success as mere pop culture fad.

One thing that made Jackson an easy target to his detractors was his lack of artistic productivity between the release of *Thriller* in late 1982 and his next album *Bad*, released in 1987. Still tied contractually to his family, Jackson toured as part of the "Victory Tour," named for the Jacksons' 1984 album. Audiences, however, wanted Michael, not the Jacksons, and his own ability to bounce back in the wake of *Thriller*'s unbridled success became suspect. Nonetheless, *Bad* became another Jackson megahit, securing another seven hit singles, five of which went to No. 1 (setting yet another record for a pop/rock album). The album debuted at No. 1 and stayed there for six weeks. Given that it would be impossible to fathom any musical artist equaling or surpassing the critical, financial, and cultural success of *Thriller*, Jackson seemed to have earned his noble nickname and his status as a true pop video icon. Since the late 1980s, Jackson's star has alternately dimmed and shone, with his personal life taking as much of the spotlight as his music.[5]

MADONNA: THE MATERIAL GIRL

The December 31, 1990, cover of *Fortune* magazine heralded the following news: "Pop Culture: America's Hottest Export Goes Boom!"[6] Ten drawings complemented that cover's headline. Included were Mickey Mouse, Julia Roberts, Levi-Strauss jeans, the Teenage Mutant Ninja Turtles, Coca-Cola, Arnold Schwarzenegger, Sylvester Stallone, MacDonald's, MTV, and Madonna. Not quite a decade since her first album, the self-titled *Madonna*, was released in 1983, the Material Girl had clearly arrived, trumping rival '80s icons Michael Jackson and Bruce Springsteen for recognition as a globally identifiable pop culture icon.

Madonna's rise to pop stardom is hardly a fairy-tale story. As an independent feminist, she is her own fairy godmother.[7] As a self-indulgent "material girl," she is her own incarnation of the American dream. As her fans' fantasy, alternately, of friend, lover,

Madonna's simulated masturbation shocked some but also introduced the first of her many reinventions. Courtesy of Photofest.

confidante, mother, daughter, sister, confessor-priest, she has become the dream goddess of pop.[8] French scholar Georges-Claude Guilbert concluded: "In some ways, Madonna proposes solutions. She incarnates the grand founding myths of America, and allows its oppressed groups to bear and contest their condition at the same time."[9] In general, she encourages the reflection about the place of women in society, the status of the artist, relations between the races, gender and sexuality issues, and so forth.[10] More specifically, she reminds us of the inherent contradictions that exist in our society, of the delicate and transitory nature of celebrity, and of our collective desire to simultaneously tear down and raise up those individuals who succeed and survive in spite of it.

Calling Madonna the biggest *female* star of the mid-late 1980s would be as limiting a profile as identifying Michael Jackson as African American or Bruce Springsteen as a New Jersey Catholic. Like Jackson, Springsteen, and countless other artists, Madonna's image has been shaped by her early life experiences and cultural background. Unlike other artists, including Jackson, Springsteen, Prince, U2, and other mega-platinum superstars from the 1980s, Madonna's star continues to shine. Her personal and professional resiliency have helped her bounce back from film debacles like *Who's That Girl?* (1987) and *Shanghai Surprise* (1986) and artistic endeavors like the critically panned *Sex* book (1992) and her follow-up album, *Erotica* (1992). Whether music fans love or hate her, Madonna's proven she has staying power, the ability to stay ahead of music trends, and media marketing savvy. The parameters of her success—or the demographics of her fans—cannot be attributed to any one area, like gender, race, social class, or religious persuasion, yet she has clearly earned the title "phenomenon."

Born Madonna Louise Veronica Ciccone on August 16, 1958, in Bay City, Michigan, to Silvio "Tony" and Madonna (née Fortin) Ciccone, Madonna's young life was touched by a childhood tragedy. Her mother succumbed to breast cancer in 1963 when little Madonna was only five years old. Many biographers[11] claim that her life was profoundly shaped by this event: "This was before pain management became an important part of cancer care," said J. Randy Taraborrelli, who wrote *Madonna: An Intimate Biography.*[12] He went on to comment on the impact of that "terrible . . . last year" (in her mother's life) for Madonna, who "felt really frustrated by the powerlessness that went along with childhood."[13] Madonna herself would later comment, "You walk around with a big hole inside you, a feeling of emptiness and longing . . . and I think a lot of times that's why you become an overachiever."[14]

Biographer Andrew Morton poignantly corroborates this notion in his book *Madonna*, recounting an episode that occurred when she was on the brink of stardom. Lying on her bed in New York, Madonna tape-recorded her thoughts about a Korean woman she had befriended, a woman who apparently had wanted to adopt her. Clearly connecting that story with memories about her mother, she can be heard plaintively saying, " 'I need a mother, I want a mother, I look for my mother all the time and she never shows up anywhere. I want a mother to hug.' "[15] Close to tears, she repeated this phrase mantralike, over and over, "I got gypped . . . I got gypped . . . I got gypped."[16] The importance of her mother's death as a driving force in her own career ambitions is hard to underestimate—or ignore.

An early indication of Madonna's career drive centered on her love of dancing: "She really worked hard to be a dancer. She was willing to practice a lot," recalled Karen Craven, who coached Madonna on her high school cheerleading team.[17] Madonna's hard work paid off when she was awarded a dance scholarship to the University of Michigan in 1976. After studying there for two years, she moved to New York City in 1978, eager to get on to bigger and better things. Picking up occasional modeling jobs and work with various professional dance troupes, Madonna had little but her own dreams on which to survive.[18] She told CNN journalist Larry King, "I danced in a lot of companies in New York for years and realized I was going to be living a hand-to-mouth existence."[19] Intrigued by casual remarks from friends, acquaintances, and passers-by who told her that her voice was not bad, Madonna decided to give singing a try: "I never wanted to be a singer. I mean, I never had any training."[20]

Perhaps part example of her relentless drive to succeed and part example of what would become her trademark ability to reinvent herself, Madonna moved from dancer to singer, coaxing an influential DJ to record a demo-tape for her in 1980. The tape featured a dance track called "Everybody," which caught the ear of record producer Seymour Stein, then president of Sire Records. He signed Madonna to a contract and, in 1982, released "Everybody" as a single, which became a hit on the New York dance club scene. The following year, Madonna recorded her self-titled debut album, which featured the single "Holiday." The success of "Holiday" garnered an invitation to appear on Dick Clark's perennially favorite teen show, *American Bandstand*, and the opportunity to make her personal and career goals known. "I want to rule the world,"[21] she giggled playfully during a postperformance interview with Clark, a remark that was more prophetic than boastful. Madonna's first album was certified platinum, producing two more hits, "Lucky Star" and "Borderline," in addition to "Holiday."

Madonna: The Image

Her unusual dress—an incongruous mix of leather and lace, rubber-band bracelets, torn rags adorning a slightly disheveled mass of hair—now immortalized on national television, Madonna realized she had sparked a fashion craze among her younger fans while she was recording her second album, *Like a Virgin* (1984). The album's title track shot to No. 1, remaining there for six weeks and providing Madonna with the opportunity to emerge as provocateur. Wearing a wedding dress adorned with a belt that read "Boy Toy" (now the name of her production company), Madonna performed "Like a Virgin" on the 1984 MTV

Video Music Awards show. During the song's choreographed dance sequence, she writhed on the floor, simulating masturbation in what would become a classically controversial rock video moment.

"It was the perfect blend of theatrics as well as this sort of psychological warfare," recalled musician Niles Rogers, who has worked as a producer for Madonna.[22] Film critic Roger Ebert later made a similar observation about Madonna in his review of her 1991 backstage/performance documentary *Truth or Dare*, adding that her provocative behavior is more about hard work and business (alluding to marketing) than sex.[23] Even Madonna's official fan club home page has anointed her "diva, mogul, icon, provocateur,"[24] though not necessarily in that order. With her gutsy, seminal MTV performance, Madonna emerged as self-made star, proving that "power is accessible to all, including women—providing they know what they want."[25] And while her childhood dreams of dance fame might have been reinvented to accommodate her pop star aspirations, her desire to be famous—and successful—has never changed.

In her 1984 video *Material Girl*, an homage to Marilyn Monroe, Madonna moved from her bohemian "virgin" look to a more sophisticated, urban retro-chic image. Courtesy of Photofest.

Like a Virgin, which included follow-up hits "Angel," "Dress You Up," and "Material Girl," went platinum within a month of its release.

In 1985, Madonna expanded her career activities to include concert tours and acting. Taking a small role in the movie *Desperately Seeking Susan*, she won early critical acclaim from many reviewers for her quirky supporting role in the offbeat comedy, which encouraged her to accept more film projects. Unfortunately, Madonna's movie career during the 1980s could hardly be called stellar, with back-to-back fiascos like the aforementioned *Shanghai Surprise* (1986) and *Who's That Girl?* (1987). It was not until 1991's concert tour documentary *Truth or Dare* or even later, with 1996's *Evita*, that Madonna's cinematic star shone again.

Her foray into concerts became an extension of her television and music video performances, "jacked up a risqué notch or two as Madonna figuratively made love to the [regularly] infatuated SRO [standing room only] crowd."[26] Wearing peacock paisley top, denim miniskirt, blue suede ankle boots, and crucifixes hanging from every possible point, Madonna was described in a *Variety* review as looking like "she stepped off the cover of Prince's psychedelic LP, *Around the World in a Day* . . . [her] singing like a soundtrack to a more visceral display of herself, her persona, her nonstop dancing and her surprisingly explicit sexual dare."[27] Somehow, the reviewer concluded, Madonna still came across as more flirtatious than naughty; more sugary sex fairy than evil menacing slut; and most important, a powerful example of the impact of early MTV on pop/rock concerts.

Madonna's Video Mastery

Her role on the MTV video front proved Madonna was a credible competitor to the formidable Michael Jackson. Like Jackson, she relied on her formative dance training to turn her videos into miniproduction numbers. Madonna used both the carefully crafted Hollywood musical dance format and the "story within a story" concept to bring new and fresh images to MTV. The *Material Girl* video is an especially good example of this fusion. Giving a playful nod and a suggestive wink to Marilyn Monroe's classic performance of "Diamonds Are a Girl's Best Friend" from the film *Gentlemen Prefer Blondes* (1953), Madonna appears in platinum-coiffed retro hair and pink satin ball gown, elegantly ogled by a troupe of male dancers, clad in top hats and tails.

Initially targeted by some outraged feminists as appallingly antifeminist, and by other political liberals as supporting Ronald Reagan–era capitalism, "Material Girl's" story within a story expresses a decidedly anticapitalist theme. Madonna's offstage character is pursued by the video's director (actor Keith Carradine), who discovers all she really wants is to be loved, not showered with expensive gifts. (Madonna has often expressed this exact sentiment when performing this song during a concert, asking the audience if they really think she is a "material girl," then responding "I'm not" while throwing handfuls of play money into the crowd.)[28] The whole Marilyn Monroe parody is done with such mockingly sweet affection (observe her facial expressions throughout the video) that Madonna's turn as sex object clearly reveals her only intention in being objectified is done exclusively on her own feminist terms. It is not surprising that many feminist writers have dubbed her "the patron saint of the new feminism."[29]

A further extension of her feminism as it applies to a comparison with Michael Jackson's performance style in music videos centers on her propensity

 VOGUE—MADONNA (1990)

Throughout the 1980s, controversy seemed to follow Madonna wherever she went. Her spontaneous mock masturbation routine performed to "Like a Virgin" during the 1984 MTV Awards was just the beginning. From homages to film legend Marilyn Monroe ("Material Girl") to debates about unwed motherhood ("Papa Don't Preach") and racism ("Like a Prayer"), Madonna used the video medium to push a variety of cultural buttons with American audiences. *Vogue*, a stylishly designed black-and-white video, underscores the song's ersatz white rap, synth-tech music, while simultaneously connecting the visual images of pop/rock's most successful female artist of the 1980s with film legends of another era.

for grabbing her crotch. In her 1993 book *Vested Interests, Cross-dressing and Cultural Anxiety*, gender scholar Marjorie Garber observed the way Madonna sometimes grabs her crotch on stage and in videos, à la Michael Jackson:

> Madonna, squeezing what she hadn't got (or *had* she?), emblematized the Lacanian triad of having, being, seeming. . . . Madonna is a famous star who is impersonating a famous male star who is celebrated for his androgynous looks and his dancing style. Why is it shocking when she grabs her crotch, repeating as she does a gesture familiar to anyone who has watched a two-year-old male child reassuring himself of his intactness?[30]

Attempts to respond to Garber's rhetorical question vary, but one source cites a fan explanation of her gesture: "I think some men hate Madonna because she has 'balls.' Some women also hate women who are powerful. Many women hate themselves and worship men."[31]

What Madonna might be saying is that her pants are better filled than Jackson's. For instance, it is often difficult to tell if she is paying tribute to him, satirizing him, or both: "When he grabs his crotch, Jackson doesn't frighten anyone, except perhaps those who believe he's an active pedophile. When Madonna imitates him, she becomes threatening. Her gender-bending terrorizes people. Jackson's antics amuse them or make them feel pity."[32] Both masters of disguise and wearers of masks throughout their careers (though some might argue, Madonna has worn hers with more panache), Michael Jackson and Madonna also embody traditional and nontraditional modes of transformation during the 1980s. Jackson's metamorphosis has been gradual and linear, his skin becoming whiter, his physical appearance more bizarre and grotesque since 1980. Madonna, as postmodern rock icon, has glided back and forth between charmingly flirtatious girl, tough sex siren, proactive feminist, and political activist. Often reiterating that she has never consciously decided, "I'm going to change,"[33] Madonna has moved effortlessly from one incarnation to another, keeping the public guessing (and interested), continuously adding to a persona that is uniquely hers.

Madonna reportedly met future husband Sean Penn, whom she wed in 1985, while filming the "Material Girl" video. Today, despite their tempestuous union of four years, which ended in divorce, Madonna still holds Penn in high regard: "He's an incredible human being," she told Larry King on his television program. "Even though things didn't work out for us, I don't regret marrying him for a minute."[34]

Madonna's Musical Style

During her marriage to Penn, Madonna released only one solo album, 1986's critically praised *True Blue*. Other hits, like 1985's "Crazy for You," were included on movie sound tracks (i.e., *Vision Quest* [1985] and *Who's That Girl?* [1987]). Madonnaphobes had predicted her exit from the pop world in 1986, equating her novelty boy-toy romp with teen idol longevity (a shelf-life of approximately two and a half years). Instead, Madonna came back strong with *True Blue*, an album that was not so much noticed for its revolutionary music as for "the obvious growth . . . in the control and character of Madonna's singing . . . and [its] imaginative, highly energized pop [music] that recognizes the limitations and pleasures of Top 40 fare."[35] Madonna, here like David Bowie, was applauded for the way she visualized music, "so that her best work seems equally designed with the stage or screen in mind, not just the jukebox."[36] Critics cited "Papa Don't Preach," the story of an unwed woman wanting her father's approval after deciding to keep her baby (written by Brian Elliot, with additional lyrics by Madonna) as "tailor-made" for video, as well as "White Heat," which confirms its connection to the 1949 gangster film of the same name by including a James Cagney clip in the video.

Like Bowie, Madonna was also acknowledged for her ability to "weave pop strains into a contemporary framework," mixing the innocence of 1950s R&B with the jolt of Phil Spector's '60s trademark "wall of sound" and the silly techno-pop harmonies of vintage ABBA.[37] Like Bowie and perhaps one other '80s artist, Annie Lennox, who have been credited with having the capacity to accept and analyze their own image creations, Madonna emerged from her *True Blue* period ready and able to integrate her growing capabilities as a singer with her business savvy and established staying-power potential as an artist. In typical Madonna fashion, she pulled herself through postmarital emptiness with another reinvention, finding refuge in her work with another expression of her Catholicism: 1989's *Like a Prayer*. In this way, the controversy that surrounded the album's title track is perhaps less about its shocking video images and more about Madonna's ability to pull them off.

The now-notorious *Like a Prayer* video, which prompted Pepsi to withdraw its companion commercial, which starred Madonna singing an edited version of the song (but with different lyrics), elicited passionate arguments from both the Liberal Left and the Christian Right. Critics accused *Like a Prayer* of sacrilege and even heresy. Donald Wildmon, then executive director of the ultra-conservative American Family Association, wrote in *USA Today*: "Madonna's new video . . . is an extension of a disturbing trend by some in the media, that of disrespect and disdain for the religious beliefs of millions of Americans."[38] Liz Rosenberg, vice president of Warner Brothers Records, countered Wildmon, saying: "[*Like a Prayer*] is about positive religious beliefs, human equality, religious symbolism. It's about being good, not about evil."[39]

The video's imagery, puns, iconography, reversals, satire, and circularities are indeed dizzying. It is the story of a white girl who learns to do the right thing—and succeeds—with the help of the black community. Madonna appears as a woman of the Deep South, perhaps of Italian or Mexican descent, with dark, curly hair (similar in countenance and style to the Virgin Mary). She witnesses a crime: A group of white men, presumably racist thugs, assault a young woman. A black man is unjustly accused. Madonna's character goes to the police and tells them what she saw. The black man is freed because of her courage, and justice is served.

Integrated into the video is a dream sequence that shows Madonna entering the doors of a white wood-framed church. As she enters, she is singing, "I hear you call my name . . . and it feels like . . . Home," whereupon she closes the church door. In his book *The Madonna of 115th Street: Faith and Community in Italian Harlem, 1880–1950*, historian Robert Orsi noted that the women of East Harlem called their church *la casa di mamma* (Momma's house), and their heavenly mother Madonna. Orsi's description of "popular religion"—and the hostile reaction it often provokes from traditionalists—is fitting here:

> When used to describe popular Catholic religiosity, the term conjures up images of shrouds, bloody hearts, bilocating monks, talking Madonnas [!], weeping statues, boiling vials of blood—all the symbols which the masses of Catholic Europe have found to be so powerful over the centuries and which churchmen have denigrated, often while sharing in the same or similar devotions.[40]

As the dream sequence continues, Madonna kneels before a statue of Saint Martin de Porres, appropriately the patron saint of social justice and played by the same actor who is the accused assailant. The statue weeps tears of blood, comes to life, and kisses Madonna, first on the forehead, then, later, more erotically, on the lips. When he leaves the church, Madonna picks up his dropped dagger and discovers stigmata have marked her hands, confirming her role in the video's redemption narrative: "Stigmata, with their obvious phallic connotations, are a sensual sign of contact with the divine, a kind of holy coupling."[41] This notion of reciprocity between the worshipper and the divine is, according to Orsi, a common feature of popular piety,[42] as is the video's depiction a statement about the union of black/white and sex/religion.[43]

The song's lyrics also reinforce its "postmodern nature": the distinctively ambiguous word "like" appearing numerous times; the blurring of distinctions between human lover and God; the unresolved relationship between Madonna and the black saint; the role of the black woman as muse/choir director/sister/savior. The music may be unambiguous with its mainstream, contemporary pop sound, but its function as the vehicle by which we can move into the world of fantasy, forward toward reality, and back into the imaginary, open to multiple perspectives and unresolved ambiguities, is clearly tied to postmodernism. We cannot help but like this prayer/virgin and all that its duality connotes, and yet "we always know that there never was/is a prayer virgin nor a virgin prayer."[44] Without doubt, Madonna's role in the concept development and creation of *Like a Prayer* (the video was directed by Mary Lambert) exemplifies her own self-professed ambiguity toward Catholicism: "She honors the memory of her deceased mother, hangs a rosary from the rear view mirror in her car and admires nuns. But she iconoclastically 'perverts' Catholic imagery."[45]

If *Like a Prayer* peaked the Madonna-shock barometer as the decade came to a close, her subsequent artistic endeavors pushed the envelope even farther. In 1990, she launched her own ambitiously developed Blonde Ambition (BA) world tour, which lasted four months and took her to twenty-seven cities. The tour coincided with the release of her fifth album, the lukewarmly received *I'm Breathless*, whose title is a reference to her character, Breathless Mahoney, in the film *Dick Tracy* (1990). Her much-publicized affair with *Dick Tracy* star/director and Hollywood lothario Warren Beatty overlapped in the BA tour and later found its way into *Truth or Dare*, the tour's acclaimed documentary. Still, critics, fans, and the general public expressed varying views of her sexually charged performances and the bold eroticism that characterized Blonde Ambition's extravagant production numbers. With her hair drawn back in severe blonde ponytail and wearing a metallic bustier with cone-shaped breast plates, Madonna was just getting warmed up for her later venture, the 1991 video *Justify My Love.*

In spite of her successes and failures (and sometimes, perhaps, because of them) Madonna has remained a viable pop artist, cultural phenomenon, and supporter of various social causes. Her assertive, often in-your-face persona has influenced the careers of artists from Janet Jackson to Courtney Love. Perhaps David Tetzlaff, a professor of theater and film studies in Connecticut, makes the most compelling argument for Madonna's enduring popularity when he recounts a story done on the television tabloid show *Inside Edition* about college professors who study Madonna or discuss her work in class: "When tabloid journalists start presenting the activities of academics to their sensation-seeking audiences, it is obvious that some very large cultural power is at hand."[46] Diva, icon, mogul, provocateur, sister, mother, feminist, lover, siren, friend, cultural phenomenon: Madonna has proven to be all of these—and more.

PRINCE

Whether he is called "His Royal Badness" or "His Purple Highness," Prince Rogers Nelson (born on June 7, 1958, in Minneapolis) could never be defined by any one phrase or symbol. Named after his father's jazz band, The Prince Roger Trio (for which his mother Mattie Shaw was often a featured vocalist), the young Nelson found an early influence in singer James Brown, whom he saw in concert in 1968. By the time he entered high school, Prince had mastered both guitar and piano and was asked to join his cousin Charles Smith's high school band, Grand Central. Within a year (and following Smith's departure), Grand Central transformed itself into a group called Champagne, with Prince as its leader.[47]

In 1977, Prince became the youngest producer in Warner Brothers history when he signed a contract giving him complete creative control over his solo

Prince directed and acted in the 1986 film, *Under the Cherry Moon*, an unsuccessful follow-up to his masterpiece, *Purple Rain*. © Warner Brothers/Photofest.

debut album. The exceptional deal did not happen by accident. Prince had spent several years learning the music business: first playing session guitar for local great Pepe Willie, then working with Chris Moon on the intricacies of recording. Moon introduced Prince to recording hustler Owen Husney, who negotiated the Warner deal and became Prince's first manager. In 1978, his debut album *For You* produced a modest R&B hit, "Soft and Wet," which merely hinted at the erotically charged efforts yet to come. Prince reportedly played twenty-three different instruments on the record, which included a broad range of styles from acoustic to rock to R&B to funk. Initially, critics were not sure how to categorize Prince's music, but a second release in 1979 clearly moved him more toward a funk-rock style.

In preparation for his self-titled second album, Prince made a number of musical and management changes. Disappointed that his January 5, 1979, hometown concert debut resulted in disappointing attendance and tickets sales, an anxious Prince took the advice of Warner record executives and agreed to let representatives from the Los Angeles firm of Cavallo and Ruffalo manage his career.[48] Prince also recruited a group of rock-influenced musicians to give his songs a harder, funkier sound: Dez Dickerson on guitar, Gayle Chapman and Matt Fink on keyboards, Andre Cymone on bass, and Bobby Z on drums. *Prince* spawned another single, the funk-pop-infused "I Wanna Be Your Lover," which was dedicated to singer Patrice Rushen and reached the U.S. Top 20. With the single's success, as well as moderately good record sales and generally favorable critical reviews, Prince took his new band, the Revolution, on the road.

Prince's early concerts were considerably tamer than his now-infamous concert forays into eroticism and spirituality, but he still pranced around the stage in ultra-tight-fitting pants, high-heeled boots, complemented by oddly dressed musicians and lingerie-clad backup singers. Unfortunately, the tour drew inconsistent crowds: a sold-out Roxy theater in Los Angeles, then only twenty fans in Dallas. Still, the concert tour proved important to Prince, who was gaining more and more confidence onstage by polishing his dance and musicianship skills. Additionally, the album's rock/new wave feel introduced a broader (read: white suburban) audience to his music.

By the end of 1979, Prince had made guest appearances on the popular *Midnight Special* and *American Bandstand* television shows, adding mystery to his demeanor and image with his cryptic answers to questions. In 1980, his third album, *Dirty Mind*, a raw, stripped-down musically collection, pushed the enveloped with explicit sexual lyrics and elicited an invitation from the Rolling Stones to join them on tour. While Prince's "soulful androgyny" did not always mix well with the Stones' more partisan audience,[49] his flirtations with synthesized new wave styles moved him farther and farther away from the R&B artist Warner Brothers had originally intended to promote. In 1981, *Controversy* sparked little, although critics were once again divided and confused over how to categorize Prince's music.

In February 1983, Prince broke impressive ground professionally with the release of his ambitious double-album *1999*, an effort that saw him cross over pop and R&B charts and demographics, "uniting a growing audience and landing himself in the top 10 and on MTV."[50] One of the first black performers on the cable music network (and rivaling Michael Jackson's popularity), Prince's musical achievements came primarily from his movement toward more melodic, pop-inspired songs like "Little Red Corvette." This fifth album release, again produced, arranged, and composed solely by the artist, was the musical breakthrough necessary to establish Prince as one of the most influential musical artists of the decade.

Prince's impact was felt most immediately by other Minneapolis-based bands, specifically the groups Time and Vanity 6, both of which Prince was rumored to have been controlling behind the scenes. He played out his role as phantom creator/muse to these groups, as well as his own climb to stardom in 1984's *Purple Rain*, a thinly disguised film autobiography that produced what is perhaps his best musical effort to date.

Portraying himself as alternately sensitive, wild, and sexy, Prince's character in *Purple Rain*, "the Kid" (a nickname coined by manager Robert Cavallo), mirrored his real-life persona. The movie made Prince a superstar, eventually selling over 10 million copies in the United States alone and spending twenty-four weeks at No. 1. "When Doves Cry," the album's mystically gospel-rooted first single release, gave Prince his first No. 1 hit. Other hits from the album included the upbeat soul-rock of "Let's Go Crazy," the lyrical "I Would Die 4 U," and the title song. Prince received two Grammy Awards for the album and an Academy Award for "Best Original Score."

His follow-up to *Purple Rain* again surprised fans and critics. Never content to be musically stereotyped, Prince veered off into a world of psycho-psychedelia for 1985's *Around the World in a Day*, the first album produced on his newly formed Paisley Park record label. (Based in Minneapolis, Paisley Park would also become the home of artists like The Family, Sheila E., and George Clinton.) Clearly a departure from the more pop-oriented *Purple Rain*, *Around the World in a Day* is best described as a "largely esoteric collection of psychedelic pop interspersed with the melodic brilliance of 'Raspberry Beret,'" possibly the finest song Prince has ever written.[51] This album was also to be the impetus for Prince's own personal reconciliation between the sexual and spiritual, a theme that would dominate his music for years to come.

In 1986, Prince announced his retirement from live performance, only to retract his pledge for the promotional tour of *Parade: Music from the Film Under the Cherry Moon*. Like *Purple Rain*, *Parade*'s sound track for *Under the Cherry Moon* contained music that stood separate and apart from an otherwise undisguised film. The album also provided Prince with his third No. 1 single, the brilliantly spare-fun hit "Kiss" (later famously covered by Tom Jones).

At the end of the *Parade* tour, Prince disbanded the Revolution and went solo for awhile, returning in 1987 with new musicians and the album that many critics believe to be his masterpiece, the ambitious double-album *Sign O' the Times*. His most thorough exploration of sex and religion to date, *Sign O' the Times* "marked the maturation of everything the artist had been working toward up to that point," incorporating the "gloriously dirty fun of the title track . . . [with] the muted musical foreplay of 'If I was Your Girlfriend.'"[52] His scheduled follow-up, the funk-based *Black Album*, was pulled (at his request) from Warner's release pool when Prince deemed the project "immoral." Instead, the less focused, musically confused *Lovesexy* was released in 1988 to tepid reviews and poor record sales in the United States (although the title track topped at No. 1 in the United Kingdom).[53]

In 1989, Prince returned to the top of the charts with the sound track for the movie *Batman*. Although not identifiably "Prince," the sound track sold well and was considered a much stronger musical effort than his sequel to *Purple Rain*, titled *Music from Graffiti Bridge*, a commercial disaster released in 1990. Prince was back on top again in 1991 with a new band, the New Power Generation, and a new album, *Diamonds and Pearls*, his biggest hit since 1985 and one that witnessed a return to his R&B roots.[54]

Since 1991, Prince has continued to explore personal issues, talents, and demons through his music. In any given decade, few artists have created the expansive and creative body of work as rich and varied as Prince. During the 1980s, he emerged as one of the most original singular geniuses of the rock 'n' roll era, "capable of seamlessly tying together pop, funk, folk and rock."[55] Not only were his compositions written for himself but for countless other artists, including Sheila E., Sheena Easton, and George Clinton. His vaults still contain hundreds of unreleased songs. While his musical experimentation sometimes met with mixed success, Prince's overall positive explorations of different musical genres distinguish him as one of those rare talents whose many diverse styles have evolved into a musically cohesive whole.

NOTES

1. A "one-hit" wonder refers to an artist/group with only one career single in the Top 40 countdown. During the 1980s, groups like A Flock of Seagulls and the Thompson Twins had just one hit; even then the music was not considered very good.

2. Joe Stuessy and Scott Lipscomb, *Rock and Roll: Its History and Stylistic Development*, 4th ed. (Upper Saddle River, NJ: Prentice Hall, 2003), 303.

3. Stuessy and Lipscomb and other rock historians, including Paul Friedlander and Dave Marsh, as well as countless rock critics, have often referred to the 1980s as a vast musical wasteland, in part because of the emergence of MTV.

4. Stuessy and Lipscomb, *Rock and Roll*, 367.

5. Like other rock greats before him, including Elvis, John Lennon, Bob Dylan, Jimi Hendrix, Janis Joplin, and Jim Morrison, Jackson continues to show how the manifestations of inner demons can both inhibit and free an artist. Like most rock stars whose excessive behavior rests outside society's norm, Michael Jackson has battled numerous personal and professional demons in his almost-forty-year career in music, defining him as more than a pop singer. The man who, in 2002, received the World Music Award as "Best Selling Pop Male Artist of the Millennium" remains an enigma to music fans and critics everywhere. His continued role as a definitive rock icon will undoubtedly be the subject of ongoing discussion, but his place as one of the most popular and innovative music and video crossover artists of the 1980s—or any decade—is undeniable.

6. Georges-Claude Guilbert, *Madonna as Postmodern Myth: How One Star's Self-Construction Rewrites Sex, Gender, Hollywood and the American Dream* (Jefferson, NC: McFarland, 2002), 152.

7. Ibid.

8. Ibid., 187.

9. Ibid.

10. Ibid.

11. Bill Holdship, as found at http://launch.yahoo.com/artist/artistFocus.asp?artist1D=1016600.

12. J. Randy Taraborrelli, *Madonna: An Intimate Biography* (New York: Simon & Schuster, 2001), as cited at http://www.geocities.com/SunsetStrip/Club/8804/bio.html.

13. Ibid.

14. MadonnaDance Web site at http://www.geocities.com/SunsetStrip/Club/8804/bio.htm.

15. Andrew Morton, *Madonna* (New York: St. Martin's Press, 2001), 36.

16. Ibid.

17. Quoted on MadonnaDance Web site.

18. Ibid.

19. Ibid.

20. Ibid.

21. Ibid.

22. MadonnaDance Web site.

23. Roger Ebert, "Truth or Dare," *Chicago Sun-Times*, May 17, 1991; found at rogerebert.com, search *Truth or Dare*.

24. Madonna's fan club Web site, 2000 version.

25. "Madonna" (unsigned article), *Photo*, November 1992; cited in Guilbert's *Madonna*, 154.

26. "Concert Review: Universal Amphitheater, Los Angeles, May 8, 1985," *Variety*, 1985; included in *The Madonna Companion: Two Decades of Commentary*, edited by Allan Metz and Carol Benson (New York: Schirmer Books, 1999), 4–5.

27. Ibid.

28. Ibid.

29. bell hooks, "Power to the Pussy: We Don't Wannabe Dicks in Drag," in *Madonnarama: Essays on Sex and Popular Culure*, edited by Lisa Frank and Paul Smith (San Francisco: Cleis Press, 1993), 65; cited in Guilbert, *Madonna*, 180.

30. Marjorie Garber, *Vested Interests, Cross-dressing and Cultural Anxiety* (New York: HarperPerennial, 1993), 126–127.

31. Guilbert, *Madonna*, 223.

32. Ibid., 151–152.

33. Sylvia Patterson, "Living in a Material World," *New Musical Express*, March 7, 1998, for example.

34. Taraborrelli, *Madonna*.

35. Robert Hilburn, "Madonna Is Nobody's Toy," *Los Angeles Times*, July 6, 1986, cited in Metz and Benson, *Madonna Companion*, 6–7.

36. Ibid.

37. Ibid.

38. Donald Wildmon, "This Video Is Offensive to Believers," *USA Today*, 1996; included in Metz and Benson, *Madonna Companion*, 183.

39. Liz Rosenberg, "Face-off: Madonna's 'Like a Prayer': This Video Affirms Religious Principles," *USA Today*, 1996; included in Metz and Benson, *Madonna Companion*, 181–182.

40. Robert Anthony Orsi, *The Madonna of 115th Street: Faith and Community in Italian Harlem, 1880–1950* (New Haven, CT: Yale University Press, 1985); cited by Carla Freccero, "Our Lady of MTV: Madonna's 'Like a Prayer,'" 1992; included in Metz and Benson, *Madonna Companion*, 184–199.

41. Freccero, "Our Lady of MTV," 184–199.

42. Orsi, *Madonna of 115th Street*, 230–231.

43. Freccero, "Our Lady of MTV," 184–199.

44. Ibid.

45. Guilbert, *Madonna*, 167.

46. Guilbert, preface from *Madonna*, quoted in David Tetzlaff, "Metatextual Girl ~ Patriarchy ~ Postmodernism ~ Power ~ Money ~ Madonna," in *The Madonna Connection: Representational Politics, Subcultural Identities and Cultural Theory*, edited by Cathy Schwichtenberg (Boulder, CO: Westview Press, 1993), 240.

47. Martin C. Strong, *The Great Rock Discography*, 6th ed. (Edinburgh, UK: Canongate Books, 2002), 831.

48. Alex Hahn, *Possessed: The Rise and Fall of Prince* (New York: Billboard Books, 2003), 28.

49. Strong, *Great Rock Discography*, 831.

50. See, for example, Jennifer Clay, "Prince," included at the following Web site: http://launch.yahoo.com/artist/artistFocuslasp/artistID=1021580.

51. Strong, *Great Rock Discography*, 831.

52. Ibid.

53. Ibid.

54. See, for example, Stephen Thomas Erlewine, "Prince," *All Music Guide*, included at the following Web site: http://www.mtv.com; search Prince.

55. Ibid.

3

WORKING-CLASS HEROES

While Michael Jackson, Madonna, and Prince dominated the pop/rock charts as well as video and concert scenes during the 1980s, there was another, equally influential and less visually driven tier of popular artists whose music defined the decade. While their fan bases, record sales, and sphere of influence were not as far-ranging or as image-defining as the first three, these artists followed in the tradition of Bob Dylan, using social issues, powerful lyrics, and a more traditional kick-ass rock 'n' roll style to reach their audiences.

Carrying Dylan's mantle into the 1980s were Bruce Springsteen, Tom Petty (with or without the Heartbreakers), and John (Cougar) Mellencamp. Already established during the 1970s as credible artists with strong elemental rock 'n' roll roots, Springsteen and Petty crossed into the 1980s with renewed musical vigor and popularity. Mellencamp followed suit, bringing a new stratum of the rock sound by utilizing his unique, sometimes ethnoregional sounds with new studio technologies and cutting-edge videos. Individually, each artist put his respective imprimatur on musical styles that impacted rock music during the 1980s and beyond.

BRUCE SPRINGSTEEN: THE BOSS

It is almost impossible to believe that one of rock 'n' roll's superstars has yet to score a No. 1 single. Bruce Frederick Joseph Springsteen, born on September 23, 1949, in Long Branch, New Jersey, the eldest of three children and only son of Douglas and Adele, has never, as of this writing, secured a No. 1 hit single recording. Albums like *The River* (1980), *Born in the U.S.A.* (1984), and *Tunnel*

After his mega-album *Born in the U.S.A.*, Bruce Springsteen returned with the more introspective, highly acclaimed *Tunnel of Love* album in 1987. Courtesy of Photofest.

of Love (1987) climbed to No. 1; singles, including "Hungry Heart," "Dancing in the Dark," "Cover Me," and "Brilliant Disguise," all made *Billboard*'s Top 10. And, to date, Springsteen has sold over 50 million records. But no, one identifiable hit, like Michael Jackson's "Beat It" or Madonna's signature "Like a Virgin," has defined his career, his image, or his music.

Perhaps that distinction is fitting, for Springsteen's classically raw rock 'n' roll sound has never really been about individual songs. The power and poetry in Springsteen's music lie in its themes: working-class aspirations and disappointments, romantic hope and disillusionment, unemployment, the readjustment of Vietnam veterans, hunger, poverty, and the angry frustration of being unable to beat "the establishment."[1] Scholars, rock journalists, and theologians have all examined his work, interpreted the richly consistent underlying messages in his lyrics, celebrated his ability to express America's deepest joys and greatest sorrows. For all the cynics who complain that the 1980s was an uninspired decade of music video fluff, Springsteen's presence alone suggests otherwise. His musical roots provide a natural link to prerock folkies like Woody Guthrie and Pete Seeger; his sense of social justice easily connects him with '60s counterculture artists like Bob Dylan or the Velvet Underground; and his musical influence on everyone from fellow New Jersey native Jon Bon Jovi to the alternative musings of Dave Matthews gives him an irrefutable tie to the future.

Springsteen, who grew up "on the wrong side of the railroad tracks"[2] in the highly segregated working-class town of Freehold, New Jersey, reportedly bought his first guitar when he was thirteen. In 1964, at the tender age of fifteen, he joined his first band, the Rogues, and by 1965 became a member of the Castiles, with whom he performed for about three years. In 1969, Springsteen failed his army physical. Graded 4-F, he was not fit for military service, due in part to injuries sustained from a prior motorcycle injury and partly from "his intentionally chaotic and confusing answers on the army questionnaire."[3] When his parents moved to California that same year, Bruce remained in New Jersey, eventually moving to Asbury Park and forming another band.

In January 1970, Springsteen and the newly organized Steel Mill performed at the Matrix in Berkeley, California, prompting *San Francisco Examiner* music critic Philip Elwood to write: "[The concert] was one of the most memorable evenings of rock in a long time. . . . I have never been so overwhelmed by an unknown band."[4] Throughout the 1970s, Springsteen performed, eventually meeting up with John Hammond, who held the previous distinction of signing Bob Dylan and who offered him a contract with Columbia Records. Springsteen spent much of the remainder of the 1970s establishing himself as a significant voice in mainstream rock, supported all the way by the superbly talented members of his group, the "E Street Band."

Although E Street members changed over the years, fans identify lead guitarist Steve Van Zandt, saxophonist Clarence Clemens, and drummer Max Weinberg as the band's core. In 1982, Patti Scialfa, who later married Springsteen, joined the group as a backup singer. The E Street band, with its elemental, blue-collar rock 'n' roll hooks, complemented by Clemen's bluesy saxophone, gave Springsteen's hauntingly poignant lyrics the sound and image that would become his signature.

By 1980, Springsteen was poised to move into superstar status but perhaps did not anticipate the phenomenal success that would come by the middle of the decade. An unassuming artist who has remained modest about his enormous talent, Springsteen was reluctant to accept some of the early accolades that followed the release and success of *Born to Run*. Rejecting labels like "the future of rock 'n' roll" and other kinds of hyperbolic nicknames that often accompany commercial success, Springsteen spent much of the late 1970s touring before returning to the studio in 1980 to record the four-dozen-odd songs he had composed on the road. The resultant double-album, *The River*, became his first No. 1 album and produced the No. 5 single "Hungry Heart."

What followed *The River* was a "stunning departure by Springsteen from rock-and-roll"[5]—his solo acoustic album *Nebraska* (released on September 20, 1982). Having used a small Teac 4-track cassette tape record to record this rather unusual, brooding set of songs based on the Starkweather-Fugate killing spree in the 1950s,[6] he reportedly recorded and mixed the songs in the bedroom of the Colt's Neck, New Jersey, farmhouse in which he was living at the time. Springsteen originally intended that his homemade recordings be used as a demo, but after many attempts to remix them, he—and the record producers—agreed that

 DANCIN' IN THE DARK—BRUCE SPRINGSTEEN (1984)

Although he had made a name in the 1970s as the new Bob Dylan, Springsteen experienced his most commercial crossover success in the rock mainstream with his 1984 album *Born in the U.S.A.* "Dancin' in the Dark," the album's first single and video, again reinforces the notion that many "real" rock artists held: that they were all about the music. *Dancin' in the Dark*'s live concert setting shows Springsteen at his muscular best; a raw, working-class Joe in jeans and white shirt (sleeves rolled up) performed with his beloved E Street Band. The video powerfully captures Springsteen's classic concert persona and seems to harness the energy produced by his standard three-plus-hour performances. Of special note in the video is the young girl Springsteen plucks out of the audience to share an impromptu dance: Courtney Cox, later of *Friends* fame, first got viewer recognition for her innocent pas de deux with "The Boss."

Bruce Springsteen performs during his *Born in the U.S.A.* tour, 1984–1985. Courtesy of Photofest.

his moody, introspective collection was best served in the crudely primitive way he had initially laid down the tracks. Despite its darkly eclectic style, *Nebraska* moved to No. 3 on the charts and is still considered to be not only among Springsteen's finest achievements but perhaps one of the most darkly poetic contemporary folk albums in recent history.

Then, on June 4, 1984, the unexpected phenomenon that would secure Springsteen's status as a rock icon, *Born in the U.S.A.*, was released. The album became Columbia Records' biggest seller to date with 13 million copies sold and, in the midst of the Reagan-era's celebration of white urban professionals, turned Springsteen into the symbol of America's newly disenfranchised, the young working class. His live-concert performance of the album's No. 2 single, "Dancing in the Dark," garnered him a new audience of MTV viewers and brought him the Grammy Award for "Best Male Rock Vocalist." His follow-up concert tour played to sold-out stadiums for over two years, reinforcing his immense popularity and establishing the marathon rock concert (over three hours) as a new standard for rock 'n' roll artists.

With Springsteen's enormous success, of course, came dissension, criticism, and confusion, as did conflict between him and the E Street Band, who, with the exception of *Nebraska*, had been an integral part of Springsteen's rise as the symbol of blue-collar rock. In the face of his newfound rock status, Springsteen's tight relationship with E Street Band members would also be challenged. *Born in the U.S.A.*'s themes clearly underscore the plight of displaced Vietnam veterans. The album's cover, which shows Springsteen's denim-clad backside in front of an America flag, was misused by the Republican committee to reelect Ronald Reagan: The committee tried to link Springsteen's working-class popularity with Reagan's elitist economic policies. Too, fans of Springsteen's pre-*Born* status as a Dylan-esque cult-figure drew criticism as well. How could America's representative of the underclass have become so popular with America's economic and political elite? And how far would Springsteen's mainstream rock go before he sold out to the pop/rock impresarios? A brief examination of Springsteen's subsequent career moves suggests that, even in the face of superstardom, he has never lost his New Jersey working-class roots nor abandoned his exploration of "underlying conflict between the promise of the American Dream, with its high ideals and comfortable affluence, and the stark disappointment felt by many who, for one reason or another, fail to realize the dream."[7]

In the October 24, 1980, issue of the *Chicago Reader*, popular music critic Don McLeese, then of the *Chicago Sun-Times*, wrote this about the paradox of Springsteen's—and any rock icon's—fame:

> [T]reating a Springsteen as something special, we threaten to undermine so much of what made him special in the first place. . . . As a reaction against pampered, postured superstars who had totally lost touch with their audiences, Springsteen brought a street-level grit and grandeur back to the music, wrenching some hope for redemption—or at least escape—out of everyday experience.[8]

Calling Springsteen a star through "sheer force of passion," McLeese acknowledged the Boss' understanding that "something vital is sacrificed when we turn our rockers into icons . . . that whatever is magic about rock and roll is gut-level; that is exists within us rather than outside us."[9] In effect, Springsteen showed us that "rock and roll is a process, an interaction, not an artifact."[10]

Proof of McLeese's assertion can be seen in 1986, with the five-record boxed set release of *Bruce Springsteen & the E Street Band Live: 1975–85*, which provided his fans with a memorable replacement for the hundreds of inferior bootleg concert recordings that had circulated for over a decade. Springsteen continued to move in new directions musically when, for 1987's *Tunnel of Love*, he replaced the E Street Band with more polished studio musicians (although members of E Street still made "guest appearances" on various tracks). *Tunnel of Love*, which won a Grammy Award for "Best Album," was Springsteen's very intimate, possibly most personal treatise on fading and broken relationships. To some, the haunting collection of songs, notably the popular track "Brilliant Disguise," was an "obvious reflection of [his] strained marriage and alienation" from first wife, actress/model Julianne Philips.[11] To others, *Tunnel of Love* was more than a personal reflection: It was an example of Springsteen's maturation as an artist, his development and evolution as a troubador/poet, and his continued struggle to express the personal demons that drive us all.

In the fall of 1988, a year after *Tunnel of Love* was released and a month after Philips filed for divorce (the divorce would become final the next year), Springsteen, along with fellow artists Sting, Peter Gabriel, Tracy Chapman, and Youssou N'Dour, embarked on a six-week world rock tour to benefit Amnesty International. He also released a four-song extended long play titled *Chimes of Freedom*. His ties with the E Street Band were officially "broken" in 1989 when he disbanded the group. It would be more than ten years before the

E Street Band would reassemble, and during that time, Springsteen's career and work underwent yet another kind of metamorphosis.

The decade between E Street Band reunions would be a time of continued interest in Springsteen as an artist. As he completed his second decade as a rock 'n' roller, he became even more interesting to the scholars and academics that began to reassess his work and his career. From the many and diverse interpretations of his personal and professional choices, one idea remains constant: No other rock artist has had "as remarkable, or as paradoxical career as Bruce Springsteen. Working-class hero. All-American sex symbol. Introspective lyricist *and* goofy showman. Compassionate chronicler of misfits, losers and loners—hard people living hard lives—but also a bastion of hope, faith and glory."[12]

Theologian and sociologist Andrew Greeley even identified him as a Catholic "meistersinger," a liturgist who "correlates the self-communication of God in secular life with the overarching symbol/narratives of his/our tradition."[13] Greeley argued that Springsteen has continually engaged in this "minstrel ministry" without ever being explicit or even necessarily aware of it:

> It might be debated how optimistic *U.S.A.* really was. But, while there is tragedy in *Tunnel of Love*, there is also hope. The water of the river still flows, but now it stands, not for death, but for rebirth. Light and water, the Easter and baptismal symbols of the Catholic liturgy, the combination of the male and female fertility principles, create life in *Tunnel of Love*.[14]

Calling *Tunnel of Love* an "exercise of . . . metaphor-making dynamisms," Greeley hailed its release, at least within the context of religion, as a more important Catholic event in this country than the visit of Pope John Paul II. Greeley's notion that "troubadours always have more impact than theologians or bishops"[15] underscores Springsteen's connection with his audience, not just Catholics but Americans: "Springsteen sings of religious realities—sin, temptation, forgiveness, life, death, hope—in images that come (implicitly perhaps) from his Catholic childhood, images that appeal to the whole person, not just the head, and that will be absorbed by far more Americans than those who listened to the Pope."[16]

Greeley's interpretations about Springsteen and the Catholic imagination[17] have been suggested and echoed by countless other writers in many different contexts. What ties these seemingly disparate threads of analysis about Springsteen's work together—whether spelling "Catholic" with a capital "C" or not— is his amazing ability to connect and reconnect with his audience, to grow, mature, and evolve over time. For over thirty years, Springsteen has carried the mantle of Chuck Berry, Elvis, Buddy Holly, Woody Guthrie, and Bob Dylan on his shoulders, but unlike Dylan or the Beatles, he remains more synthesizer than innovator: "I like the whole idea of a rock and roll lineage," Springsteen has said. "I was interested in becoming part of people's lives and growing up with them."[18] His songs, then, offer that "wonderfully bewildering problem of how to keep up. Words tumble over another, phrases mysteriously *feel* right, then disappear,"[19] making the power of his imagery—and his presence—almost as elusive as the driving force behind his imagination.

What might be even more impressive during his decade-spanning career is Springsteen's "extraordinary facility for growth. The person who created the dazzling wordplay of *Greetings from Asbury Park, N.J.* differs greatly from the person who, years later, penned the largely somber songs of *The Rising,* separated by time, certainly, but also by vast degrees of maturity and worldly experience."[20] Indeed, many fans—even those who were not born when he first entered the rock arena—have watched him change over the years and have changed with him.

Since the 1980s, Springsteen has experienced ups and downs in his musical experiments, with releases of various CDs, including a return to his somber folk roots with *The Ghost of Tom Joad* in 1995. In March 1999, after a reunion tour with the E Street Band, Springsteen celebrated his much-deserved induction into the Rock and Roll Hall of Fame and Museum.[21]

And so his legend continues into the new millennium. Married since 1991 to backup singer Patti Scialfa, "The Boss" has remained true, not only to his musical principles "but to the historic principles of mainstream rock and roll: to express popular sentiments in a hard-driving, uncomplicated, but musically proficient style."[22] Unlike the elusiveness of Michael Jackson or the mercurial transformations of Madonna, Springsteen's artistic constancy has never kept him from exploring new territories in the depiction of human nature, whether celebrating our differences or examining the joys and sorrows that connect us all. Ultimately, it is Springsteen who perhaps best explains the key to rock 'n' roll's longevity and viability:

> I believe that the life of a rock and roll band will last as long as you look down into the audience and can see yourself, and your audience looks up at you and can see themselves. . . . The biggest gift your fans can give you is just treatin' you like a human being because anything else dehumanizes you.[23]

TOM PETTY

It is perhaps both ironic and appropriate that in 1989 Tom Petty released his first solo album, *Full Moon Fever,* a critical and fan favorite that became one of the most influential albums of the decade, without the full musical assistance of his band, the Heartbreakers. For Petty, *Full Moon Fever* capped a decade and a half of playing rock 'n' roll "in the very finest American tradition,"[24] a career that thus far had taken him from his university hometown of Gainesville, Florida, to concert halls around the world. Born on October 20, 1950, Petty began playing music while still in high school. In 1968, he formed a school band

Tom Petty, performing here in about 1990, continued in the tradition of mainstream rock 'n' roll during the 1980s. Courtesy of Photofest.

called the Sundowners, who later became the Epics. By 1971, the group evolved into Mudcrutch, which included future Heartbreakers Mike Campbell (guitar; born February 1, 1954, in Panama City, Florida) and Benmont Tench (keyboards; born September 7, 1954, in Gainesville).

After playing in and around Florida without gaining much national attention, Petty and Mudcrutch relocated to Los Angeles, where the band soon broke up. Unfazed, Petty continued to pursue a musical career, eventually landing a record deal with Leon Russell's Shelter Records label. By 1976, Campbell and Tench, plus LA musicians Ron Blair (bass; born September 16, 1952, in Macon, Georgia) and Stan Lynch (drums; born May 21, 1955) reemerged as the Heartbreakers and, together with Petty, recorded their debut album, *Tom Petty and the Heartbreakers*. From the opening chords of "Rockin' Around (With You)" to the now-classic singles "Anything That's Rock 'N' Roll" and "American Girl," Petty established himself as a rock 'n' roll artist in the tradition of the Beatles, the Byrds, and the Stones. The album climbed to No. 55 in the United Kingdom and ultimately went gold. In an age overblown by disco and pop-inspired new wave, Petty and the Heartbreakers were a musical breath of fresh air.

By 1978, after a second album release—*You're Gonna Get It!*—and a nasty contract battle with MCA Records over rights to the band's next project, Petty and the Heartbreakers released what would be their most accessible masterpiece to date, *Damn the Torpedoes* (1979). Produced by Petty and recording master Jimmy Iovine, *Damn the Torpedoes* "boasted a booming contemporary sound" that spawned two of Petty's best singles: the Top 15 hits "Don't Do Me Like That" and "Refugee," co-written by Petty and Campbell. The album peaked at No. 2 in the United States, staying there for several weeks.[25]

The success of *Damn the Torpedoes* sparked another clash between Petty and MCA Records when the company decided to raise the price of his next album (part of the company's "superstar product" initiative). Petty threatened to withhold the album from the label until MCA relented, issuing 1981's *Hard Promises* at the standard price. Both *Hard Promises* and its 1982 follow-up, *Long After Dark*, cracked the Top 10, producing three Top 25 hits between them: "The Waiting," "You Got Lucky," and "Change of Heart." The year 1981 also saw Petty's first collaboration with what would become a "Who's Who" of rock superstars. He and Fleetwood Mac singer Stevie Nicks recorded a duet, "Stop Draggin' My Heart Around," another Petty/Campbell effort. The song gave Petty his first Top 5 hit, peaking in the United States at No. 3. Petty also exercised his producer's muscles, working on Del Shannon's release *Drop Down and Get Me*, backed by the Heartbreakers.

The mid-'80s were a mixed bag of events for Petty and the Heartbreakers, characterized alternately by incredible professional accomplishments and disappointments. In 1985, Petty broke his hand during a frustrating moment of recording the complex and ambitious *Southern Accents*, which furthered his songwriting collaborations with musicians outside the Heartbreakers, including Dave Stewart of the Eurythmics and the Band's Robbie Robertson. *Southern Accents* "marked a newfound maturity [for Petty], both musically and lyrically, [with] the brooding 'Don't Come Around Here No More' furnishing Petty with his biggest UK hit single to date."[26] In 1986, Petty and the Heartbreakers joined rock great Bob Dylan for a major world tour that resulted in "Jammin' Me," a Top 20 Petty-Dylan composition that opened 1987's *Let Me Up (I've Had Enough)*.

If Petty had, indeed, had enough, critics and fans would not have known it. His auspicious meeting and subsequent tour with Bob Dylan introduced him to the company of rock's older aristocracy, forming more new musical partnerships. In 1988, Petty joined Dylan, former Beatle George Harrison, ELO's Jeff Lynne, and the legendary Roy Orbison to create a fictitious band called "The Traveling Wilburys." The Wilburys' first release, *The Traveling Wilburys:Vol. 1*, received much critical acclaim and fan approval and provided jump-starts to Harrison's, Lynne's, and Orbison's careers. Tragically, Orbison's sudden and unexpected death (of a heart attack) on December 6, 1988, ended the supergroup's recording life, although former Byrd Roger McGuinn substituted for Orbison on the band's second release, confusingly titled *The Traveling Wilburys:Vol. 3*.

Nonetheless, the Wilburys sound became the blueprint for Petty's next release, 1989's aforementioned solo effort *Full Moon Fever*. Produced by Lynne and featuring the support of most of the Heartbreakers, Petty's solo debut became "[his] commercial pinnacle," climbing to No. 3 on the U.S. charts, going triple platinum and generating the hit

HANDLE WITH CARE—THE TRAVELING WILBURYS (1988)

Originally recorded as a joke for the "B" side of a George Harrison single, "Handle with Care" became such a hit that it spawned an entire album and, in the process, created one of rock 'n' roll's greatest supergroups, the Traveling Wilburys. In addition to Harrison, the Wilburys consisted of Jeff Lynne, Tom Petty, Bob Dylan, and Roy Orbison, and their first album, *Traveling Wilburys, Vol. 1*, immediately found a spot on *Rolling Stone Magazine*'s "Top 100 Albums of All Time" list. The video for "Handle with Care" befit the quintet and the old-fashioned, elemental style of rock it represents. Set in a recording studio, the video focuses on each of the band's members and on their collaborative performance, reminding viewers that, at its best, rock 'n' roll is all about the music and the artists who create it.

singles "I Won't Back Down," "Free Fallin'," and "Runnin' Down a Dream."[27] While all three singles contain strong rock 'n' roll components and memorable guitar riffs, it is perhaps "I Won't Back Down" that provides the most fitting description of Petty's attitude and career choices.

Following *Full Moon Fever*'s release, Petty seemed to gain renewed energy as he teamed up once again with the Heartbreakers for 1991's *Into the Great Wide Open*, "another highly melodic opus previewed by the impassioned 'Learning to Fly' single."[28] The 1990s saw Petty branch out in a variety of directions, switching record labels (to Warner Brothers), penning songs for Ed Burns's 1986 film *She's the One*, and recording another solo album. Throughout his entire career, highlighted by intriguing musical projects, pairings, and collaborations, Petty has remained true to his rock 'n' roll roots and to a sense of artistic and commercial integrity rarely seen with such consistency. In 2002, Tom Petty and the Heartbreakers were deservedly inducted into the Rock and Roll Hall of Fame. Their musical story lives on.

JOHN (COUGAR) MELLENCAMP

Name changes notwithstanding, John Mellencamp's (born October 7, 1951, in Seymour, Indiana) climb to rock stardom was a treacherous uphill battle. Beginning with his debut album, Mellencamp struggled to gain both recognition and respectability. The 1976 fledgling effort, *Chestnut Street Incident*, was credited to a Johnny Cougar. Unbeknownst to Mellencamp, his manager, MCA impresario Tony De Fries, had changed his name to something more catchy and marketable. No matter. The album's poor sales and mostly unoriginal compositions or covers of songs previously sung by the Doors, Roy Orbison, and Elvis Presley seemed to indicate that neither Johnny Cougar nor John Mellencamp had much of a career ahead of him. Yet, sixteen years later, "when many of the world's most prestigious recording artists gathered together at Madison Square Garden to pay tribute at Bob Dylan's 30th Anniversary Concert,"[29] it was Mellencamp who opened the show with a rousing cover of "Like a Rolling Stone."

Rock from America's heartland was led by John (Cougar) Mellencamp here in 1985. Courtesy of Photofest.

The success of John (Cougar) Mellencamp can be traced to his dogged determination to be taken seriously as an artist—and to do so on his own terms. And the transition from the cartoonish Johnny Cougar to the respectable John Mellencamp is an important lesson of how

> 1) far an artist will compromise himself to break into the music business; 2) [how] much manipulation of image a manager or record label will [exercise]; 3) [how] all the manipulation in the world can't help a flawed record, and finally, 4) [how] long it can take to repair a reputation once it becomes nearly irreparably damaged by all the above."[30]

For John Mellencamp, the story is as compelling professionally as it is important to the music development of the 1980s.

After the debacle of his debut album, Mellencamp signed a new deal with England's Riva Records label, which released his second effort, *A Biography*, in 1978. Though *A Biography* never saw an American release, two of its tracks could be found on 1979's self-titled American release *John Cougar*: "Taxi Dancer" and "I Need a Lover," the latter cracking the Top 30 for Mellencamp later that year. With his less-than-auspicious entrance into the rock world, Cougar Mellencamp was all but dismissed as a straight rock 'n' roller from the heartland, much in the tradition of Bob Seger or Bruce Springsteen. But within a year, Mellencamp's next album, *Nothin' Matters and What If It Did*, landed in the Top 40 and spawned two hits: "This Time" and "Ain't Even Done with the Night," proving the Indiana native was more than a one-hit wonder and an artist with far more creativity than a three-chord rock 'n' roller.

In 1982, still saddled with the "Cougar" moniker, Mellencamp finally managed to combine "hard-bitten authenticity with epic anthem-rock" (à la Tom Petty)[31] with the release of *American Fool*, which shot to No. 1 and stayed there for nine weeks. The album further boasted No. 1 hits "Hurt So Good" and "Hand to Hold on To," as well as the Top 5 Midwest paean to young love "Jack and Diane." ("Hurt So Good" and "Jack and Diane" held Top 5 slots simultaneously that year.) With his musical clout and viability no longer in question—*American Fool* was 1982's biggest-selling album—Mellencamp insisted that his next release, 1983's *Uh-Huh* include his real surname, Mellencamp, on its cover.

In addition to getting busy with the Indiana farmhouse he had converted to a recording studio, Mellencamp also embarked on new artistic ventures. *Scarecrow*, in 1985, a triple-platinum success, took on the plight of the American farmer and produced five hit singles, including the Top 10 triple-threat of "Lonely Ol' Night," "Small Town," and "R.O.C.K. in the U.S.A." Later that year, Mellencamp helped organize and participated in Farm Aid (created along with Willie Nelson and Neil Young). He later returned to perform in Farm Aids II and III in 1986 and 1987, respectively. Mellencamp continued to explore new musical territory and social commentary in 1987's *The Lonesome Jubilee*, which featured not only new band members but new instruments as well. Violins, accordions, pedal steel guitars, and dulcimers were featured on many of the tracks, giving it the most mature and sophisticated sound of any of its predecessors. Peaking at No. 7 on the album charts, *The Lonesome Jubilee* also generated three hit singles, "Check It Out," "Paper in Fire," and "Cherry Bomb," with the latter two cracking the Top 10. This "melancholy elegy for the forgotten middle America"[32] proved to be Mellencamp's most eloquent musical statement to date.

In 1989, his appeal crossed over to the British market with the release of *Big Daddy*, perhaps his most subtle and introspective effort "utilizing a distinctively more subdued musical approach, the rosy, melancholy backing echoed the more intensely personal lyrical fare."[33] *Big Daddy*'s critical success and musical growth pushed Mellencamp into a period of reevaluation and solitude. The end of the '80s and early '90s solicited little work from him, spurred partly by the untimely death of friend and keyboard player John Cascella at the age of thirty-five. Mellencamp himself was suffering from emotional and physical exhaustion, culminating in his own confrontation with mortality: a 1994 heart attack at the age of forty-three.

Since his fight to stardom in the 1980s, Mellencamp continues to explore new musical horizons and to champion various human rights causes. His 1993 effort *Human Wheels* is considered his finest album ever: "certainly the most forward-looking—perhaps due to the touch of co-producer Malcolm Burn."[34] Whatever the reason, Mellencamp's unique blend of folk-rock and hard-rock, his insights into the heart of Midwestern America, and his unfailing conviction to stand by his sense of artistic and personal integrity made him one of the most creative, marketable, and substantive artists of the 1980s—or any decade.

AND ALL THE REST

J. Geils Band

Many artists who had already established themselves as working-class, kick-ass, or "pub" rockers continued to rock or reemerged during the 1980s. One of the most popular touring acts of the 1970s, the J. Geils Band was, pure and simple, a bar band "churning out greasy covers of obscure R&B, doo wop and soul tunes, cutting them with [a] healthy dose of Stonesy swagger."[35] Lead singer Peter Wolf vamped the group right into the MTV era with what become their high water mark, 1981's *Centerfold*. Featuring the memorable video for the title track's hit single (which spent six weeks at No. 1), *Centerfold* also spawned the No. 4 follow-up single, "Freeze Frame." Unfortunately, *Centerfold*'s success could not sustain the ongoing volatility among band members, another carryover from the 1970s. When the band refused to record material written by Wolf, he left the group, which disbanded shortly after.

John Fogerty

If *Centerfold* produced popular radio and video hits, America's fascination with being in the middle of things continued with former Creedence Clearwater Revival (CCR) lead singer John Fogerty. A solo act since 1975, Fogerty (born May 28, 1945, in Berkeley, California) spent nine years in recording silence while working out leftover business problems with CCR before emerging with his megahit, 1985's *Centerfield*. The album's catchy title track, whose theme seemed as much a metaphor for Fogerty's career as it did for American pop culture, boosted the album to No. 1. Fogerty's 1986 follow-up effort *Eye of the Zombie* failed to capture America's sporting imagination, and Fogerty went into seclusion.[36]

Bob Seger

Another bar band perennial, Bob Seger (born May 6, 1945, in Dearborn, Michigan) continued to enjoy his status as one of America's top working-class rockers with 1982's *The Distance*. The album featured Seger's biggest hit single to date, "Shame on the Moon." As the 1980s moved on, so did many members of Seger's Silver Bullet Band—some over creative differences, others over his increased use of studio musicians during recording sessions. *The Distance* also signaled a shift in Seger's popularity, plateauing at a million copies sold, despite the hit "Shame on the Moon." Seger released only one other album, 1986's *Like a Rock*, and saw one more hit single, "Shakedown," from the *Beverly Hills Cop II* sound track.[37]

Dire Straits

Sometimes associated with post-punk rather than pub rock, Dire Straits became both puckish pranksters for the MTV era and international stars. After years of experimenting with various musical styles and consolidating a motley fan base, their 1985 summer release, *Brothers in Arms*, became their breakthrough album. Underscored by the groundbreaking animated video for the MTV-mocking single "Money for Nothing," the album spent nine weeks at No. 1 in the United States and sold over 9 million albums in England, making it the country's biggest seller of the decade. Led by guitar impresario and creative spirit Mark Knopfler (born August 12, 1949, in Glasgow, Scotland), Dire Straits also included Knopfler's kid brother David (born 1951) on guitar as well as John Illsley (born June 24, 1949, in Leicester, England) on bass and Pick Withers on drums. Singles like "Walk of Life" and "So Far Away" kept *Brothers in Arms* on the charts throughout 1986 while the band played over 200 concert dates for its promotion. After the tour, Dire Straits went on hiatus for several years as band members pursued solo projects. The band reconvened briefly in 1990 but never recaptured the enormous success of *Brothers in Arms*.[38]

Rolling Stones

Without doubt the quintessential bar band, the Rolling Stones continued to rock 'n' roll and brawl throughout the 1980s. Kicking off the decade with the No. 1 album *Tattoo You*, which touted the commercially and critically praised "Start Me Up" and "Waiting on a Friend," the Stones appeared to be on yet another rockin' roll. But *Tattoo You* proved to be the last time the Stones dominated the charts. Lead singer Mick Jagger (born July 26, 1943, in Dartford, Kent, England) and rhythm guitarist Keith Richards' (born December 18, 1943, in Dartford) ongoing personal feud had a negative impact on their music.[39] By the time the two patched up their differences in 1988, their subsequent release *Steel Wheels* (1989) seemed overshadowed by the album's supporting tour, which grossed over $140 million. Following the tour's live release *Flashpoint*, bassist Bill Wyman (born William Perks, October 24, 1936, in London) left the group, and the legacy of the Stones moved into its fourth decade.

Unlike other rock genres that often experienced brief, if lucrative, popularity, the ongoing themes of the working class permeated rock in fresh variations of traditional rock/blues styles throughout the 1980s. The emergence of Bruce Springsteen as a superstar, combined with the continued viability of legends like the Rolling Stones, reinforced the notion that in spite of (and because of) MTV rock music as an expression of social issues and class differences remained an integral part of the network's, life and artistic growth.

NOTES

1. Dave Marsh, *Glory Days: Bruce Springsteen in the 1980s* (New York: Pantheon, 1987), 30–31; also noted in Joe Stuessy and Scott Lipscomb, *Rock and Roll: Its History and Stylistic Development*, 4th ed. (Upper Saddle River, NJ: Prentice Hall, 2003), 372–374.

2. June Skinner Sawyers, ed., *Racing in the Street: The Bruce Springsteen Reader* (New York: Penguin Books, 2004), xix.

3. Ibid.

4. Ibid., xxi.

5. See, for example, http://home.att.net/~S1.schofield2/springsteein/life.html.

6. Springsteen's album *Nebraska* was based, in part, on stories and themes taken from the Starkweather-Fugate killing spree of the 1950s and taken from the 1973 cult film about these murders, *Badlands*, starring Martin Sheen and Sissy Spacek and directed by Terrance Malick.

7. Stuessy and Lipscomb, *Rock and Roll*, 374.

8. Don McLeese, "Abdicating the Rock 'n' Roll Pedestal: Bruce Springsteen Gets Down," *Chicago Reader*, October 24, 1980; included in Sawyers, *Racing*, 99–102.

9. Ibid., 99–100.

10. Ibid.

11. Ibid.

12. Sawyers, *Racing*, 1.

13. Andrew Greeley, "The Catholic Imagination of Bruce Springsteen," *America*, February 6, 1988; included in Sawyers, *Racing*, 151–165.

14. Ibid.

15. Ibid., 159.

16. Ibid.

17. The "Catholic Imagination" has been defined by Greeley and others as a Catholic perspective on the world that focuses on an individual's role within a community and often using sacramental or liturgical symbols to express secular or global ideas.

18. Neil Strauss, "The Springsteen Interview," *Guitar World*, October 1995; cited in Sawyers, *Racing*, 1.

19. Peter Knobler, with Greg Mitchell, "Who Is Bruce Springsteen and Why Are We Saying All These Wonderful Things about Him?" *Crawdaddy!* March 1973; included in Sawyers, *Racing*, 31–39.

20. Sawyers, *Racing*, introduction.

21. See, for example, "Inductees" at the Rock and Roll Hall of Fame and Museum Web site: http://www.rockhall.com.

22. Stuessey and Lipscomb, *Rock and Roll*, 374.

23. McLeese, from introduction to "Abdicating"; cited in Sawyers, *Racing*, 99.

24. See, for example, Dave DiMartino, "Tom Petty," included at the following Web site: http://music.yahoo.com; search Tom Petty.

25. Ibid.

26. Martin C. Strong, *The Great Rock Discography*, 6th ed. (Edinburgh, UK: Canongate Books, 2002), 799.

27. See, for example, Stephen Thomas Erlewine, "Tom Petty," *All Music Guide*, included at the following Web site: http://www.vh1.com/artist/az/pett_tom/bio.jhtml.

28. Strong, *Great Rock Discography*, 799.

29. Dave DiMartino, "John Mellencamp," included at the following Web site: http://music.yahoo.com; search John Mellencamp.

30. Ibid.

31. Strong, *Great Rock Discography*, 684.

32. See, for example, Stephen Thomas Erlewine, *All Music Guide*, included at the following Web site: http://www.vh1.com; search John Mellencamp.

33. Strong, *Great Rock Discography*, 684.

34. See, for example, Web site listed at note 32.

35. See, for example, Web sites like these that offer biographies of selected bands: http://www.mobstastic.com/artists_bio_ringtones_logos_picture_messages/j/jgiles/band.

36. See, for example, William Ruhlmann, "John Fogerty," *All Music Guide*, included at http://www.vh1.com; search John Fogerty.

37. See, for example, Stephen Thomas Erlewine, "Bob Seger," *All Music Guide*, included at http://www.vh1.com; search Bob Seger.

38. See, for example, Stephen Thomas Erlewine, "Dire Straits," *All Music Guide*, included at http://www.vh1.com; search Dire Straits.

39. See, for example, Stephen Thomas Erlewine, "The Rolling Stones," *All Music Guide*, included at http://www.vh1.com; search Rolling Stones; and Strong, *Great Rock Discography*, 881–883.

4

PUNK, UNDERGROUND, AND ALTERNATIVE ARTISTS

In September 1991, a little-known Seattle grunge band called Nirvana released an album called *Nevermind*, which, in a matter of weeks, pushed Michael Jackson's *Dangerous* from its No. 1 spot on *Billboard*'s album chart. For Jackson's fans, *Dangerous*' fairly quick exit from the top spot, even in light of its sales success, was one more indication that Jackson's staying power after *Thriller* remained elusive. For fans of underground, indie[1] artists, Nirvana's score at No. 1 was more than a success for the band: It was a victory for all those artists, musicians, and record producers who were not part of the industry's big corporate conglomerate.

Nirvana's remarkable achievement is really a culmination of work that began with other punk, underground, and alternative artists a decade earlier. An undeniably "seminal"[2] year for modern American underground rock, 1981 marked the formation of Sonic Youth and the release of first albums from the Replacements and the Minutemen. That same year, Henry Rollins joined Black Flag, Mission of Burma and Minor Threat released their first albums, and an obscure group from Atlanta called R.E.M. released the "epochal" debut single "Radio Free Europe"/"Sitting Still" on the equally obscure Hib-Tone Records.[3] It is perhaps with a touch of appropriate pop culture irony that Ronald Reagan, both the inspiration and evil enemy of what would become much of the underground movement's discontent, began his first term as president.

While some histories of America's indie rock movement during the 1980s exclude R.E.M. because of their eventual signing with Warner Brothers records in 1988, the Georgia-based group was as instrumental in shaping the sounds of underground rock as they were influential in defining subsequent alternative rock styles. R.E.M. became a powerful catalyst for the mainstreaming of many new independent and punk bands whose music often ran counter to more commercially successful artists. But even before R.E.M. opened more venues to less mainstream artists, another band from across the Atlantic set the standard for the indie post-punk movement that would define much of the 1980s American rock scene: U2.

U2

Perhaps the most exciting rock band to emerge from the 1980s, U2 stood tall in a decade that threatened to compromise rock 'n' roll's musical integrity to the whims of MTV. *Rolling Stone* editor John Swenson has described the hauntingly plaintive, intensely visceral sound of the band as "informed by the spirit of the punk revolution of the mid-1970s, but inspired by the heroic gestures of the 1960s who tried to make rock the medium for the self-realization and spiritual growth of a generation."[4] Swenson's description aptly summarizes a 1982 proclamation in the British publication *NME* (which hit American newsstands just before U2's first concert at New York City's The Ritz) about the band's music: "transcendentally eclectic, refreshingly realist, naively passionate."[5] Music critics called the *NME* assessment equivalent to Jon Landau's prediction about Bruce Springsteen more than a decade earlier: "I have seen rock and roll's future."[6] Clearly, U2's unique combination of innocence, passion, and eclecticism would become the defining words in mainstream rock for some time to come.

U2 is considered one of the greatest rock bands of the 1980s. Courtesy of Photofest.

Before their 1982 debut concert in the United States, U2 had won equally rave reviews in their native Ireland. In the fall of 1976, drummer Larry Mullen (born Lawrence Mullen, October 31, 1961) reportedly posted a note on the bulletin board at the Mount Temple Comprehensive School in Dublin, soliciting interested musicians to join a band. Four friends responded: Bono Vox (vocals; born Paul Hewson on May 10, 1960), "The Edge" (guitar and keyboards; born David Evans on August 8, 1961, in Barking, Essex), Dik Evans, and Adam Clayton (bass; born March 13, 1960, in Chinnor, England). Dik quickly left to join the Virgin Prunes, leaving Mullen and his three comrades to form a group called Feedback, which was later changed to the Hype before the quartet finally settled on U2.

In 1978, U2 won £500 at a St. Patrick's Day talent contest in Limerick, a victory Bono attributed to the band's "spark" that seemed to overshadow some of their competitors' technical superiority. One of the contest's judges was CBS representative Jackie Hayden, who was impressed enough with what he heard to arrange the band's first demo session. Again, U2's lack of experience was apparent, but their reputation for "intense and electrifying live shows" helped them win a dedicated fan base early on.[7]

Having secured Hayden's support, along with the attention of famed manager Paul McGuinness, the band signed a three-year deal with CBS Records and released its first record, a three-song album titled *U2-3*, in September 1979. A second single the following year, "Another Day," brought a new contract with Island Records, and an extensive tour followed. Still, with all its initial promise and contract viability, U2 seemed to make little impact cultivating an audience base or attracting much critical attention.

That lack of fame changed late in 1980 with the release of their first album, *Boy*, which received wide critical acclaim that suggested the band had begun to nurture an emerging cult status: "Strikingly original, the group carved out their own plot of fertile territory within the suffocatingly oversubscribed rock format, cultivating a watertight, propulsive minimalism to partner their politically direct lyrics."[8] Equally balanced by Bono's "crusading vocal theatres," The Edge's "serrated guitar cascades," and the driving rhythms of Clayton and Mullen, songs like "I Will Follow" became a "blueprint for the U2 formula."[9] And it was that formula—along with the band's focused commentary on global issues—that drew a fan base as devoted to their humanitarian causes as to their music.

U2's second album, the more mellow and spiritually centered *October*, released in the fall of 1981, failed to produce any Top 10 hits, so it appeared that the band surfaced out of nowhere early in 1983 when its single "New Year's Day" cracked the Top 10. A highly emotive tribute to Lech Walenska's Polish Solidarity Union, "New Year's Day" prepared the way for *War*, released the following month in February 1983. *War* entered the UK charts at No. 1 and became the band's first No. 1 album. Considered their first masterpiece, *War* established the band's mainstream status on both sides of the Atlantic, almost breaking the Top 10 album charts in the United States and praised for being consistently compelling, alternatively rousing and celebratory, meditative and evocative.[10]

In addition to garnering critical praise of and fan approval for its early efforts, U2 had also begun to gain a reputation as one of the most exciting and innovative live acts to emerge from the post-punk's musical quagmire. The band capitalized on its concert image by following up *October* with a live mini-album, *Under a Blood Red Sky*, which consisted of seven songs recorded while on tour. Besides the already praised "New Year's Day," *Under a Blood Red Sky* included the movingly intense anthem "Sunday Bloody Sunday," which, interpreted by many

SUNDAY BLOODY SUNDAY—U2 (1983)

Rock 'n' roll has often been linked to political issues or causes. In the aftermath of Vietnam, America's global awareness seemed to lay dormant. U2 jump-started that malaise through many of its music videos, perhaps most memorably in 1983's *Sunday Bloody Sunday*. The song, which opened their 1983 album *War* (considered by many to be the band's most focused album), pays tribute to "Bloody Sunday," a violent encounter between the British Army's First Parachute Regiment and a group of unarmed civilian demonstrators. The incident, which took place on January 30, 1972, in Bogside, Erry, Ireland, saw thirteen demonstrators killed and several others wounded. The march, which had begun as a protest against a recently passed British statute upholding "internment without trial," was dubbed "illegal" by the British government, and a subsequent trial of the British soldiers found them not guilty of shooting thirteen civilians. U2's undeniable connection to the English-Irish conflict gave them a powerfully haunting voice in the fight for global human rights and pushed MTV beyond its tendency toward vapid, meaningless video fodder. An early video foray for the Irish band, *Sunday Bloody Sunday* reminded audiences of how music and social issues are intrinsically linked, setting the stage for other, seriously minded videos by the group that would culminate in the group's landmark 1988 concert tour documentary *Rattle and Hum*.

as being a republican rebel song, was memorably declared otherwise by lead singer Bono when he introduced the song on the live track. Touring followed *Blood Red Sky*'s release, which also marked the end of an era for the band. *Under a Blood Red Sky* was the last record made before Brian Eno and Daniel Lanois were engaged to collaborate on future projects.[11]

Under a Blood Red Sky hinted at U2's potential power to energize a world audience with its sound and message. With that in mind and using Eno's creative guidance, the band moved in a different, more complex direction with its next release, 1984's exquisitely atmospheric album *The Unforgettable Fire*. Featuring only one anthem—the powerfully driven tribute to the late Dr. Martin Luther King Jr., "Pride (in the Name of Love)"—reminiscent of earlier work, *The Unforgettable Fire* solidified U2's commercial and creative maturity and provided fans with "a collection of more exploratory, occasionally near-ambient excursions, the highlight arguably being the stunning title track."[12] The subsequent promotional tour traveled to both Europe and America and produced yet another live mini-album, 1985's *Wide Awake in America*. By the spring of that year, John Swenson declared U2 was "the most exciting rock band to emerge in the 1980s."[13]

U2's commercial success, coupled with *Rolling Stone*'s somewhat dubious title, set the stage for two major events that would define the band's career and legacy. In summer 1985, U2 was among the artists asked to participate in the Live Aid concert. They accepted, playing a now-historic rendition of "Bad" (from *The Unforgettable Fire*) at London's Wembley Stadium, a performance that introduced them to the world. The "almost hymn-like incantation"[14] lasted almost twelve minutes, mostly because of Bono's stage antics that included dancing with members (read: girls) in the audience. The song's unplanned extended version forced concert producers to drop "Pride (in the Name of Love)," due to time constraints, a move that almost caused Bono to leave the band.

Although U2's popularity and acclaim had only grown since its first release, its celebrity did not come without a price. Some fans and critics viewed Bono's humanitarian activism as self-aggrandizing and arrogant. Bono reportedly became embarrassed that his own self-indulgence might have cost the band an opportunity to perform another song and feared he had ruined the band's set. After a friend told him that "Bad" had truly been a highlight of the show (second only in importance perhaps to Queen's performance, which helped rejuvenate their career and engender a new audience), Bono reconsidered his place in the band and stayed on. The following year, U2 performed at Self Aid, a benefit concert for Ireland's unemployed. U2 also joined the Conspiracy of Hope tour for Amnesty International.[15]

If their performance at Live Aid gave them an entrée to a global audience, U2's next project would secure their place on rock's world stage. In light of their near-cult-turned-mainstream status, it was understandable that anticipation for U2's next album was high. And the fever-pitch with which fans and critics waited was undeniably justified upon the release of 1987's iconic masterpiece, *The Joshua Tree*. This seventh album release was U2's best-selling album to date and became the fastest-selling album ever in the United Kingdom, additionally topping the album charts at No. 1 in twenty-two countries, producing the band's first American No. 1 single, the hauntingly cerebral "I Still Haven't Found What I'm Looking For."

The song, which perhaps best expresses the album's overall undertow of spiritual soul searching, "struck a chord in a decade . . . concerned with ruthless material gain," while other tracks, notably "With or Without You" and "Running to Stand Still," evoked an air of "soft-focus melancholy [that] further enhanced the album's almost tangible warmth."[16] Even more poignant were "Where the Streets Have No Name" and "In God's Country," both of whose sounds seemed to "emanate from a deep-seated yearning through which the shards of The Edge's guitar scream."[17] Like other such rock masterpieces, including *Blonde on Blonde*, *Sgt. Pepper's Lonely Hearts Club Band* or *Dark Side of the Moon*, *The Joshua Tree*'s brilliance "lies in its creative and subtle balance between panoramic euphoria and hushed reflection, between the personal and the political and between insinuation and crystal clarity."[18]

And like other rock albums elevated to the elite category "greatest of all time," *The Joshua Tree* elicited its share of detractors, most of whom lambasted U2 more for its perceived "pomposity and preaching self-importance" than for its musical shortcomings. Suddenly, Bono's stage persona was equated with that of a self-declared messiah, his increasingly lengthy political commentaries between songs a sign of his own distorted sense of self-worth.[19] Undaunted, Bono and Co. continued their 100-plus performance concert tour, selling out every show and cementing their reputation with what *Time* magazine appropriately terms "rock's hottest ticket."[20] Band members even played a bit with their audiences during the third leg of the tour, opening some of their own shows as a country-western band known as "The Dalton Brothers."

During the tour, director Phil Joanou was chosen to capture the band's tour, especially its perceptions of America. Filmed primarily in the West and Southwest (that is, Denver, Colorado, and Tempe, Arizona), *Rattle and Hum*, a half-live/half-studio produced rockumentary released in 1988, provided fans with a video remembrance of the group's tour (a sound-track companion was also available) and allowed the band one gentle chuckle at critics who had derided their political message. The album produced the band's first No. 1 single in the United Kingdom, the drivingly impassioned "Desire." Other highlights included a set with blues great B. B. King, who joined the boys in Australia, New Zealand, and Japan. Shot in dramatic black and white, *Rattle and Hum*, a self-effacing, sometimes self-deprecating behind-the-scenes and onstage view of the band, stripped away some of the undercurrent surrounding the band having a not-so-hidden political agenda while simultaneously maintaining the group's elusive ethereal image.

At the end of the 1980s, U2 played a series of four concerts at The Point Depot in Dublin, culminating the concert set with a New Year's Eve show that was broadcast worldwide. At that final concert, Bono announced that "it was time to go away and dream it all up again,"[21] causing some fans and critics to conclude that the band was breaking up. Not so. Following the four-concert stint in their native Ireland, U2 went underground, emerging three years later with a new album, 1991's *Achtung Baby*, and a new look, accessorized with wraparound sunglasses and skintight leather. With that, another exciting and creative musical phase for the band had begun.

R.E.M.

If U2 can be called the "last great rock band," then R.E.M. can certainly claim title to an encore. Easily the greatest American rock band of the '80s and '90s, R.E.M.'s musical roots reach as far back into the folk, blues, and jazz roots of an earlier time; their creative branches extended to spawn most of the indie punk and alternative bands that came after. From mythical stories of their humble beginnings touring the United States in a van to promote their first single "Radio Free Europe" to their now-legendary arena tours that play to thousands of fans in a single night, Athens, Georgia's most famous quartet has been credited with paving the way for artists as diverse as Nirvana and Hootie and the Blowfish. Members from both groups have acknowledged R.E.M.'s influence on their individual sounds as well as on the whole rock world.[22]

R.E.M.'s rise from an indie band heard mostly on college radio stations to mainstream popularity and commercial success is often looked to as a model for young rock bands to emulate. What separates R.E.M. from other artists who have followed similarly slow but steady paths to stardom is how the band has remained on the cutting edge of alternative rock without selling out its sound, artistry, or personal philosophy.[23] The band formed in 1980 when former high school marching band buddies Mike Mills (bassist; born December 17, 1958, in Orange County, California) and Bill Berry (drummer; born July 31, 1958, in Duluth, Minnesota) met shy record store clerk Peter Buck (guitarist; born December 6, 1956, in Oakland, California) and army brat Michael Stipe (singer and lyricist; born John Michael Stipe on January 4, 1960, in Decatur, Georgia). Lyricist Stipe and record-collector-turned-fledgling-guitarist Buck had already hooked up as collaborators, having met at Athens' Wuxtry record store.

In April 1980, the band formed to play a party for a mutual friend, rehearsing a number of garage, psychedelic bubblegum and punk covers in a converted Episcopal church. They played under the name Twisted Kites, but by the summer they had secured a new name, R.E.M., and found their first manager, Jefferson Holt. For the next year and a half, R.E.M. toured throughout the South, playing mostly garage and folk rock covers. It was during this time, as band members were learning how to play individually as well as together, that Buck began to develop his distinctive, arpeggiated jangle and Stipe ironed out his cryptic lyrics.[24] By July 1981, the band's first single, the Mitch Easter–produced "Radio Free Europe," was released on the independent Hib-Tone label, and the group embarked on a cross-country promotional tour. Back home in Athens, Georgia, college radio stations contributed to marketing the single with its constant airplay. What began as an experimental recording with only 1,000 initial presses, "Radio Free Europe" topped the year-end record polls, receiving honors from the *Village Voice* as "Best Independent Single."

With its "soaring melody and jangly guitar playing off Stipe's low-key vocals,"[25] "Radio Free Europe" established the band's unique sound and caught the attention of I.R.S. label boss Miles Copeland, who immediately signed the band to a contract. "Radio Free Europe" was followed by a string of other original songs that continued to touch a responsive chord among college listeners: 1982's album, *Chronic Town*, which included "Gardening at Night," "Wolves, Lower," and "Carnival of Sorts (Boxcars)," was received with much enthusiasm by both critics and audiences, solidifying the band's niche in defining the sound of American college radio in the early 1980s.

As the band matured musically, altering itself to stay fresh artistically while simultaneously keeping its fans guessing as to what their next release might sound like, R.E.M.'s audience grew beyond its initial college-age base and into the broader record-buying mainstream. Their first full-length album, 1983's momentous *Murmur*, "was a stunning debut which sharpened the hooks, honed the pealing guitar sound and generally engendered a compelling air of mystique. . . . [M]uch of this was [attributed] to Stipe's impenetrable lyrics and vague execution which enhanced rather than detracted from the melodic melancholy of [the] songs."[26] In addition to their breakthrough debut single "Radio Free Europe," *Murmur* included more somber, haunting pieces like "Moral Kiosk" and "Talk About the Passion."

Their sophomore effort, 1984's *Reckoning*, failed to solidify the inventiveness of *Murmur*; nonetheless, what *Reckoning* may have lacked in inventiveness was

Rock band R.E.M.'s 1983 debut album, *Murmur*, holds a deserved and respected slot among the decade's most influential albums. © S.I.N./Corbis.

 THE ONE I LOVE—R.E.M. (1987)

Leading the way for alternate and independent groups, R.E.M. became the first group to experience mainstream commercial success. Michael Stipe's mysteriously eccentric personality and random, sometimes incoherent enunciation of the song's lyrics gave this otherwise upbeat-sounding jangle rock hit an edge. The video, which begins with overhead shots of the group performing, quickly dissolves into the kind of visual, overlapping stream-of-conscious imagery that became synonymous with the band's musical and video style. Too, the ethereal quality that would later find its way into what is perhaps the group's most stunning and enigmatic video, *Losing My Religion* (1991), has its roots in *The One I Love*'s lyrical impressionism.

more than made up for in the band's increasingly sophisticated songwriting technique. *Reckoning*'s slot among the Top 30 albums that year indicated that R.E.M.'s sound had become slightly more accessible to American audiences. Still not content with critics' plaudits for poignant efforts like "(Don't Go Back To) Rockville" nor eager to settle into mainstream complacency, the band traveled to London in 1985 to record their next album with veteran folk producer Joe Boyd. An edgy, heavily atmospheric sound dominated the eleven-set album, *Fables of the Reconstruction*. Again, fans applauded the group's undeniably assured poise evident in its recordings and credited to its almost nonstop touring and crescendoing critical acclaim.

By 1987, R.E.M. seemed to find its focus with the release of *Document*, which produced the "sardonic, brooding"[27] single

"The One I Love," the band's first American Top 10 hit. Even Stipe's vocals seemed more comprehensible on this album, a shift from his previously notorious, dense, mysterial style. Thanks to the invited intervention of Don Gehman, who cleaned up the band's sound, Stipe's vocals were clearer; the band's musicianship more coherent.[28] The uncharted success of "The One I Love" opened up another door to the band: a new recording contract with Warner Brothers Records at the end of the year. With Warners Brothers, R.E.M. gained its first sense of mainstream popularity with its first release under the new contract, 1988's *Green*: "The unashamed jaunty pop of 'Stand' (1989) gave the band their biggest hit to date while 'Orange Crush' (1989) echoed the muted moodiness of 'The One I Love.'"[29] Other songs, like "World Leader Pretend" and "The Wrong Child," were proof of the band's skill in creating subtle, intelligent songs that were still "annoyingly hummable."[30]

R.E.M.'s irritatingly irresistible ability that brought underground music to a mainstream audience is unparalleled in the 1980s—or any other era's—rock 'n' roll history. The enormous undertaking of a world tour in the immediate aftermath of *Green*'s release stalled their next project until its 1991 release. Still, *Out of Time* would relinquish the group's most ethereally delirious single to date: the enigmatic, yet mournful polemic "Losing My Religion": With its plaintive mandolin refrain, the "starkly melancholy" single sent *Out of Time* into multimillion-selling status and paved the way for the group's unquestionable masterpiece: 1992's darker, harsher *Automatic for the People*.

R.E.M. signals the point when post-punk turned into alternative rock. While they never courted the widespread audience appeal that eventually followed them, the band nonetheless laid the groundwork for indie rock groups to gain mainstream success. R.E.M. was a key component in an important shift in American musical taste. Bands like REO Speedwagon, Journey, and Styx, which had dominated pop/rock audiences in the late 1970s and early 1980s, were replaced by a new generation of bands, led by R.E.M. and followed by groups as unique and diverse as Nirvana, Sonic Youth, the Gin Blossoms, the Replacements, and Pearl Jam.

THE REPLACEMENTS

Originally formed in 1979 in Minneapolis, Minnesota, when vocalist/songwriter Paul Westerberg (born December 31, 1960) joined a garage punk band led by guitarist brothers Bob (lead guitar; born December 17, 1959) and Tommy Stinson (bass; born October 6, 1966) and drummer Chris Mars (born April 26, 1961), the Impediments became the Replacements after being banned from a local club for disorderly behavior.

Notorious for their drunken, chaotic concert sets, the Replacements soon cultivated a considerable local following and landed a recording contract with the Minneapolis-based Twin/Tone label in 1981, a "local stalwart" among indie

The Replacements, shown here in 1989. Their hit album *Let It Be* became a mainstay among alternative fans. © Corbis.

producers.[31] Their first album, 1981's *Sorry Ma, Forgot to Take Out the Trash*, deemed a "sloppy, hardcore collection by several critics," generated little national attention, but the band's "raw-nerve attitude, cathartic melodies and twisted humor"[32] seemed to outshine their minimalist three-chord punk rock style. The following year, an album titled *Stink* "stepped on the gas and upped the nihilism"[33] with songs like "Gimme Noise" and "Fuck School."

The Replacements' third album *Hootenanny*, released in 1983, "used the[ir] hormonal energy to more satisfying and constructive ends"[34] and set the stage for what would become their breakthrough effort, 1984's *Let It Be*. *Let It Be* showed that the band had grown musically, establishing Westerberg as one of the top singer/songwriters of the genre, second only perhaps to Hüsker Dü, and the band as commercial enough to attract a major recording label contract. In 1985, the band released *Tim*, a big-budget production led by former Ramone Tommy Erdelyi, with a resulting set that tempered the band's ragged edges without compromising its signature razor-sharp hooks.

Both poised for and reluctant to venture into the arena of mainstream popularity, the Replacements accepted an invitation to perform on *Saturday Night Live*. Unfortunately, the band sabotaged itself by appearing drunk and disorderly on the show, culminating with Westerberg uttering "fuck" on the air. Subsequent concert appearances magnified this sloppy behavior, as band members were often too drunk to play or finish playing their songs. Even MTV could not salvage any respectability when their video for 1985's "Bastards of

Young" consisted of nothing but a stereo system playing the song. Any mass exposure MTV might have provided was cut off by the band's bold snubbing of the music video format.

Following the tour to promote *Tim*, guitarist Bob Stinson was fired from the band, a somewhat ironic move, as the reasons for his departure centered on his inability to control his drug and alcohol addictions. Stinson later died (February 18, 1995) from an apparent drug overdose. Robert "Slim" Dunlap (born August 14, 1951) came onboard as the band's new guitarist and promptly participated in another critical and fan favorite, 1987's *Please to Meet Me*. The album ventured farthest into the band's growing musical eclecticism, while Westerberg's songwriting prowess was at its demonstrated best with both "Skyway" and "Can't Hardly Wait," the "killer pop song he'd been threatening to pen since the band's inception."[35] Unfortunately, critic and fan appreciation did not translate into large record sales, and the Replacements were once again teetering on the verge of mainstream success.

The band's final bid for a mainstream audience came in 1989 with the release of *Don't Tell a Soul*. The album barely broke a Top 60 chart niche (peaking at No. 51 as a pop/rock album), even with an attempt to assuage the MTV audience with a viewer-friendly video for "I'll Be You." By 1990, the Replacements seemed to be more of a backup to Westerberg's solo work than a cohesive unit, and the band's impending breakup occurred quietly in the summer of 1991.

THE MINUTEMEN

Formed in San Pedro, California, in 1979 as the Reactionaries, singer/songwriter D. Boon (born Dennis Dale Boon on April 1, 1958) and bassist Mike Watt (born December 20, 1957, in Portsmouth, Virginia) wrote music to promote their own revolutionary left-wing politics. Joining Boon and Watt were drummer George Hurley (born September 4, 1958, in Brockton, Massachusetts) and front man/vocalist Martin Tamburovich. The Reactionaries' short life—seven months—ended when Boon and Watt decided that having a traditional front man was too "bourgeois" and "rock 'n' roll" and so created the Minutemen in 1980. Hurley left the band briefly to work with another group (Frank Tonche replaced him) but rejoined the newly reorganized Minutemen in time to record their first album.

Contrary to popular opinion, the Minutemen were not named for the length of their songs, many of which lasted less than a minute. The "eye-blink" brevity of their material came primarily from two sources: the English art-punks Wire and post-punk band Pop Group. Wire, whose debut album *Pink Flag* (1977) featured twenty-one songs in thirty-five minutes, suggested the idea that a band's musical shortcomings might be compensated by brief compositions that did not allow for much improvisation or elaboration. Said Watt,

"With the short rhythms, you'd be out faster; you wouldn't have to groove on it. We were trying to find our sound. . . . So we just said let's go the other way and just stop 'em up really big time."[36]

Reinforcing Wire's nontraditional influence was Pop Group, whose "caustic guitars and elemental dance rhythms supported explicit harangues about racial prejudice, repression and corporate greed in the most didactic terms."[37] Together, the iconoclasm of Wire and Pop Group taught Watt and Boon an important lesson: "You didn't have to have choruses, you didn't have to have lead guitar solos, you didn't have to have *anything*."[38] What the Minutemen did have, after just two concert gigs: the first, opening for Black Flag in March 1980; the second, a solo effort the following May.

On July 20, 1980, the Minutemen, now reunited with Hurley (Tonche left after punks spat on him during the band's second concert), recorded a seven-song album called *Paranoid Time* for SST Records. The six-minute, forty-one-second set established the group's left-wing political consciousness with Boon's defiant shout on "Paranoid Chant": "'I try to talk to girls and I keep thinking of World War III!'"[39] An eerily prophetic rant, given that Ronald Reagan would take office as president only six months later, both "Paranoid Chant" and *Paranoid Time* began to define the unique signature sound Boon and Watt desired: "Although the agile, skittering drums, trebly guitar, and twanky bass had nothing to do with hardcore punk, the relatively straight-up rhythms and hyper tempos did."[40]

Paranoid Time sold out its 300-copy pressing, prompting SST producer Greg Ginn to invite the trio to make another record. That fall, the Minutemen recorded *Punch Line*, a lightning-round set that boasted eighteen songs in fifteen minutes. Essentially funky in style and sound, "like a highly caffeinated Captain Beefheart running down James Brown tunes, the songs railed against injustice, materialism, ignorance and war; the lyrics could have been written by an idealistic young intern at *The Nation*."[41] *Punch Line* attracted attention from both critics and college radio stations, which began playing the album regularly. Soon the Minutemen were playing out of town, usually opening for fellow indie comrades like Hüsker Dü and Black Flag.

By 1982, the band had built a modest but loyal local following, often headlining small LA clubs on off nights. Early in February 1983, they recorded the first of two albums that year, *What Makes a Man Start Fires?* Later that year, *Buzz or Howl Under the Influence of Heat* was released. The formidable, if idiosyncratic, sound of their recordings was often unusually replicated in their live act:

> They were just one of the oddest bands you ever could have seen. . . .
> Here's these three goofy-looking guys playing in this totally stripped-down
> manner—these really, really short songs. So maybe at first you're not really
> sure if they're playing them well. . . . But after about four or five songs . . .
> you were like, "Yeah, this is cool! This is really neat! Why didn't I think of
> that?"[42]

What Makes a Man Start a Fire? became an important turning point for the Minutemen. The funky, offbeat quality of their abbreviated songs suddenly took on uniquely crisp tones, and the band's signature sound was firmly established by "little songs, high-end guitar, melodic bass, lots of toms."[43]

The Minutemen toured only once more with Black Flag before embarking on the project that would confirm their status among indie rock bands, 1984's *Double Nickels on the Dime*. A take-off on Pink Floyd's 1969 double-album *Ummagumma*, where each band member had his own featured side, *Double Nickels* gave each member of the trio an album side, with rejected cuts collected on the fourth, cleverly labeled "chaff." Boon and Watt reportedly wanted to eradicate all the bad music from their past, especially the jazz fusion of their youth, "[s]o they chased out those demons with ideas from folk music, specifically the realistic, autobiographical nature of it."[44] Perhaps, "Take 5, D" provides the ultimate, almost oddly moving expression of that purge.

Double Nickels caught the attention of Michael Stipe, who invited the Minutemen to tour with R.E.M. in 1985. The Minutemen, whose tour schedule after the release of *Double Nickels* was similar to their musical style—fifty-seven concerts in sixty-two days, accepted the offer, although the tour at times was problematic: the Minutemen's quirky personal style and political activism offstage as well as on sometimes created problems with the roadies and members of R.E.M. Still, touring with a former indie band with rising mainstream accessibility was promising to the California trio.

But that accessibility would never materialize. On December 23, 1985, a few days after returning from an overall triumphant tour with R.E.M., D. Boon was killed in an automobile accident. The Minutemen's final album recorded shortly before Boon's death, *3-Way Tie (For Last)*, was released in January 1986.

The Minutemen's lasting significance far outlived their short songs, which perhaps best expressed American culture during the 1980s. In *Our Band Could Be Your Life*, Michael Azerrad writes,

> America was in nothing if not a catatonic state through the Eighties, and the Minutemen's music—all angular stops and starts—was a metaphor for the kind of alertness required to fight back against the encroaching mediocrity. Short songs not only reflect a state of dissatisfaction and non-complacency; they simulate it.[45]

SONIC YOUTH

Considered one of the most unlikely success stories of American underground rock during the 1980s, Sonic Youth first formed when guitarists Thurston Moore (born July 25, 1958, in Coral Gables, Florida) and Lee

Sonic Youth led the way of the aggressive, post-punk, indie sound. Courtesy of Photofest.

Ranaldo (born February 3, 1956, in Glen Cove, New York) united with bassist Kim Gordon (born April 28, 1953, in Rochester, New York) in New York City early in 1981. Moore and Gordon had already named the group The Arcadians, after trying out several others, including Male Bonding (then a new phrase) and Red Milk. The Arcadians made their debut at the "Noise Festival" in the summer of 1981. After recruiting drummer Richard Edson and keyboardist Ann De Marinis, the newly reorganized quintet rechristened itself Sonic Youth, a move that better identified the sound that was more of what Moore wanted to do musically. That sound "took the heady, transcendent discord that [Glenn] Branca had extracted so purely from rock and injected it back into a gracing stew of the Stooges, MC$_5$, Television, noise-jazz guitarist Sonny Sharrock, Public image, LTd., and no wave."[46]

De Marinis made a quick exit from the band, and the remaining quartet recorded its first album, *Sonic Youth* (*live*), released with little fanfare by Neutral Records in 1982. But Moore wisely sent promotional kits to the U.S. press, so that whatever reviews the album received were uniformly favorable and ultimately encouraging to the then-obscure band.

Shortly after the album's release in the summer of 1982, Richard Edson left the group to pursue an acting career. He was replaced by Bob Bert, who traded Edson's "little syncopations for an explosive tribal stomp."[47] Perhaps less the hardcore style Moore had hoped for, Bert's percussive eruptions nonetheless merged seamlessly with Gordon's simple bass lines, giving the band's sound a much more visceral effect.

Sonic Youth's small hipster following was very supportive of Bert's rhythmic contribution to the band and turned out in force for his debut at CBGB's in the fall of 1982. Soon after Bert's debut, the band embarked on what would be two unsuccessful tours with the Swans, a "dire, noisy East Village band that was as brutally slow as it was slowly brutal."[48] Low audience turnouts, no pay, little food, and unpleasant weather and working conditions contributed to the tours' failing. As soon as the second tour was finished, Moore, angered and irritated by what he considered a lackluster rhythm performance, decided to fire Bert. Gordon inherited the unenviable task of giving Bert the bad news. New drummer Jim Sclavunos, a less inspired but technically better player than Bert, joined the group briefly, leaving after two months. Shortly thereafter, Bert rejoined the group.

The band's 1983 debut album *Confusion Is Sex* features both Bert and Sclavunos on drums. Like its debut album, *Confusion* received little notice, although, again, the few reviews given were favorable overall. In spite of a small but ardent following and low record sales or artistic recognition, Sonic Youth was creating a new language for the electric guitar: "Throughout the record, the guitars make uncannily unique sounds and chords, [at one point] resembl[ing] Balinese gamelan music."[49] Unlike collegial indie bands R.E.M. or Hüsker Dü, who relied heavily on fairly conventional pop song structures, Sonic Youth abandoned any of rock 'n' roll's identifiable musical traditions, opting instead to fuse the "freeform noise experimentalism of the Velvet Underground . . . [with] a performance-art aesthetic borrowed from the New York post-punk avant garde."[50] Sonic Youth's radical approach to music not only gave it its unique sound, but it allowed the band to explore a limitless number of creative, compositional options. Still, a contract with a major record label was not in the offing.

In 1985, after several failed attempts the previous year to land a deal with British indie label Doublevision, Sonic Youth released the album *Bad Moon Rising*, its first effort for Black First Records. Decidedly different from their previous recordings, *Bad Moon Rising* integrated their signature experimentations with dissonant, feedback-drenched resonance with a more straightforward pop song structure. The result provoked overwhelmingly strong reviews from the underground press that led to offers from several major record labels. But instead of pursuing a more mainstream label, Sonic Youth eventually signed with SST, already the musical home of fellow indie bands Hüsker Dü and Black Flag.

A trio of increasingly significant albums—and the steady support of permanent drummer Steve Shelley—followed: 1986's *EVOL*, which made the group mainstays on college radio; 1987's *Sister*, heavily praised by mainstream publications like *Rolling Stone*; and 1988's Ciccone Youth side-project, *The Whitey Album*, a tongue-in-cheek tribute to Madonna and other aspects of pop culture that widened their fan base. By 1988, Sonic Youth was poised and ready for its breakthrough effort, its masterpiece double-album released by Enigma Records titled *Daydream Nation*. Hailed as a tour de force, *Daydream Nation* yielded the college radio hit "Teenage Riot" and elicited high praise from both mainstream and indie critics. Unfortunately, Enigma Records, plagued by poor marketing and distribution, went bankrupt, often making the album difficult to find in record stores. Given its uneven history with various indie record companies, Sonic Youth's move to major-label DGC (David Geffen Company) in 1990 was not surprising.

Signing a contract with a major record label that gave them complete artistic control over their product established a precedent for Sonic Youth and alternative bands in general. Proving that it was possible to preserve indie integrity and credibility while working under the auspices of a mainstream record company, Sonic Youth released *Goo* in 1990. Boasting a more focused sound that did not compromise the group's "noise aesthetics," *Goo* spawned a college radio hit, "Dirty Boots," that cracked the Top 100 and generated an invitation from Neil Young to join him on his *Ragged Glory* tour. Though the group would never attract a mainstream rock audience, their inclusion on Young's tour brought them wider audience exposure and gave Young a natural niche with the alternative crowd.

In the 1990s and beyond, Sonic Youth continued to perform at such mainstream productions as Lollapalooza, as well as smaller, individual concert venues. However, the late 1980s releases of *EVOL*, *Sister*, and *Daydream Nation* continue to signal Sonic Youth's status as "touchstones for indie-rockers, who either replicated the noise or reinterpreted it in a more palatable setting."[51] As its career progressed, Sonic Youth's sound became more palatable, its free-form songs more like identifiable compositions, and its performance style more attuned with rock 'n' roll. But despite its roots in the anti-rock indie underground, Sonic Youth emerged as perhaps *the* indie archetype: "They made records that were not only artistically respected but popular; they helpfully provided at least the illusion that rock still had some fresh tricks up its sleeve."[52]

MISSION OF BURMA

The only sin that Mission of Burma might be legitimately accused of committing is bad timing. Far ahead of the indie movement that would support underground bands a decade later, Mission of Burma maintains a pivotal role in shaping the indie rock movement that flourished during the 1980s. Taking elements of free jazz, psychedelia, and experimental music and infusing them into anthemic punk rock, Mission of Burma produced, according to one critic, the kind of "avant-garde music you could shake your fist to,"[53] a concept not lost on subsequent efforts by R.E.M., Sonic Youth, or Hüsker Dü.

The band formed in 1979, when two Boston-based groups merged: Moving Parts guitarist Roger Miller and bassist Clint Conley joined with Molls' drummer

Peter Prescott to form Mission of Burma, adding Martin Swope to coordinate tape loops and live sound. The band's legendary determination to beat the odds and compete with more established mainstream rock bands would define the mantra of a generation of indie bands in the 1980s. Their 1980 debut underground anthem, "Academy Fight Song," recorded for the Ace of Hearts label, became the battle cry other indie bands would embrace. The single was followed with the 1981 album *Signals, Calls, and Marches*, a brightly intense expression of their eclectic musical brilliance.

Despite critical acclaim and limited fan support, Mission of Burma's promotion remained an uphill battle. For one thing, Boston—with all its traditional upscale education and money—seemed an unlikely place to launch a group whose sound was clearly unconventional and edgy. For another, Miller's growing battle with tinnitus threatened the group's existence. A second album, *Vs.* (1982), tried to capture the band's "rich overtones and deafening resonance,"[54] but it neither captured the group's primal live sound nor cultivated a broader audience.

Miller's volume-damaged ears forced the group to disband in 1983 after a tour that produced their last live album, *The Horrible Truth about Burma*. Two planned farewell concerts did not garner much public interest initially, until a Boston newscast closed a nightly show with a brief clip of the band and information about Miller's degenerative ear ailment. Filled mostly with curiosity seekers who did not understand nor appreciate the band's cutting-edge musical style, the concert halls seemed an unsentimental, anticlimactic end to a band whose music never really took off—until later.

In 1988, R.E.M. opened its *Green* tour with a cover of "Academy Fight Song," partly in tribute to Burma's enduring significance in the American indie rock movement and partly to promote a comprehensive set of reissues of the Burma catalogue. *Musician* magazine identified Roger Miller as one of the most important guitarists of the last forty years. In addition, Mission of Burma's practice of spotlighting local bands by including them as opening acts in their concerts is one that has continued in both the underground and mainstream rock arenas. So it is with a touch of wistfulness that Burma's band members recall their eclipsed moment in indie rock celebrity. A world-weary Clint Conley has said, in retrospect, that despite the band's cutting-edge style that included aggressively noisy guitars, pounding drums, and intense pop melodies: "I suppose it's an honor, in a way, to be ahead of your time. . . . But on the other hand, it would be nice to be right *with* your time."[55]

Mission of Burma helped lay the groundwork for the rise of indie rock bands in the 1980s and after, developing both the creative and commercial environments indie and alternative groups needed to survive. Molding such a foundation is easily identified by both fans and critics as the band's enduring legacy, but there is more to its musical worth than heralding the dawn of a new indie rock age. Mission of Burma's greatest accomplishment and enduring musical legacy is simple and perhaps best expressed by drummer Peter Prescott, "We never sucked."[56]

BLACK FLAG

An icon among the American indie rock movement, Henry Rollins of Black Flag performs in California in 1981. © Alison S. Braun/Corbis.

In an interview for *Flipside* fanzine, Black Flag founding guitarist Greg Ginn (born June 8, 1954, in Hermosa Beach, California) responded to a question about whether or not the band made a profit in this way, "We try to eat."[57] Having defined both the image and aesthetic for what later would be identified as the underground punk scene, Black Flag was the definitive Los Angeles–based hardcore punk band. In addition to founders Ginn and bassist Chuck Dukowski, Black Flag, which formed in 1977, originally included drummer Brian Migdol and lead singer Keith Morris. That same year, Ginn and Dukowski began the independent SST Records label, which would serve as host to other indie punk bands, including Sonic Youth, Minutemen, and Hüsker Dü.

In 1978, the band released its first album, *Nervous Breakdown*, on its own SST label (an earlier effort to release the single via the indie label Bomp fell through). By the time a second album, *Jealous Again*, was completed in 1980, Black Flag had endured several band member changes. Morris and Migdol had left the group and were replaced by Chavo Pederast and Robo, respectively. A promotional tour for the new album cultivated a small but dedicated fan base. Then Pederast left the group shortly after *Jealous*' release. Pederast's replacement, Dez Cadena, preferred to play guitar, so Henry Rollins, a Washington, D.C. fan who jumped onstage to sing with the band during a New York performance, became the group's new lead singer. Cadena's shift to guitar gave the group a heavier sound and eventually led to a contract with MCA-Unicorn Records.

In 1981, Black Flag recorded their debut album, *Damaged*, and delivered it to Unicorn, only to have the company refuse to release the record because executives did not approve of some of the tracks' outrageous content. Unfazed, Ginn released the album on his own SST label. The album went on to receive considerable critical praise, especially from the European and British press, who were fascinated by California's burgeoning hardcore punk scene. Unfortunately, early praise was cut short when Unicorn sued Black Flag and SST over the unlawful release of *Damaged* as soon as the album appeared in record stores in America. For the next two years, the band was not permitted to use its name or logo on any records.

During those two years, Black Flag toured extensively and secretly released a double-album retrospective appropriately titled *Everything Went Black* (1983) that made no mention of the group's name but did list band members' names on the front cover. Black Flag's battle with Unicorn Records ended in 1983 when the latter filed for bankruptcy, reinstating the band's rights to its name and logo. By that time, Cadena had left the band to form his own group. Ginn took over on both guitar and bass (listing the pseudonym Dale Nixon for his bass alter ego), and drummer Bill Stevenson took over for the departing Robo.

In what seemed like a determined effort to make up for lost time, Black Flag released three albums in 1984: *My War*, *Family Man*, and (with new bassist Kira Roessler) *Slip It In*. In addition, the group released a cassette-only version of their while-in-recording-exile concert tour, *Live '84*, as well as *The First Four Years* (1984) compilation album and the rerelease of *Everything Went Black*, this time with all credits properly restored.[58] But in spite of their prolific recording and touring, Black Flag did not seem to be cultivating a new or broader fan base. Constantly experimenting with the group's seminal two-third chord punk sound, Ginn insisted that he would give the audience what it *needed*, not necessarily what it wanted. That attitude, in the eyes of many fans and critics, became problematic from both an artistic and marketing point and would lead to the band's eventual breakup. In her review of *Live 84*, *Puncture* magazine critic Patty Stirling addressed both the merits of the album and the impact of Ginn's experimentation: " 'Black Flag's music creates itself best when the band has an audience, they unleash emotions at each other. It's violently sensual at best and irritatingly childish fighting at worst.' "[59] By the end of 1985, the band had released three more records, *Loose Nut*, *The Process of Weeding Out*, and *In My Head* and lost drummer Stevenson, who had left to join the group Octoberfaction. Anthony Martinez replaced Stevenson.

Early in 1986, another live album—*Who's Got the 10 ½?*—came out. After its release, Ginn broke up the band, concentrating instead on running SST Records and recording two albums with the even more avant-garde Gone. Henry Rollins formed his own group, the Rollins Band, and went on to become one of the most recognizable figures in alternative music during the 1990s. As for Ginn, he has remained adamant that ending Black Flag when he did was the right thing to do: "I was real proud of what Black Flag had done from the beginning to the end. . . . I have been fortunate enough to never have played a note of music that I didn't really want to play at the time, and I wasn't going to change that."[60] Instrumental in defining what hardcore punk—with its unabashed noise, experimental sounds, tough image, and controversial lyrics—would come to mean, Black Flag's story promoted the notion that in the world of indie rock sometimes jumping off a ledge and doing it is the best path to follow.

HÜSKER DÜ

Another Midwestern punk band hailing from the Minneapolis/St. Paul area, Hüsker Dü formed late in 1978 and consisted of vocalist/guitarist/ keyboard-percussionist Bob Mould (born October 12, 1961, in New York), guitarist/bassist Greg Norton (born March 13, 1959, in Rockford, Illinois), and drummer Grant Hart (born Grantzberg Vernon Hart on March 18, 1961). While critics generally typify the trio's early hardcore sound as "often tediously workman-like in its adherence to the steadfast confines of the genre,"[61] Hüsker Dü's melding of pop and punk has also been credited as having the most profound impact on modern alternative music.[62]

Hüsker Dü's quirky name and unique sound added to the evolution of American independent rock. Courtesy of Photofest.

The band's name is taken from a Norwegian board game and means "Do you remember?" in that language. Clearly, punk fans and musicians alike do remember the lasting significance Hüsker Dü has had on the indie genre. In addition to its unique combination of pop and punk and experimentation beyond the hardcore thrash sound, Hüsker Dü's strength lay in Mould and Hart's songwriting collaboration, which remained consistently complementary throughout the band's life.

Their first single, "Statues," was released on the tiny Reflex label in 1981. The following year, a debut live album *Land Speed Record*, was released on its own label, New Alliance Records, and is considered one of the "lousiest albums ever made" by some critics: "Without pause, the band pummels through song after similar song without break. No melodies come to the surface and the noise has neither dynamic nor ferocity; much like a vacuum cleaner, it merely whirrs endlessly."[63] Despite such negative reviews, the band pushed, releasing another album that same year, *In a Free Land*.

Poor reception to their early efforts, coupled with a small fan base and ineffective marketing, forced the band back to the Reflex label, which released their second album, *Everything Falls Apart*, in 1982. Reviews were moderately better, but it was not until 1983's *Metal Circus* that Hüsker Dü gained critical respectability and fan appreciation. *Metal Circus*, the band's first effort for new label SST, saw Mould and Hart's songwriting take shape. Within six months of *Circus*'s release, Hüsker Dü consolidated its previously fleeting glimmers of noise-pop greatness by "cross-fertilizing the . . . polarized worlds of psychedelia and hard-core punk"[64] in an electrifying single release, an energized cover of the Byrds' "Eight Miles High."

A follow-up double-concept album, *Zen Arcade* (1984) solidified Mould and Hart's songwriting abilities as sharp and focused, if still a bit uneven and sprawling. The album tells the tale of a young alienated punkster who leaves home only to discover life even more difficult on his own. A fourteen-minute closing song, which reveals the boy's entire journey has been a dream, completely broke all the rules of punk's hardcore reality base. In the words of some critics, "The concept falls apart somewhere in the middle, but the epic scope proved that indie-rock bands had options other than copying each other ad infinitum."[65]

Hüsker Dü made two more albums for SST in 1985, *New Day Rising* and *Flip Your Wig*, before violating yet another unspoken indie code and signing with a major record label, Warner Brothers. *Candy Apple Grey*, released in 1986, culminated the razor-sharp Mould-Hart collaboration, perfecting the melodic discord that defined them while simultaneously showcasing their dark introspection. Another double-album, 1987's *Warehouse: Songs and Stories* signaled the last release from Hüsker Dü, as Hart was fired from the band in 1988. Conflicting stories about his dismissal abound, from ego struggles with Mould to Hart's growing heroin addiction as possible causes. Both Mould and Hart worked as solo artists before working with new musicians: Mould created the similar-sounding band Sugar; Hart formed Nova Mob. Bassist Norton reportedly returned to Minnesota and began parallel careers as a real estate agent/chef. Like other indie rock meteors, Hüsker Dü's lightning-bolt arrival on the punk scene led to an equally fast exit, leaving fans and musicians a pop/punk fusion to explore and develop.

DEAD KENNEDYS

Merging revolutionary politics with hardcore punk, the Dead Kennedys became synonymous with hardcore bands. Part of their legacy—and their intention—was to make their politics as important as their music. Even though many non-punk fans know little about indie rock or its respective icons, the Dead Kennedys in name alone conjure up images of a hardcore rock scene. Perhaps it is because the Kennedy name itself represents so many images and conflicts of unfulfilled dreams in postmodern American culture. Perhaps, too, it is because the Dead Kennedys lived in an age when British punk and the Sex Pistols had already established the fiery rock politics of the genre.

Formed in San Francisco early in 1978, the Dead Kennedys included founder vocalist Jello Biafra (born Erick Boucher on June 17, 1958, in Boulder, Colorado), who recruited guitarist East Bay Ray (born Ray Glasser in Castro Valley, California) and bassist Klaus Flouride (born in Detroit, Michigan) through a magazine ad. Drummer Bruce Slesinger (aka Ted) joined soon after, and the band began playing locally throughout the Bay Area, occasionally venturing outside their local neighborhoods.

Within a year, the Dead Kennedys released their first single, "California Uber Alles," a scathing attack on then-California governor (and former Linda Rondstadt paramour) Jerry Brown. The band easily became identified as the most dangerous band in hardcore punk because of their (read: Biafra's) "raging, razor-sharp satire of America and everything it stood for."[66] In 1979, Biafra ran for mayor of San Francisco and came in fourth. The following year, a second satiric single, "Holiday in Cambodia," was released on Miles Copeland's Faulty label. "Holiday in Cambodia" remains "the Dead Kennedy's most realized moment, a dark, twisting diatribe on American middle-class liberal trends."[67] Later that year, the band released its first album, *Fresh Fruit for Rotting Vegetables*, which landed unexpectedly (since punk was considered dead in England) on Britain's Top 40 album chart.

Perennial favorites on the band's debut album include hardcore punk classics like "Let's Lynch the Landlord," "Drug Me," and "Kill the Poor," the latter of which became a hit single in Britain. Drummer Ted left the band shortly after *Fresh Fruit*'s release and was replaced by Darren H. Peligro (born in East St. Louis, Illinois). In 1981, Biafra and Co. formed their own label, Alternative Tentacles, and released their second album on that label, *In God We Trust, Inc.* A controversial single from the album, "Too Drunk to Fuck," managed to chart in the UK Top 40, in spite of the fact that the record had been banned in England, making it the first single using the word "fuck" to chart in the United Kingdom.

In 1982, the band released its second album on the Alternative Tentacles label, *Plastic Surgery Disasters*. After its release, band members—notably Flouride—embarked on various side projects. Biafra concentrated on building up the Alternative Tentacles label, which became a major force in American underground recording. By 1985, the band had regrouped and released its most controversial work to date, an album titled *Frankenchrist*. Included in the album packaging was a poster of Swiss artist H. R. Giger's *Lanscape #XX*, a graphic landscape of penises and anuses.

For the next two years, the Dead Kennedys and Alternative Tentacles were embattled in a bitter legal battle with the state of California, prosecuted for allegedly violating the state's newly revised antiobscenity laws that prohibited distributing pornography to minors. Other opposition came from the PMRC (Parents' Music Resource Center), who worked to ban adult content in music from open marketing and distribution. Biafra emerged as an articulate advocate for free speech and one of the most intelligently vocal opponents of the

PMRC. In the summer of 1987, the case against the Dead Kennedys ended with a hung jury and was subsequently dismissed.[68]

Nonetheless, the cost of the trial had dire consequences for the band. Their final album, the aptly titled *Bedtime for Democracy*, was released just before the trial began and proved to be their poignant finale. The Dead Kennedys broke up almost immediately after the trial ended, releasing a posthumous compilation, *Give Me Convenience or Give Me Death*, in 1987. Biafra embarked on a solo career, recording both musical and spoken-word projects over the next two decades.

OTHER INDIE BANDS OF THE 1980s

If there is a legacy to the Dead Kennedys story, it is one that makes an appropriate bookend to this chapter. With the possible exception of R.E.M., the Dead Kennedys are perhaps the only other indie band with name recognition outside their immediate fan base. Most indie rock bands, whether artistically motivated like Sonic Youth or politically challenged like Hüsker Dü, were confined by social mores or marketing restraints. An example of the latter, sometimes called the "textbook" cult band of the 1980s, was the Violent Femmes, who perhaps best captured the raw and jittery essence of cult punk but found little commercial success. The Milwaukee-based trio, whose name comes, in part, from a local slang word for "wimps," formed in the early 1980s after being discovered by the Pretenders' James Honeyman-Scott. Violent Femmes consisted of lead singer/guitarist Gordon Gano, bassist Brian Ritchie (who is credited with giving the band its paradoxical name), and percussionist Victor DeLorenzo. The band's self-titled 1983 debut album, a "melodic folk-punk collection which struck an obvious chord with young listeners,"[69] never charted a hit but has remained a rite-of-passage experience for three generations of teenagers. In true indie style, the album went platinum a decade after it was released.[70]

Tales like these of "art for art's sake" musicians parallel biographies of pre-indie movement artists from the 1970s, including Tom Waits (born Thomas Alan Waits; December 7, 1949, in Pomona, California), whose "downtrodden Jack Kerouac–meets–Charles Bukowski persona"[71] made popular a kind of retro paean to an earlier generation and served as an early role model for artists like Bruce Springsteen. Waits, whose raspy voice captured with dissonant

 WHIP IT—DEVO (1980)

Fans of this 1970s cult group (formed in 1972 at Ohio's Kent State University) thought this early contribution to MTV was totally cool. Outfitted in oddly retro clothes complete with red flowerpot hats, the band appears at a dude ranch, whipping the clothes off beautiful women. Some feminists were outraged; most viewers were mildly amused by Devo's foray into video with this quirky, sexual parody. Today the film's kitschy imagery holds up, even if the music has gone the way of Pringles commercials.

elegance the desperation of society's lowlifes, had already won critical acclaim (and a cult audience) for albums like *The Heart of Saturday Night* (1974), *Nighthawks at the Diner* (1975), and *Blue Valentine* (1978). By the 1980s, Waits' experimentation continued with projects like *Swordfishtrombones* (1983), "a surrealistic cut up of mutant jazz, skewed rhythms and wildly inspired lyrics,"[72] and culminated in what might be the apex of his eccentricity, 1985's *Rain Dogs*. Indie artists like Waits, Violent Femmes, and others were usually less interested in chart success than they were in finding new creative outlets; thus, they often moved from project to project without growing a large fan base.

U2's rise from punk to post-punk celebrity gave the indie movement of the 1980s the impetus to exist. R.E.M. gave underground music the hope of mainstream acceptability without losing its avant-garde core. The Dead Kennedys remind us that even the most articulate cutting-edge artists can be cut down by societal perceptions that threaten the very heart of our democratic system.

The indie underground movement of the 1980s paved the way for the grunge and alternative movements that would help define the 1990s rock scene in both musical experimentation and lyric content. So it is appropriate and fitting that Nirvana's *Nevermind* topped Michael Jackson's *Dangerous* in 1991. A decade after R.E.M.'s first single release and the quiet emergence of Sonic Youth, Hüsker Dü, Black Flag, the Replacements, Mission of Burma, and the Minutemen, rock music had surreptitiously moved to a new era, one that would invite alternative music to cultivate a larger audience and redefine rock 'n' roll in the process.

NOTES

1. "Indie" bands refer to those artists whose musical style and experimentation went outside the conventional pop/rock mainstream, often recording for smaller recording labels and garnering a narrower, often college-aged fan base.

2. Michael Azerrad, *Our Band Could Be Your Life: Scenes from the American Indie Underground 1981–1991* (Boston: Little, Brown, 2001), 3–4.

3. Ibid.

4. John Swenson, "The Last Great Rock Band," in *The U2 Reader: A Quarter Century of Commentary, Criticism, and Reviews*, compiled and edited by Hank Bordowitz (Milwaukee, WI: Hal Leonard, 2003), xvii.

5. Bordowitz, *U2 Reader*, xv.

6. Ibid.

7. See, for example, the following Web site: http://www.threechordsandthetruth.net.

8. Martin C. Strong, *The Great Rock Discography*, 6th ed. (Edinburgh, UK: Canongate Books, 2002), 1093.

9. Ibid.

10. See, for example, Web site listed in note 7; and ibid., 1093.

11. See, for example, "three chords" Web site listed in note 7.

12. Strong, *Great Rock Discography*, 1093.

13. John Swenson, "Foreword: The Last Great Rock Band," in *The U2 Reader: A Quarter Century of Commentary, Criticism, and Reviews*, edited by Hank Borowitz (Millwaukee, WI: Hal Leonard, 2003), xvii.

14. Strong, *Great Rock Discography*, 1093.

15. See, for example, "three chords" Web site listed in note 7.

16. Strong, *Great Rock Discography*, 1093–1094.

17. Ibid., 1094.

18. Ibid.

19. Ibid.

20. *Rolling Stone* (April 1985); included at the "three chords" Web site in note 7.

21. See, for example, "three chords" Web site listed in note 7.

22. See, for example, Craig Rosen, "R.E.M.," included at this Web site: http://music.yahoo.com; search R.E.M.

23. Ibid.

24. See, for example, Stephen Thomas Erlewine, "R.E.M.," *All Music Guide*, included at this Web site: http://www.vh1.com; search R.E.M.

25. Strong, *Great Rock Discography*, 868.

26. Ibid.

27. Ibid.

28. See, for example, Craig Rosen at Web site listed in note 7.

29. Strong, *Great Rock Discography*, 868.

30. Ibid.

31. See, for example, Stephen Thomas Erlewine, "The Replacements," included at this Web site: http://www.mtv.com; search The Replacements; Strong, *Great Rock Discography*, 871.

32. Strong, *Great Rock Discography*, 871.

33. Ibid.

34. Ibid.

35. Ibid.

36. Azerrad, *Our Band*, 67.

37. Ibid.

38. Ibid.

39. Ibid., 68.

40. Ibid.

41. Ibid.

42. Ibid., 70–71.

43. Ibid., 71.

44. Ibid., 82.

45. Ibid., 71.

46. Ibid., 236.

47. Ibid., 239.

48. Ibid., 240.

49. Ibid., 242–243.

50. See, for example, Stephen Thomas Erlewine, "Sonic Youth," *All Music Guide*, included at this Web site: http://www.mtv.com; search Sonic Youth.

51. Ibid.

52. Azerrad, *Our Band*, 233.

53. Ibid., 95.

54. See, for example, Tristram Lozaw, "Mission of Burma," included: http://music.yahoo.com.

55. Azerrad, *Our Band*, 118.

56. Ibid.

57. Ibid., 13.

58. See, for example, Stephen Thomas Erlewine, "Black Flag," *All Music Guide*, included at this Web site: http://www.mtv.com; search Black Flag.

59. Azerrad, *Our Band*, 45.

60. Ibid., 60.

61. Strong, *Great Rock Discography*, 495.

62. "Hüsker Dü," in *The Encyclopedia of Popular Music*, compiled and edited by Colin Larkin (London: Muze, 1998).

63. See, for example, Rob O'Connor, "Hüsker Dü," included at: http://music.yahoo.com; search Hüsker Dü.

64. Strong, *Great Rock Discography*, 495.

65. O'Connor; see Web site listed in note 63.

66. Strong, *Great Rock Discography*, 268.

67. Ibid.

68. See, for example, Stephen Thomas Erlewine, "Dead Kennedys," *All Music Guide*, included at http://www.vh1.com; search Dead Kennedys.

69. See, for example, Jason Ankeny, "Violent Femmes," *All Music Guide*, included at http://www.vh1.com; search Violent Femmes.

70. Ibid.

71. Strong, *Great Rock Discography*, 1111.

72. Ibid.

5

A NEW PHASE FOR NEW WAVE ARTISTS

If punk, post-punk, and independent artists attracted fans primarily from college campuses and the arty worlds of New York and Los Angeles, another, less musically defiant class of musicians began to tap into that same audience, becoming known as "new wave." Where punk rock took pride in the fact that it garnered low record sales and elicited little American radio play, new wave artists often bridged the gap between the harder, less accessible punk sound and more commercial pop artists. By the mid-1980s, the inherently self-destructive punk sound had been sublimated by new wave, although punk, in its raw, seminal form, would go on to be the most direct musical influence on the grunge and alternative movements that dominated the 1990s.

In the early 1980s, many bands, notably the Cars or the Go-Go's, that were identified as new wave were really pop bands dressed up in new wave regalia;[1] other artists including the Police and Elvis Costello, turned their punk-pop-new wave fusion into long and distinguished careers. Still others, like pop favorite Billy Joel, morphed onto the new wave scene, infusing typically trite pop melodies with jazz, funk, or techno riffs to breathe life, if not substance, into less-than-critically-acclaimed careers. This chapter will focus on those artists who brought new wave into the 1980s by defining and perpetuating its movement with a successful and creative integration of punk's social defiance with pop's melodic availability.

THE POLICE

If leaving the stage before an encore with an SRO audience begging for more is a formula for success, then the Police definitely balanced its musical

The Police, a post-punk, new wave group, fused jazz and reggae with definitive rock rhythms and haunting lyrics. Courtesy of Photofest.

equation. Epitomizing the "veni, vidi, vici" of rock 'n' roll, the Police's less-than-a-decade life span does not compare with the lasting impact the band has had on rock music. Combining punk with jazz and reggae, the Police were the most popular rock band in the world before U2 ascended to that throne and were no less influential than their Irish folk-punk counterparts or even America's R.E.M. Unlike U2 or R.E.M. who learned much of their musical skill along on their way to mainstream success, the Police began with three technically proficient and superbly talented musicians.

The Police were formed early in 1977 by drummer Stewart Copeland (born June 19, 1952, in Alexandria, Egypt) and vocalist/bassist Sting (born Gordon Sumner, October 2, 1951, in Wallsend, England). After releasing their debut single, the punk-based "Fall Out" on the indie label Illegal (owned by Stewart's brother Miles), original guitarist Henry Padovani left the band and was replaced by guitarist Andy Summers (born Andrew Somers, December 31, 1942, in Blackpool, England). The newly reformed trio was clearly overqualified musically for the ethos of punk that espoused the notion than anyone who can pick up an instrument can play it. Copeland had drummed for many progressive rock bands and could play polyrhythms effortlessly. Sting had played bass for the jazz group Last Exit and, with his high-reaching vocals, was capable of constructing infectiously memorable pop songs. And Summers, who had already participated in several studio recordings, "had a precise guitar attack that created dense, interlocking waves of sounds and effects."[2] Despite their anti-punk expertise, the Police succeeded by "infusing their complex reggae-tinged pop/rock with insidiously catchy hooks and radio friendly melodies while keeping most of their songs down to an acceptable post-hipp[ie] playing time."[3] They also adopted a post-punk look—bleached blonde hair—that added to their Euro-hip image.

In 1978, the Police signed a contract with A&M Records and released its debut single, "Roxanne." The single, a thinly disguised punk-hymn narrative about a prostitute, failed to chart but landed at No. 12 when it was released in the United Kingdom the following year. Their follow-up single "Can't Stand

Losing You" was another minor success, as was their debut album, *Outlandos d'Amour* (1978). Still, critics were impressed with the band's effort, "an impressive collection with a strong rhythmic thrust and a few token nods to punk."[4] On the strength of such critical praise, A&M rereleased the album the following year, and in the spring of 1979, *Outlandos* reached the UK Top 10 and the U.S. Top 30.

The Police captured the No. 1 single spot for the first time in the summer of 1979 with "Message in a Bottle," followed quickly by a second album that same year, *Regatta de Blanc* (aka *White Reggae*). *Regatta* also peaked at No. 1 on the album charts, making the band two for two in releases that year. With their masterful understanding of dynamics and appealing use of time changes, the band continued to chart new musical territory. At the dawn of the 1980s, the Police seemed poised to break through to a worldwide audience, including the desirable American market.

That breakthrough came in the form of *Zenyatta Mondatta*, their 1980 album release that included the "lyrically rhythmic genius" of "De Do Do Do, De Da Da Da" and the eerie eroticism of "Don't Stand So Close to Me." A season of global touring followed, including gigs at the likes of Madison Square Garden. By the 1981 release of *Ghost in the Machine*, the Police were a world-class act that consistently delivered its musical goods with instrumentally diverse compositions like the "exotically effervescent 'Every Little Thing She Does Is Magic.'"[5] Lyrics were also taking on new depth, as evidenced on "Invisible Sun" wherein Sting commented on the tension in strife-torn Northern Ireland. The fact that Sting's songs dominated the group's recordings was both a blessing and a curse, as tensions among band members were beginning to surface.

Following the success of *Ghost in the Machine* that included garnering British and American recording industry awards (and three Grammys), the Police took a break in 1982, returning the following year to release what would be their undisputed masterpiece and final album, *Synchronicity*. The album's summer release sparked huge record sales, with the album entering both the UK and U.S. charts at No. 1 (and staying at its U.S. niche for eight weeks). With *Synchronicity*, the "brooding atmospherics" of the seductively perverse "Every Breath You Take" (a global No. 1 hit), the "pummeling" "Synchronicity II," and the album's melancholy centerpiece single, "Wrapped Around Your Finger" illustrated "the band's ability to craft a consistently satisfying but varied musical palate."[6]

 EVERY BREATH YOU TAKE—THE POLICE (1983)

Was it erotic voyeurism or creepy stalkerism? The song's moody chords overlaid with Sting's alternately menacing and plaintive vocals create an intriguingly sexual oxymoron, one that is heightened by the video's stark black-and-white imagery. Instead of the sometimes jarringly in-your-face visual bytes found in many early music videos, *Every Breath You Take* used floating images that flowed with Sting's voice but seemed, at times, oddly out of sync with the persistent rhythms that subliminally intensify as the song progresses. The Police's new wave jazz-rock fusion was never more enticing, sexy, or captivating, as this video demonstrates.

The band followed *Synchronicity*'s release and multiplatinum success with a huge international tour that set standards and records for all subsequent tours of the decade. When the tour was completed, band members announced their decision to go on sabbatical to pursue outside interests. Internal tensions had reached an almost unbearable level, and the trio needed a break. They never returned from their self-imposed sabbatical. They reunited briefly in 1986 for an Amnesty International concert, but any hopes of a sustained reunion, as with several sessions to record tracks for a Greatest Hits album, failed. In 1986, *Every Breath You Take: The Singles* was released and quickly reached No. 1 on the UK and U.S. album charts. The Police quietly disbanded after the compilation's release.

Sting, who had already appeared in feature films, continued to explore more adventurous musical paths, releasing a solo jazz–based effort, *Dream of the Blue Turtles*, in 1985. Picking up most of the Police's fan base, Sting went on to become an international superstar. Copeland and Summers, both respected musicians, dabbled in various individual projects but never cultivated a following like Sting's and generally faded from the rock spotlight.[7] In 2003, the Police were inducted into the Rock and Roll Hall of Fame. The sound the Police had chased and caught, "an alluring mix of new wave and reggae, with touches of Lou Reed . . . Dylan . . . and even Bo Diddley,"[8] appealed to fans and critics alike, creating an edgy brilliance that shone long after the group's members had parted. Their success story, perhaps much like new wave's unique fusion of punk's defiance and pop's accessibility, remains one of rock's most poignant tales of a kind of flashing musical brilliance that continues to shine amid rock 'n' roll's diverse legacy.

ELVIS COSTELLO

A self-professed member of the Beatles fan club and the son of a jazz bandleader who grew up listening to the jazz greats of his father's era as well as the artists of his own time, Elvis Costello (born Declan McManus, August 25, 1954, in Liverpool, England) created a new wave fusion that combined jazz, Motown, and the late 1960s British Invasion sound of The Who and The Kinks. A computer operator during the day who peddled his musical wares in London clubs during the mid-1970s (Costello's trademark glasses were a result of the eye strain he suffered at the computer), McManus became another kind of pop wave fusion in 1974 when he became Elvis Costello, a name created both as a challenge to rock royalty and in honor of his mother's maiden name.

Signing a contract with the newly formed Stiff Records label, Costello made his first album in twenty-four hours, backed by a local country and western bar band called Clover, whose leader was a then-unknown Huey Lewis.[9] When two single releases, "Less Than Zero" and "Alison," failed to chart, Costello took desperate action, playing outside the London Hilton while a CBS international records conference took place inside. In spite of being arrested for his antics, Costello landed a contract with Columbia records, who released his first album *My Aim Is True* in July 1977. Hailed as one of rock's finest debut albums, *My Aim Is True* was voted "Album of the Year" by *Rolling Stone* magazine's annual poll and climbed to No. 14 on the British charts. A single, "Watching the Detectives," reached No. 15 in the United Kingdom.

A superficial listening of Costello's first effort might result in the assumption that his "bristling cynicism and anger" were clearly connected to the punk explosion. In reality, Costello's only link to punk may be the uninhibited passion with which he writes and performs music, borrowing liberally from country, Tin Pan Alley pop, and reggae as well as ripping through the back pages of early rock 'n' roll.[10]

Costello continued to connect with punk-obsessed critics and fans with his second album, a rawer, harder-rock-sounding collection titled *This Year's Model*, released in 1978 with his newly formed group The Attractions. *This Year's Model* reached No. 4 in Britain and cracked the U.S. Top 40, peaking at No. 30. Three more albums—*Armed Forces* (originally titled "Emotional Fascism"), which cracked the U.S. Top 10 in 1979, the soul-influenced Motown-sounding *Get Happy!!* in 1980, and the more subdued *Trust* in 1981—came out before Costello released his sixth, and easily most ambitious, project, *Imperial Bedroom*, in 1982.

Often cited as Costello's best album, *Imperial Bedroom* was produced by former Beatles' engineer Geoff Emerick. Not surprisingly, the album has been compared to masterpieces from artists ranging from the Beatles to the Beach Boys and produced several memorable tracks, including "Man out of Time" and "The Long Honeymoon." Despite its critical acclaim, *Imperial Bedroom* failed to produce any Top 40 singles, and Costello responded with the much more pop-based *Punch the Clock* in 1983, which climbed to No. 3 in the United Kingdom (No. 24 in America) and boasted the single "Everyday I Write the Book," which cracked the Top 40 in the United States. Hoping to repeat his budding commercial success, Costello released *Goodbye Cruel World* the following year, which proved to be his biggest critical and commercial failure, threatening to end his heretofore undefinably eccentric career.

Costello spent the next years redefining his musical style and reinventing his own musical image. A collaboration with singer/songwriter T-Bone Burnett produced the 1985 single "The People's Limosine," as well as a separate album, *Rum Sodomy and the Lash*, by punk-folkies The Pogues. His next effort, 1986's *King of America*, recorded without The Attractions, was mostly a country-folk album that received more positive reviews than any of his releases since *Imperial Bedroom* and suggested that Costello was moving toward a more stripped-down musical style.

But ever the creative enigma, Costello instead negotiated a new contract with Warner Brothers records in 1987 and embarked on a songwriting collaboration with perennial Beatle Paul McCartney. Two years later in 1989, Costello released *Spike*, perhaps the most diverse collection he had ever recorded. *Spike* featured his collaborations with McCartney, including the single "Veronica," which became his biggest American hit, peaking at No. 19. In 1991, he followed *Spike* with another, equally diverse but substantially darker collection called *Mighty Like a Rose*.

Though stylish eclecticism has clearly defined Costello's long-established recording career, he has equally distinguished himself with substantive, challenging lyrics and richly diverse music. Easily one of the most versatile and talented artists since the early days of rock 'n' roll, Elvis Costello remains one of the most innovative and influential artists in rock music and, arguably, one of the best songwriters since Bob Dylan.[11]

TALKING HEADS

Their first gig was supporting the Ramones at New York City's famous CBGB's club in mid-1975. Famed recording impresario Seymour Stein spotted them soon after and promptly signed them to a contract with Sire Records. An intriguing, if not infectious, mix of "nervous energy, detached emotionalism and subdued minimalism,"[12] Talking Heads' new wave funk immediately caught on with New York's art-punk scene. Led by the eccentric Scotsman David Byrne (vocals, guitar; born May 14, 1952, in Dumbarton, Scotland) and supported by original American members Tina Weymouth (bass, vocals; born November 22, 1950, in Coronado, California) and Chris Frantz (drums; born Charton Christopher Frantz on May 8, 1951, in Fort Campbell, Kentucky), the trio became a quartet soon after their first recording with the addition of keyboardist Jerry Harrison (born February 21, 1949, in Milwaukee). Combining extensive, and sometimes expensive, acoustic and electronic instruments with carefully constructed arty pop songs and Byrne's odd post–Buddy Holly geekiness and jerky vocals, Talking Heads established themselves as one of the most subversively intellectual anti-rock establishment bands, taking their post-punk foundation to new heights that matched—and then went beyond—early new wave styles.

Relying as heavily on African-inspired rhythms as the Police did on jazz-inspired reggae, Talking Heads created a credible funk sound that manifested itself most strongly in their 1980's release *Remain in Light*. Three years—and several concert tours—later, Talking Heads went back to the studio and returned with another innovative masterpiece, *Speaking in Tongues*, which juxtaposed the "trace-rock" single "Slippery People" against the more jittery "Burning Down the House," with the latter cracking the United Kingdom's Top 10.[13]

Back on tour, equally eccentric filmmaker Jonathan Demme directed their live-concert performance for the movie *Stop Making Sense* (1984), which contained "some of the most innovative live footage ever committed to celluloid."[14] The band's biggest chart—and video—hit "Road to Nowhere" followed, as did its parent album, 1985's *Little Creatures*, the band's most straightforward pop album. Although Talking Heads' audience and reputation continued to grow, band members became involved in other, solo projects, and *Little Creatures* became their last original group effort. Byrne's fascination with world music continued, and he (in collaboration with Ryuichi Sakamoto and Cong Su) won an Academy Award for Best Original Score in 1988 for Bernardo Bertolucci's epic *The Last Emperor.*

THE HUMAN LEAGUE

Riding into new wave (from a techno-indie perspective) on a crest of synthesizers and electronic rhythms, The Human League's merger of state-of-the-art technology with infectious melodies proved enormously influential on countless 1980s video and pop artists. Boasting a trio of vocalists and synthesizer technicians led by Phil Oakey (born October 2, 1955), Ian Craig Marsh (born November 19, 1956), and Martyn Ware (born May 19, 1956), the Sheffield, England natives demonstrated, though slightly differently than Elvis Costello, how computer technology could turn into recording stardom.[15] Signing their first contract in 1978 with indie label Fast, The Human League scored several underground hits (and several band member changes)[16] before achieving mainstream success with their 1981 breakthrough album *Dare*, which shot to No. 1 and included the No. 1 single "Don't You Want Me?"

By the mid-1980s, the group's early Kraftwerk-inspired industrial electronic leanings had turned to a kind of new wave romantic synth that made *Dare* and its much-anticipated follow-up, 1984's *Hysteria*, defining albums of the decade. When *Hysteria* failed to generate more airplay than its predecessor, The Human League went on an indefinite hiatus, with the duo of Jimmy Jam and Terry Lewis resurfacing briefly in 1986 with the single "Human." All too quickly, the mullet-shorn, pseudoromantics of pop/rock were gone, leaving countless other rock 'n' roll hopefuls to pick up the pieces of their plaintive new wave romance.

MEN AT WORK

A surprising addition to new wave's success was the irreverent Police-inspired Australian band Men at Work. Incorporating Sting & Co.'s erotically charged reggae-styled rhythms with wailing saxophones, catchy guitar hooks, and an offbeat sense of humor, the band's 1982 debut album *Business as Usual* became an international hit. In America, the album broke the record for the most weeks spent by a debut album at the top of the charts. Pairing their somewhat off-kilter humor with equally irreverent music videos, Men at Work became the darlings of MTV, sending "Who Can It Be Now?" and "Down Under" to No. 1.

The quintet originally began as an acoustic duo in 1979, consisting of founder Colin Hay (who had moved to Australia from his native Scotland at the age of fourteen) and Ron Strykert (guitar and vocals). Within a few months, the duo expanded to five with the addition of John Rees (bass), Greg Ham (saxophone, flute, keyboards), and Jerry Speiser (drums). The remarkable success of *Business as Usual* delayed the group's second album release, *Cargo*, which had been recorded during the summer of 1982 during *Business as Usual*'s global success. *Cargo*, released in 1983, spawned two Top 10 singles, "Overkill" and "It's a Mistake." After a profitable concert tour and a co-headliner stint at the U.S. Festival with The Clash and the Stray Cats, Men at Work took an extended break in 1984 and never fully regrouped. Speiser and Rees left the band and were replaced with session musicians for the group's third album, 1985's *Two Hearts*. Although the album went gold in the United States, the album was considered a commercial disappointment, forcing the group to disband. Hay went on to a solo career, reforming with Ham in 1998 for a live release titled *Brazil*.[17] Like many new wave artists who failed to find an original voice for its blend of pop, punk, and international rhythms, Men at Work remains a brief, if engaging, blip on the 1980s pop/rock video scene.

New wave artists were a hodgepodge of pop, reggae, jazz, techo-synth, and post-punk. Most, with the exception of career workhorses like Elvis Costello or reinvented solo artists like Sting, did not enjoy extended or sustaining commercial success. Inviting countless imitations and reconfigurations of their sound, new wave initially labeled 1980s rock as bland. Ultimately, the decade both blurred and redefined rock 'n' roll genres, inspiring the edgier alternative grunge movements of the 1990s.

NOTES

1. See, for example, general articles on major rock 'n' roll movements, including "new wave," found at http://en.wikipedia.org/wiki/Rock_music.

2. See, for example, Stephen Thomas Erlewine, "The Police," *All Music Guide*, included at the following Web site: http://www.vh1.com; search The Police.

3. Martin C. Strong, *The Great Rock Discography*, 6th ed. (Edinburgh, UK: Canongate Books, 2002), 813.

4. Ibid.

5. Ibid.

6. Ibid.

7. See, for example, VH1 Web site: http://www.vh1.com.

8. Christopher Sandford, *Sting: Demolition Man, a Biography* (New York: Carroll and Graf, 2000), 55.

9. At Stiff, Costello also met two men who would become longtime collaborators, Nick Lowe and Jake Rivera. Clover is credited as the Shamrocks on Costello's 1977 album *Less Than Zero*; Huey Lewis never performed with the group during Costello's recording sessions; included in Strong, *Great Rock Discography*, 232–233.

10. See, for example, "Elvis Costello," by Stephen Thomas Erlewine, *All Music Guide*, included at http://www.vh1.com; search Elvis Costello.

11. Ibid.

12. See, for example, "Talking Heads," by Stephen Thomas Erlewine, *All Music Guide*, included at http://www.vh1.com; search Talking Heads.

13. Strong, *Great Rock Discography*, 1029.

14. Ibid.

15. See, for example, Jason Ankeny, "Human League," *All Music Guide*, included at http://www.vh1.com; search Human League.

16. In 1978, the Human League added Adrian Wright (b. December 30, 1956) on synthesizers and visuals; founding members Ware and Marsh left in 1980, replaced by vocalists Joanne Catherall (b. September 18, 1962) and Susanne Sulley (b. March 22, 1963); Ian Burden (b. December 24, 1957) was also added at that time on bass and synthesizers. Finally, in 1981, Jo Callus (b. May 2, 1955, in Glasgow, Scotland) was added on guitar. See Strong, *Great Rock Discography*, 492.

17. See, for example, "Men At Work," by Stephen Thomas Erlewine, *All Music Guide*, included at http://www.vh1.com/artists/az/men_at_work/bio.jhtml.

6

HEAVY, THRASH, AND POWER METAL BANDS

Describing heavy metal has been likened to trying to "aim at a moving target."[1] The style of music whose name was suggested lyrically in Steppenwolf's 1968 hit "Born to Be Wild," with the phrase "heavy metal thunder," was also used to describe Jimi Hendrix's seminal power blues-rock guitar, which to some sounded "like heavy metal falling from the sky,"[2] and also referenced the title of a short story by counterculture author William S. Burroughs, "The Heavy Metal Kid." In the 1970s, heavy metal described the harder, pumped-up power sound associated with American bands like Steppenwolf, Iron Butterfly, and Grand Funk Railroad, and British artists like the Who, Deep Purple, and Led Zeppelin. The initial introduction of power chords through blues-rock guitar virtuosos like Hendrix and, later, the classically infused riffs of Eddie Van Halen and Quiet Riot's Randy Rhoads, along with more aggressive percussion styles, formed the foundation of a musical genre that would, by the 1980s, morph into subcultures, including power metal, thrash metal, and hair metal. In addition to a harsher, tougher, more distorted sound, the metal experience also included the pageantry of the concert, with '70s shock rock acts like Alice Cooper and theatrical bands like KISS blurring the line and skewing the musical definition of what "heavy metal" really meant.

Yet even with technological changes that might make the sound heav*ier*, or the speed faster, the most popular metal acts of the 1980s broke little new ground musically[3] but did alter some of their extramusical elements, like image and theatrics. Later in the decade, bands like Metallica and Megadeth gained mainstream popularity for what became known as "thrash" or "speed" metal. These variations on the heavy metal genre generally included "blistering drum beats . . . [and a] punk-rock sensibility . . . [that] played loud and hard, growling

Before his reality TV series on MTV and after his days with the band Black Sabbath, Ozzy Osbourne was reborn as a solo artist during the 1980s. Courtesy of Photofest.

or screaming . . . [and delved into] the psychological and pathological."[4] But earlier in the decade, metal fans saw the genre's dark baton carried in by two artists from the 1970s, Ozzy Osbourne and Iron Maiden.

OZZY OSBOURNE BAND

Born John Michael Osbourne on December 3, 1948, in Aston (a suburb of Birmingham, England), Osbourne first gained fame as the lead singer of Black Sabbath (1968–1979, with a brief exit in 1976). In 1979, after ongoing creative differences with guitarist Tony Iommi, whose musical experimentations began to take the group in a more progressive direction, Osbourne was fired from Black Sabbath. Having signed away all his rights to the band, Osbourne reportedly locked himself in a room at Los Angeles' La Park Hotel where, with curtains shut, "he drank and snorted blow all alone in the dark."[5] Enter Sharon Arden, daughter of former Black Sabbath manager Don Arden, who made Ozzy's career as a solo artist her primary project. Not only would she launch and manage his solo career, Sharon would later marry Ozzy (on July 4, 1982). Together they began to put a new band together.

By 1981, Ozzy's newly designed solo career saw him releasing two, now iconic albums: *Blizzard of Ozz* and *Diary of a Madman*. Ozzy's collaborator on both albums was former Quiet Riot guitar virtuoso Randy Rhoads. There are many versions of how Rhoads and Osbourne actually met, but all agree that the musical connection between the two was almost instantaneous. Often compared to Eddie Van Halen for his creative fusion of "classically-inspired and blues-oriented melodic ideas in improvisation,"[6] Rhoads was willing to stay within the hard-rock/metal genres with which Osbourne was comfortable. Rounding out the band were bassist Dana Strum (formerly of Slaughter) and drummer Frankie Bannalli (Rhoads' friend and former Quiet Riot band mate). Although the group began rehearsing in Los Angeles, they were scheduled to record the album in England. When Ridge Farm Records could only obtain one work permit for a non–English band member, Rhoads was quickly tapped as the band member Osbourne most wanted on the recording.

Working at Osbourne's home in Wales, the two began to write the *Blizzard of Ozz* album during Thanksgiving 1979. Rumors that the two would audition potential band members at a local pub became legend and also served as the venue by which they previewed some of their songs. By the spring 1980, with ex-Uriah Heep members Lee Kerslake (drums) and Bob Daisley (bass), the newly reconstructed Ozzy Osbourne Band entered Ridge Farm's Surrey studios, recording for almost a month. Disagreements over one of the sound engineer's initial mixing of the music eventually led to the acquisition of Ridge Farm's resident engineer Max Norman, who would play an integral part in many of Osbourne's subsequent recordings.

Back in California, Rhoads teamed up one last time with Quiet Riot before joining Osbourne for the U.S. "Blizzard of Ozz" tour. Also included in Osbourne's tour band was Rhoads' Quiet Riot bassist Rudy Sarzo. When the Ozzy Osbourne Band returned to the United Kingdom to play their first "official" show at the Apollo Theatre in Glasgow, Scotland, on September 12, 1980, 4,000 fans broke the box-office record and sent *Blizzard of Ozz* straight to No. 7 on the UK charts. The band toured the United Kingdom for almost three months, playing thirty-four shows. Still, they had not secured a major record deal.

In February and March 1981, the Osbourne band returned to Ridge Farm Studios to record their second album, *Diary of a Madman*. Sandwiched between finishing the recording and embarking on a U.S. tour to promote *Blizzard*, the band rushed *Diary*'s recording and were unable to remain to participate in the album's mixing. Although *Blizzard* and *Diary* were written and recorded almost simultaneously, they sounded completely different. Record companies were reluctant to take a chance on two albums of material. Warner Brothers, Osbourne's label when he was a member of Black Sabbath, turned him down before Jet Records, a division of CBS, gave him a one-album deal for *Blizzard of Ozz*.

Meanwhile, record and concert ticket sales for *Blizzard* took off. Unfortunately, so did Ozzy's now trademark bizarre behavior. During a marketing meeting with CBS Records, Osbourne allegedly bit the head off a dove, ruining Sharon's idea that releasing doves during the conference would soften his bad-boy image with record executives. Although the incident drew lots of attention, CBS officials were not amused, "threaten[ing] not to promote the album if he pulled another stunt like that."[7] Clearly, Osbourne did not take their warning seriously.

More stories about outrageous onstage behavior surfaced, some claiming that the band used dead or fake animals and raw meat as part of their concert schtick. Such antics drew strong criticism from some members of the American and British national presses, although few could top Osbourne's most notorious act: biting the head off a live bat. The incident took place in 1982 in Des Moines, Iowa, during the *Diary of a Madman* tour. Constricted by limited stage space (and with orders from Osbourne that no band member upstage him), bassist Rudy Sarzo noticed something rubbery had been thrown on the stage and motioned to Osbourne to check it out. Thinking it was a Halloween toy, Osbourne bit off its head, realizing seconds later that it was not a toy at all. While band members scrambled to recover the remains of the animal so it could be tested for rabies, Osbourne was hospitalized for rabies vaccinations. Later, he was arrested in Texas after urinating on the Alamo while wearing one of Sharon's dresses. As a result, he was banned from San Antonio, Texas, for the next ten years.[8]

If American fans were shocked by Osbourne's unique blend of heavy metal and shocking behavior, European fans witnessed even more craziness. During their tour in Hamburg, Germany, band members stopped at a sex club. Decorated with tables shaped like penises, the club featured live sex shows. The following evening during a dinner with Sony executives, Ozzy "climbed on top of the table, stripped naked and re-enacted the sex show. He capped his performance by urinating in a carafe of wine. Several minutes later, a waiter entered, took the carafe in the next room and served it to another table."[9] Despite his bizarre and often disgusting antics, Osbourne's solo career was thriving. With strong album sales and even stronger notoriety for exhibiting behavior that far exceeded anything any other bad boys of rock had done, Osbourne's career—and ego—were flying high. Not too far removed from his self-imposed three-month hotel confinement after being exiled from Black Sabbath, Osbourne became bigger than his former band.

Not so for guitarist Randy Rhoads, who remained humble and low-key even as his own stature as a guitar virtuoso was growing. Guitar magazines bestowed accolade upon accolade upon him for his guitar-playing genius, but Rhoads was growing tired of the rock music industry. Eager to return to his classical roots, Rhoads planned to enroll at a university following the *Diary of a Madman* tour to earn a doctoral degree in music. Even his mother was scouting appropriate schools to which her son could apply.

Rhoads was said to be unusually superstitious about guitars and, on three occasions, elicited the help of designer Grover Jackson to create the custom-made instruments he desired:

> [H]e didn't want to know too much about how a guitar was made because he liked the mystery of what made a guitar special. He refused to see his guitars until they were finished, and once a guitar was completed, he would take it out of the case every day and look at it, bonding with the instrument before he would play it.[10]

Jackson was working on a third guitar for Rhoads when tragedy struck.

On March 19, 1982, the band's bus stopped for repairs outside Orlando, Florida, the next stop on the tour. Andrew Aycock, the bus driver, wanted to remove some of the bunks from the bus so that band members might travel more comfortably. The repair shop was adjacent to an airplane hanger, which housed a small plane. A licensed pilot, Aycock offered to take the band up for a ride while the bus was being fixed. What band members did not know was that Aycock's pilot's license had been revoked after he had crashed a helicopter, killing a young boy who had been onboard with him.

Rhoads, along with Rachel Youngblood—the band's seamstress—joined Aycock for a ride. Several minutes later, Sarzo was awakened when the private plane piloted by Aycock grazed the roof of the tour bus. A loud explosion followed, then silence. After clipping the bus, Aycock apparently lost control of the plane, crashing it through a tree and then into a garage. The plane exploded on impact, killing all three aboard. Randy Rhoads was twenty-five years old. The guitar that Jackson was working on for the young impresario remains uncompleted and hangs on a wall in his home.

Rhoads' death impacted all members of the band, especially Ozzy: "I suppose when he died, part of me died with him. . . . He was the first person that came into my life who gave me hope."[11] Indeed, Osbourne's sense of survivor's guilt haunted him for years. He refused to play the Orlando gig, "Rock Super Bowl XIV," where the band was heading when Rhoads was killed, and concert promoters were forced to refund tickets to fans. Ten days after Rhoads' death, Osbourne's band fittingly returned to the concert stage at the one place Rhoads had dreamed about playing his whole life: Madison Square Garden. Had it not been for Sharon's encouragement, Osbourne claims he would never have set foot onstage again.

Osbourne upheld Rhoads' memory—and artistic integrity—in other ways. Before Rhoads' death, the band was contracted to put out a double live album: Side one was to have contained Osbourne's solo material; side two consisted of Black Sabbath songs. Osbourne and Rhoads had already recorded the double-album, although Rhoads had never been pleased about recording Black Sabbath songs. Still, Sharon's father and Jet Records owner Don Arden insisted that the double-album be released. Osbourne owed Jet Records $1.5 million, and Jet would not let him out of the deal until he repaid them. The album would have made Osbourne—and Jet Records—a fortune, but the shock metaller refused to back down: "The record company had me by the balls," he recalled, "[but] there was no way I was going to let the record company make a whore out of Randy."[12] Osbourne did not release the album until 1987 when he received permission from Rhoads's mother Delores. *Tribute*, which had been recorded live in Cleveland, Ohio, on May 11, 1981, also contained Rhoads' memorable solo from the band's Montreal concert in July of that same year.[13]

While *Tribute* became a Top 10 (and critical) hit, Osbourne went on to fulfill his contractual obligations by performing two nights of Black Sabbath songs at the Ritz and releasing an album of his own versions of Sabbath's hits called *Speak of the Devil*. Ozzy's battle with Don Arden took its toll on Arden's relationship with daughter Sharon, who became estranged from her father after Ozzy's legal obligations to Arden's company were complete. They have since reconciled.

Though Rhoads could never be replaced, Osbourne secured several fine guitarists during the 1980s, notably Jake E. Lee and Zakk Wylde, who joined the band in 1988. First guitar replacement Bernie Torme had difficulties coping with live performance and never recorded with Osbourne. Second recruit Lee, formerly of Ratt and Rough Cutt, was more successful than Torme, recording 1983's *Bark at the Moon* and 1986's *The Ultimate Sin*. Lee also toured behind both albums.

Musical differences ultimately caused Osbourne and Lee to part ways but then allowed Osbourne to discover yet another young guitar talent, Wylde, whom Osbourne supposedly plucked from a New Jersey bar. Wylde joined Osbourne for his 1988 effort *No Rest for the Wicked*, which also included drummer Randy Castillo and former Osbourne band bassist Bob Daisley. For the follow-up tour, Osbourne reunited with Black Sabbath bassist Geezer Butler, and a live album featuring Osbourne, Wylde, Butler, and Castillo—*Just Say Ozzy*—was released in 1990.

Osbourne's struggle during the 1980s—to carve out a successful solo career, then continue after Rhoads' death—was compounded by repeated efforts to get clean and sober. In 1986, he became embroiled in yet another legal battle. This time, the issue involved two teenagers who had committed suicide, allegedly because of subliminal lyrics contained in one of Osbourne's songs, "Suicide Solution." Osbourne contended that the song, written about his friend, former AC/DC singer Bon Scott, who died from alcohol abuse, was really a warning about not turning to alcohol to solve personal problems. Judges agreed that Osbourne could not be held accountable for any fan's actions, but the allegations fueled other social concerns that heavy metal music encouraged teenage fans to engage in inappropriate behavior.

Since the 1980s, Osbourne has continued to fight the alcohol and substance abuse problems that have plagued him throughout most of his career, although he appears to be handling these demons more effectively. His albums continue to be commercially viable, as was his 1990s heavy metal concert marathon venture, *Ozzfest*. In March 2002, Ozzy, wife Sharon and children Jack and Kelly (but not daughter Aimee, who declined to participate) embarked on a new, appropriately bizarre, brand of reality television. *The Osbournes* featured the not-so-traditional domestic life of the Osbourne family and quickly became MTV's greatest hit, reminding fans that regardless of his age or his fans Osbourne remains an important, if outrageous, part of heavy metal history and American culture.

IRON MAIDEN

After disco's glittering, if ubiquitous, dust had settled, rock music was in dire need of reinvention. Faced with the challenge of maintaining heavy metal's popularity amid fears that the genre was approaching extinction, early metal bands of the 1980s often fused the growing insurgency of punk with staple elements of both heavy metal and hard rock. Like the second generation of many rock genres, heavy metal needed to reinvent itself. One of the most successful bands in crossing both the cultural and musical bridge from the 1970s to the 1980s became one of the most influential bands of the heavy metal genre: Iron Maiden.

Originally formed in 1976 by bassist Steve Harris (born March 12, 1957), the East London–based band included (briefly) rhythm guitarist Tony Parsons, drummer Doug Sampson and vocalist Paul Di'Anno (born May 17, 1959, in Essex, England). Before releasing their self-titled debut album in 1980, guitarist Dennis Stratton (born November 9, 1954) replaced Parsons, and Clive Burr (born March 8, 1957) replaced drummer Sampson. *Iron Maiden* landed in the Top 5 on the UK charts, establishing

Iron Maiden was a staple among heavy-metal innovators. Courtesy of Photofest.

the group as "the leading lights of the New Wave of British Heavy Metal; carrying on where Black Sabbath and Uriah Heep left off."[14] Iron Maiden would help to "create and embody the cartoon caricature that the genre would become."[15] The album's Top 40 single "Running Free" has been described as "100 horsepower outlaw fantasy"[16] and easily foreshadows the lone cowboy dreams later celebrated by American bands like Bon Jovi. And despite production problems, the group's debut album, with its tightly raw metal riffs and ample punk-inspired melodies, remains one of the most important of their career, hinting at the possibilities of speed and thrash metal that were yet to come. Anthrax guitarist Scott Ian confirms, "You listen to those first two Iron Maiden albums, and they're right up there with anything on early Anthrax or Metallica."[17]

Maiden's 1981 follow-up album *Killers* evoked an even harsher metal sound, with Di'Anno's vocals more "guttural punk than metal warbling."[18] Though lacking the tight focus of its first effort, Iron Maiden managed to capture a huge audience, who bought the sophomore effort in droves. The second album also saw the departure of guitarist Stratton, who was replaced by Adrian Smith (born February 27, 1957). Soon after *Killers'* release, lead singer Di'Anno was forced to leave the group due to his inability to control his alcohol addiction.

Bruce Dickinson (born Paul Bruce Dickinson on August 7, 1958, in Sheffield, England) stepped in as the new lead singer, heralding what would become the group's groundbreaking release, 1982's *Number of the Beast*.

With *Beast*, Iron Maiden placed its first Top 10 single, "Run to the Hills," on the charts. Though more melodic and audience accessible than earlier albums, *Number of the Beast* turned Iron Maiden into international rock stars, complete with iconic heavy metal anthem "Hallowed By Thy Name" and an eerily ghoulish album cover mascot named Eddie. Like many metal bands to follow, Iron Maiden instituted the visual link that, in the years right before MTV, connected each of their albums. Eddie, "a giant, rotting ghoul with green skin,"[19] appeared on their album covers and T-shirts. Created by artist Derek Riggs, Eddie was drawn as "a punk with red hair splayed in all directions like a Rorschach test."[20]

Following in the musical tradition of *Number of the Beast* were two more albums, 1983's *Peace of Mind* and 1984's *Powerslave. Piece of Mind* spawned two major tours, while *Powerslave*'s eleven-month tour spawned a double live album featuring all their biggest hit singles, 1985's *Live after Death*. After *Live*'s release, the band went back to the studio to record the first of two concept albums, 1986's *Somewhere in Time*. A bit different from earlier releases, *Somewhere in Time* showcased synthesized guitars and complementary, thematic songs. And 1988's *Seventh Son of a Seventh Son* featured two masterfully written and executed singles, "The Evil That Men Do" and "The Clairvoyant." This eighth album was easily Iron Maiden's most critically acclaimed album since *Number of the Beast*. After another grueling tour, tensions between Harris and Smith over the musical direction the group should take resulted in Smith's departure and a year long hiatus for the band.

Smith's departure introduced new guitarist Janick Gers, who helped the band resurface in 1990 with *No Prayer for the Dying*, which boasted their first No. 1 single in the United Kingdom, "Bring Your Daughter . . . to the Slaughter." Interestingly, the hit also garnered the group the Golden Raspberry award as "Worst Song of the Year."[21] Perhaps the dubious "raspberry" was another kind of signal: that Iron Maiden's ghoulish mystique had finally worn thin with fans. Despite lead singer Dickinson's attempts to move the band in a different direction after 1985's *Powerslave* tour, founding bassist Harris, who called the artistic shots for the band, refused to include some of Dickinson's acoustic songs on *Somewhere in Time*. Ditto for Smith's more melodic efforts which could have had crossover appeal. Indeed, neither Harris nor producer Martin Birch ever envisioned the band "as anything other than what they were."[22]

What Iron Maiden became was an influential metal band whose time had passed. Its core members, by the 1990s, came and went. Their sound stagnated and eventually faded, and the band dissolved into heavy metal legendry, paving the way for groups like Metallica, Megadeth, and Anthrax to take speed and thrash metal to the next level.

Best known for their defining speed and thrash metal style, Metallica cast a dark shadow over 1980s heavy metal. Time Life Pictures/DMI/Time Life Pictures/Getty Images.

METALLICA

Giving Guns N' Roses their stiffest commercial competition among both hardcore and hair-metal fans for being the late 1980s quintessential heavy metal band was Metallica. Formed in the summer of 1981 by drummer (and British new wave heavy metal fanatic) Lars Ulrich, the original California-based trio also included lead singer/bass guitarist James Hetfield and lead guitarist Lloyd Grant. By 1982, after recording several unreleased demos, playing various gigs, and securing new band members, the trio became a quartet, adding Cliff Burton (born February 10, 1962) on bass and Kirk Hammett (born November 18, 1962) on lead guitar (replacing Grant's successor Dave Mustaine, who had left to join Megadeth). Metallica's first album *Kill 'Em All*, a reference to their contempt for record producers who had nixed their original title, "Metal Up Your Ass," was released in July 1983. A two-month tour followed, and by the fall of that year, band members were back in the studio recording their second album, *Ride the Lightning*.

Lightning's June 1984 release, which peaked at No. 100 on the album charts, was followed quickly in November by the 12" single release of one of the album's songs, "Creeping Death" and established them as heavy metal's purveyors of doom and gloom. That attitude was solidified in August 1984 at a Monsters of Rock concert, when, sandwiched between Ratt and Bon Jovi, Hetfield told the 70,000-plus fans assembled at Castle Donnington just what Metallica was all about: "If you came here to see spandex, eye make-up, and the words 'O baby' in every fuckin' song, this ain't the fuckin' band."[23] Clearly, heavy metalers were not dissuaded by Hetfield's candor. The group spent the next three months recording album number three, *Master of Puppets*, released in March 1986, the same month they began a critical tour with Ozzy Osbourne.

Although the tour would mark the group's last stint as a supporting act, it would also be marked with tragedy. Early on the morning of September 27, 1986, while traveling between Stockholm and Copenhagen, twenty-four-year-old bassist Cliff Burton was killed when one of the tour busses hit a patch of black ice and overturned. Years after, fellow band member James Hetfield remembered the scene:

> I saw the bus lying right on him. I saw his legs sticking out. I freaked. The bus driver, I recall, was trying to yank the blanket out from under him to use for other people. I just went, "Don't fucking do that!" I already wanted to kill the guy. I don't know if he was drunk or if he hit some ice. All I knew was, he was driving and Cliff wasn't alive anymore.[24]

The shaken band members dealt with this tragedy in typical rock star fashion: Hetfield broke two hotel windows; Hammett and his guitar tech stayed up all night with their room light on. Two days later, they all returned to the United States. The following month, after interviewing five candidates, Jason Newstead, who'd prepared for the audition by learning all of the band's songs, became Metallica's newest member.

Newstead was immediately included in Metallica's tour and studio schedule, but the group did not release any new material until the summer of 1988. (*Note:* 1987's *The $5.98 E.P.: Garage Days Re-Visited*, now a rare collector's item, included only cover tunes to introduce Jason to the fans. It rose to No. 28 on the charts.) With . . . *And Justice for All*, released in August 1988, Metallica finally cracked the Top 10, settling in at No. 6. The album also produced a No. 4 single, the un–heavy metal almost-ballad "One." Not only did it contain all the requisite heavy metal characteristics—pounding, heavy rhythms, distorted guitar riffs, and growling vocals—the album also reiterated Metallica's pessimistic nature. Song titles included "Blackened," "The Frayed Ends of Sanity," and "Harvester of Sorrow," while lyrics were peppered with words like "obscurity," "agitation," "mutilation," "hypocrisy," and "death." Most of the songs focused on society's cruel overpowering of helpless victims, presumably the kind of themes that would appeal to its predominantly male teenage audience.[25]

In 1990, after filming their first music video for "One," and after losing the previous year to Jethro Tull, Metallica won a Grammy Award for "Best Metal Performance" for the single "One." They continued through the 1990s with music that suggested grunge and alternative influences and an eclectic live performance with the San Francisco symphony in 1999.

In 2004, a documentary co-directed by Joe Berlinger and Bruce Sinofsky titled *Metallica: Some Kind of Monster*, was released. Hailed by the *New York Times as* a "psychodrama of novelistic intricacy and epic scope,"[26] the film chronicles the band's transformation and healing after Burton's death, "a relationship that is, superficially, both an artistic bond and a business partnership but that is also a deep, bubbling source of identity and anxiety for each man."[27] Far beyond a large screen "Behind the Music," *Monster* reminds fans that, in spite of its adolescent rebelliousness, rock 'n' roll is still a business, and Metallica's ability to survive and overcome the challenges of substance abuse, violence, and death is testament to their professional survival and personal maturation.

MEGADETH

In 1987, former Metallica guitarist Dave Mustaine recalled how the concept for his new band materialized:

 ONE—METALLICA (1988)

The standard heavy-metal video boasted a bevy of beautiful women, with Mötley Crüe often considered the winner in the "best-looking babes" category. This video, considered one of the decade's metal achievements, is considerably more substantive in both its audio and visual components. Inspired by Dalton Trumbo's anti-war novel *Johnny Got His Gun* (1939), and using clips from a subsequent film based on the novel, *One* incorporates disturbing war-torn images with clips from the movie, creating an impressive, effective—if ultimately depressing—existential video. There are three versions of the *One* video. The first version, with movie clips and scenes from the band's jam session, is the longest. The second version, also containing film and jam sequences, is shorter than the first, and the third version is the shortest, with no movie scenes. *One* is the first video Metallica ever made and also won the group its first Grammy Award. In a video medium often overflowing in a sea of breasts, babes, and sophomoric sexual innuendo, Metallica's *One* showed the brass from which heavy metal was made.

> Megadeth represents the power of annihilation. We spell the name phonetically because the meaning to us is the same you get out of the dictionary—it's a hypothetical body count after [a] nuclear fallout. . . . [I]t represents extreme power. . . . It's a million deaths, and we want to leave our audience shell-shocked wherever we go.[28]

"Shell-shocked" may be an understatement to describe the heavy metal beast most closely connected to Metallica in terms of its musical doom-and-gloom philosophy. More than a spin-off band, Megadeth has been described as "vital . . . in continuing to define and redefine the sound and fury of metal music."[29] Co-founders Mustaine and David Ellefson devised, beginning in 1983 (shortly after Mustaine's departure from Metallica), "a musical creature that, with each new album forges new ground and stretches the very boundaries where metal lives."[30] Those boundaries have reached beyond the usual cynicism against modern society to embrace issues of divorce and teenage loneliness

Companions to Metallica's sound, Megadeth also helped to define speed and thrash metal.
© S.I.N./Corbis.

(Mustaine's own latchkey childhood looms large here) as well as musical fusions with blues, jazz, and thrash metal.

Megadeth's rise to the heavy metal forefront started shortly after their 1985 debut release, *Killing Is My Business . . . and Business Is Good*. The success of this first, Combat records–produced album pushed the group right into a second release in September that same year. *Peace Sells . . . But Who's Buying?* went gold, and Megadeth signed a contract with the larger, more powerful Capitol Records, who took over distribution and promotion of their sophomore effort. Touring followed, as did conflicts among band members. By 1987, original group members Chris Poland (guitar) and Gar Samuelson (drums) had been replaced with Jeff Young and Chuck Behler, respectively.

In January 1988, the band released the *So Far, So Good . . . So What!* album, which unleashed the power hits "Mary Jane" and "Set the World Afire," and took off on a world tour that included opening the Monsters of Rock tour at Castle Donnington and playing with KISS, Anthrax, and Iron Maiden. Additionally, Megadeth was featured in the critically acclaimed documentary *Decline of Western Civilization II: The Metal Years* (1988). By 1990, inspired by new members Nick Menza (drums) and Marty Friedman (guitar), Megadeth entered what might be called its most creative and controversial period: "When the four of us got together and made the record *Rust in Peace* (1990), we knew we were on to something special," says Ellefson. "Since then we have really honed our sound and we have learned how to write and record together."[31]

In 1989, Mustaine was arrested for driving impaired and spent a month in rehab. A year later, he recalled the experience:

> I realized that I'm seriously addicted to drugs only when I hit the very bottom. I was sitting in a jail cell looking at my hands full of needle holes. I was in the joint because I drove into a parked car. . . . A while before that I injected myself with some heroin, I was already on some cocaine, a couple of drinks and some other shit. In the hospital they counted nine of the other shit. In my pockets they found a jar of hard drugs, a spoon, needles, and a sack of pot. I stayed in the hospital for a month and started the process of quitting; not that it was really my decision. Some drug users can force themselves to do it. These are the ones that hadn't gone over the edge yet. I was in the other group. Now I'm sober for the fourth strait [sic] month. I don't even drink coffee; I don't smoke. I watch out for sugar and other white powders.[32]

While in rehab, Mustaine was visited by shock rocker Alice Cooper, an encounter that resulted in an important personal and artistic connection: "Alice is actually my godfather. . . . We are one and the same as far as being fascinated with sex, drugs, and rock 'n' roll, life, death, blood and guts. The only difference between he and I is that his music has been out a lot longer and he's been more successful. I hope that I can learn a lot from him."[33] Soon after, Megadeth recorded a cover of Cooper's "No More Mr. Nice Guy," which was included on Wes Craven's *Shocker* sound track. The almost simultaneous release of *Rust in Peace* in October 1990 confirmed the band's status as an innovative metal band destined to last.

Since then Megadeth has continued to perform and record. While some members, including Menza, have come and gone, the group's cofounders Mustaine and Ellefson have remained, now an old married couple in rock vernacular, husbands and parents in a more traditional venue.

ANTHRAX

If thrash metal pioneers Anthrax had not chosen such an appropriately menacing name, they might have called themselves "Survivor." Unlike

Proponents of the "death" metal legacy, Anthrax, shown here in 1986, appealed to thousands of American teenagers. Courtesy of Photofest.

many metal bands that grind out the same sound over and over again until the sound has been wasted, Anthrax has moved beyond its niche alongside fellow thrash/speed metallers Metallica and Megadeth to forge crossovers with rap and punk. And unlike many metal bands' gruesome preoccupation with death and destruction, Anthrax maintained a macabre sense of humor about themselves and their songs. They were, for example, the first metal band to wear shorts onstage, breaking the metal uniform of leather and spandex and, in the process, allowing fans to separate their music from the stereotypical metal image.

Formed in mid-1981 in their native Queens, New York, Anthrax consisted of a quintet of "nice Jewish boys"[34]: lead singer Neil Turbin (born December 24, 1963), lead guitarist Dan Spitz (born January 28, 1963), rhythm guitarist Scott "Not" Ian (born December 31, 1963), bassist Dan Lilker (born October 18, 1964), and drummer Charlie Benante (born November 27, 1962). Spotted and signed to a Megaforce contract by the legendary Johnny Z, the band made its debut in 1984 with the album *Fistful of Metal*. The album's cheesy, almost cartoonish cover did little to melt the hearts of hardcore metal fans, nor did the music. However, a few tracks, notably "Metal Thrashing Mad" and a cover of Alice Cooper's "I'm Eighteen" brought a few smiles from fans and critics.

By the time the group released its next effort, 1985's *Armed and Dangerous*, Joey Belladonna (born October 30, 1960, in Oswego, New York) had replaced vocalist Neil Turbin (Matt Fallon also took a brief turn in the lead singer spot before Belladonna took over), and ex-roadie-turned-bassist Frank Bello (born September 7, 1965) replaced Dan Lilker. With Belladonna's more traditional-sounding vocals, *Armed and Dangerous* seemed to have "a modicum of style and sophistication"[35] that was missing on the first album. Over the next five albums, with the possible exception of 1988's uninspired and less-than-intoxicating *State of Euphoria*, Belladonna led the band to new and creative heights, avoiding the usual musical clichés that often infiltrate the heavy metal genre. Arguably, between 1985 and 1990, Anthrax became the leaders of speed metal.[36]

But there was more than good speed metal that gave this band its uniqueness and also turned the metal community on its ear. In 1985, as a side project to *Armed and Dangerous*, Scott Ian solicited the help of just-signed lead singer Belladonna and original bassist Dan Lilker to turn some of Ian's cartoon doodles and accompanying guitar riffs into an album. Ian had created a ghoulish character in an army uniform named Sergeant D. and had decided to make a band out of Sgt. D and his unusual riffs, calling it Stormtroopers of Death (or S.O.D. for short). After recruiting one imposing roadie named Billy Milano to sing the part of Sgt. D, Ian, Lilker, Benante, and Belladonna recorded an album inspired by Ian's cartoons and riffs called *Speak English or Die*, which Island Records released in 1985. The set of politically incorrect songs included titles like "Fuck the Middle East," "Pre-Menstrual Princess Blues," and "Pussy Whipped" and clearly satirized everything from immigrants to domineering women.[37] Anthrax fans embraced the bold, political incorrectness of this effort, although some critics were less than kind. Ian defended the project (and the band's sense of humor): "We just did what we did. . . . There was no responsibility to anything except just doing something that we had fun with."[38] In spite of the band's misunderstood satire, many fans, critics, and artists credit *Speak English or Die* with initiating the crossover between heavy metal and punk. Their 1987 single "I'm the Man" further solidifies Anthrax's cutting-edge fusion of heavy metal and punk styles.

One of the band's heaviest and most popular albums was 1987's *Among the Living* and provides another example of Anthrax's creatively enduring success. Two songs on the album, the title track and "A Skeleton in the Closet," were based on Stephen King's *The Stand* and "Apt Pupil" from the *Different Seasons* anthology, respectively. To Ian's delight, King is, in turn, a fan of Anthrax, having cited the group in several print interviews and admitting to cranking up Anthrax when he needs private time to write.[39]

Anthrax's peak during the last half of the 1980s did not extend far into the next decade. In 1992, the band fired Bellandonna and replaced him with ex-Armored Saint John Bush (born August 24, 1963, in Los Angeles). Bush's sound was gruffer and deeper, much more like other metal bands. Consequently, Anthrax's sound became less unique, and its audience base diminished. A contract with Elektra Records produced 1993's *Sound of White Noise* and 1995's *Stomp 442*. After leaving Elektra, the band—now a quartet consisting of Ian, Bush, Bello, and Benante—built their own studio in Yonkers, New York. Since then, both new releases and concert appearances (including a proposed reunion with Belladonna in 2000) have been sporadic. In spring 2004, a CD/DVD set called *Music of Mass Destruction: Live from Chicago* arrived in record stories, celebrating the band's twenty years in rock 'n' roll.[40]

HEAVY METAL'S LEGACY TO ROCK MUSIC

While many rock historians argue that heavy metal rose to prominence during a period of "cultural mistrust" in America during the 1970s, heavy metal's forays in thrash, speed, power, and even hair metal during the 1980s allowed for new energy, classical and blues–infused innovations, and crossover potential with rival genres rap, punk, and—even though metal fans might cringe—pop. The mainstreaming of heavy metal during the 1980s infused new life and vitality into this sometimes static-sounding musical style. Together with MTV, heavy metal found a broader base among fans that included women and minorities without alienating their core fan base of suburban white male teens. The popularity of a genre that celebrates a life led with no social convention or restriction is perhaps best summed up by former Van Halen lead singer David Lee Roth: "We're not like this because we're in a rock band . . . we're in a rock band because we're like this."[41]

Aside from any other psychological or sociological connections, heavy metal artists upped its musical ante during the 1980s, setting new standards for speed, technological sound, and musicianship in a genre that originally required three distorted chords and lots of noise.

NOTES

1. Joe Stuessy and Scott Lipscomb, *Rock and Roll: Its History and Stylistic Development*, 4th ed. (Upper Saddle River, NJ: Prentice Hall, 2003), 380.

2. See, for example, Web sites that explain how heavy metal got its name: http://www.campusprogram.com/reference/en/wikipedia/h/he/heavy_metal_music.html.

3. Ibid. Also see Ed Ward, Geoffrey Stokes, and Ken Tucker, *Rock of Ages: The Rolling Stone History of Rock and Roll* (New York: Rolling Stone Press, 1986).

4. See, for example, "The History of Heavy Metal," included at http://myuselessinfo.com/uhistorymetal.html. This Web site is part of the *St. James Encyclopedia of Popular Culture*, 2002 Gale Group.

5. David Konow, *Bang Your Head: The Rise and Fall of Heavy Metal* (New York: Three Rivers Press, 2002), 114.

6. See, for example, Web sites like the following: http://encyclopedia.thefreedictionary.com/Ozzy%20Osbourne.

7. Konow, *Bang Your Head*, 118.

8. See, for example, Web sites like that listed in note 4.

9. Konow, *Bang Your Head*, 119–120.

10. Ibid., 121.

11. Ibid., 122.

12. Ibid., 124.

13. See, for example, Randy Rhoads–based Web sites, including: http://www.hotsotditigal.com/WellAlwaysRembmer.4/RandyRhoadsBio.html.

14. Martin C. Strong, *The Great Rock Discography*, 6th ed. (Edinburgh, UK: Canongate Books, 2002), 508.

15. Ibid.

16. Ibid.

17. Konow, *Bang Your Head*, 128.

18. Strong, *Great Rock Discography*, 508.

19. Konow, *Bang Your Head*, 128–129.

20. Ibid., 129.

21. Barry Weber, "Iron Maiden," *All Music Guide*, included at the following Web site: http://www.mtv.com; search Iron Maiden.

22. Konow, *Bang Your Head*, 224–225.

23. See, for example, the Encyclopedia Metallica Web site at http://www.encycmet.com/biography.

24. Ibid.

25. Stuessy and Lipscomb, *Rock and Roll*, 384.

26. A. O. Scott, "Heavy-Metal Headshrinking and Other Secrets of the Rock and Roll Business," *New York Times*, July 9, 2004; found at http://www.nytimes.com; search archives.

27. Ibid.

28. See Megadeth Web site: http://www.megadeth.com/biography.

29. See, for example, http://www.singers.com/ar/m/megadeth/biography.htm.

30. Ibid.

31. Ibid.

32. See Web site at note 28.

33. Ibid.

34. Konow, *Bang Your Head*, 237.

35. Strong, *Great Rock Discography*, 29.

36. See, for example, Web sites like the following: http://www.vh1.com; search Anthrax.

37. Konow, *Bang Your Head*, 237–239.

38. Ibid., 239.

39. Ibid., 237–238.

40. Stephen Erlewine and Greg Prato, "Anthrax," *All Music Guide*, included at http://www.vh1.com; search Anthrax.

41. See, for example, "Godz Useless Music: The History of Heavy Metal," found at http://myuseless-info.com/uhistorymetal.html.

7

GLAM-METAL HAIR BANDS

The splintering of heavy metal during the 1980s was not surprising, considering its enormous commercial success a decade earlier. Seminal metallists of the late 1960s and early 1970s—Deep Purple, Led Zeppelin, and Black Sabbath—earned heavy metal's historic connection to the radioactive elements or powerful artillery units, where the term originated. Heavy metal during the 1980s was as much about lifestyle as it was about music, the artists better groomed personally and less gloomy musically than their predecessors. Heavy metal was played as often on MTV as it was on the radio, with pop and rap artists integrating metal's signature blues-rock guitar riffs and power chords into their music. Additionally—and for the first time—metal artists found a market among women and minorities.[1] By 1986, MTV's *Headbangers' Ball* easily became its top-rated show, and metal concerts dominated the summer music scene. Despite its expanded fan base, metal's core audience remained white suburban male teenagers, although audience diversity clearly helped record sales (including the hair bands). Record sales of heavy metal artists were more stable than any other genre of the 1980s.

While many bands of this period—Bon Jovi, Poison, and Warrant—softened their look, toned down the volume, and infused more sexually suggestive lyrics into their songs as a way of broadening the fan base, other bands tried to maintain some of the rawness and grittier appearance associated with heavy metal's forefathers.

Metal bands from this decade clearly shared as much of a proclivity toward big hair, sexy, muscular bodies, and chiseled good looks as they did a tougher, hard-edged sound, giving rise to the term "hair metal" or "glam-metal" bands. To some, these terms were not complimentary, as they suggested that the

Often targeted for their good looks, excessive "big" hair and muscular appearance, Van Halen's musical virtuosity and integrated rock/metal sounds created one of the most popular crossover bands in the 1980s. Courtesy of Photofest.

band's image superceded its musical quality. A closer look at some of the 1980s most successful and popular hair-metal groups shows they contributed as much to the music of the decade as they did to the changing video image associated with heavy metal and rock 'n' roll.

VAN HALEN

The hair-metal band that came closest (some would argue, surpassed it) to achieving the kind of superstar status associated with Michael Jackson, Madonna, or Bruce Springsteen was Van Halen. The Van Halen family, including brothers Alex (born Alex Arthur Van Halen on May 8, 1953) and Eddie (born Edward Lodewijk Van Halen on January 26, 1955), emigrated from the Netherlands, where both brothers had received early training in classical piano, to California in 1967. Their father, Jan, was an accomplished clarinetist who, interestingly, was the featured clarinet soloist on "Big Bad Bill (Is Sweet William Now)," from the group's 1982 *Diver Down* album.

As the brothers' interest in music grew, Alex took an interest in guitar and Eddie in playing the drums. Legend has it that in order to pay for his drum set Eddie took a job delivering newspapers. While he was working, Alex used to practice on Eddie's drum set. When Eddie realized Alex had real skill as a drummer, he decided to learn to play guitar instead, a switch that fans know changed rock history. Today, Alex is considered one of the finest rock drummers, and Eddie remains one among a handful of innovative rock—not just heavy metal—guitarists in the music industry.

Original band members included bassist Michael Anthony (born Michael Anthony Sobolewski on June 20, 1954, in Chicago) and lead singer David Lee Roth (born David Lee Roth on October 10, 1954, in Bloomington, Indiana), plus Alex and Eddie. The group became a hit on the Los Angeles club scene in the early 1970s under a series of names, including "The Broken Combs," "Mamooth," and "Rat Salade." Eventually, the band members decided upon the name Van Halen, after its founding brothers and Roth's suggestion that their name just sounded "heavy like a German tank."[2] In 1976, KISS' Gene Simmons attended one of their shows and financed their first demo tape, which led to a recording contract with Warner Brothers. The signing of Van Halen's first recording contract provided a bit of drama itself. Warner executive Mo Ostin officiated the signature ceremony, which took place after one of their concerts at Los Angeles' famed Starwood Club.

The self-titled *Van Halen* became the group's first album release in 1978. Each of the band's first five albums, released between 1978 and 1982, rose progressively higher on the charts,[3] culminating with 1984's phenomenal *1984 (MCMLXXXIV)*. Climbing to No. 2 (unable to topple Michael Jackson's *Thriller*) as a critical and fan favorite and yielding the No. 1 monster hit "Jump," plus two other Top 20 singles ("Panama" and "House of Pain"), *1984* culminated the first decade of the band's extraordinary musical evolution, establishing Van Halen among heavy metal *and* rock bands and breaking the stereotype that heavy metal bands were not musically innovative.

On both *Van Halen* and *1984*, the group experimented with new instrumental soloing techniques, distinctive styles that would become part of its musical trademark. For example, "Eruption," a track off the first album, introduced a technique called "tapping," where Eddie used both right and left hands on the guitar neck. *Van Halen* also introduced what became notoriously known in the guitar world as the "brown sound," "a nickname given to the combination of Eddie's own relaxed style coupled with his experimentation in guitar tweaking and effects processing that produced a distinctive tone sought after by

 JUMP—VAN HALEN (1984)

As flamboyant visually as it is musically, *Jump* pushed Van Halen to No. 1 status on the *Billboard* Charts and secured its spot as heavy metal's most successful pop-infused band to date. With front man David Lee Roth demonstrating his trademark high kicks and high jinks in sync with Alex Van Halen's insistent drums and Eddie Van Halen's legendary guitar riffs, *Jump* catches Van Halen at doing what it did best: creating infectiously good, solid rock hits sung by Roth with impishly sexual innuendo that reminded audiences not to take them— only their music—seriously. Visually, *Jump* is a celebration of life, where everyone is encouraged to "roll with the punches" and not let anything get them down.

other musicians."[4] Again, folklore plays a role in the history of how this technique evolved. Supposedly done in order to keep other musicians from imitating his technique prior to the release of their first album, Eddie played his concert solos with his back to the audience.

If *Van Halen* inaugurated a new age for the electric guitar, *1984* initiated parallel groundbreaking for the electric keyboard, heretofore unheard of as a heavy metal/hard-rock instrument. The hit "Jump" was based on a series of "syncopated chords on the synthesizer over a pounding, steady eighth-note bass."[5] Complementing the synthesizer's catchy hooks and octave-reaching bridge were "Diamond Dave's" energetic vocals and Eddie's harmonically virtuoso guitar solo. Both "Jump" and "Runnin' with the Devil" (from *Van Halen*) are listed as two of the Top 500 most influential rock 'n' roll songs in the Rock and Roll Hall of Fame and Museum.[6] To date, both *Van Halen* and *1984* have achieved "diamond" status, each having sold over 10 million copies.

The innovative musical styles of Van Halen's recordings were equaled by the theatrics of their concert performances. Alex's "shimmering hi-hat attack" has been as much a part of their onstage antics as Eddie's "hammer-on-crazy solos." Soon, phrases like "ribboning leads" and "guitar pyrotechnics" became part of rock 'n' roll's vernacular.[7] And then, of course, there was David Lee Roth, with flowing blonde hair and randy bad-boy image, who exuded much of the group's charisma. His outrageous, over-the-top personality, coupled with the tradition of having attractive women plucked from the audience and carried to his dressing room for post-concert partying, became legend. But so, too, did Eddie's guitar-playing genius and his tabloid romance (and subsequent marriage) to popular television actress Valerie Bertinelli. Eddie and Valerie's 1981 marriage signaled a change in the air for Van Halen's image, with Eddie's new lifestyle downplaying the group's wild bachelor reputation. Then, Roth's solo album *Crazy from the Heat*, released in 1985 and securing a No. 15 spot on the album charts, produced two hit covers: his sexy, playful rendition of the Beach Boys' "California Girls" (also topping at No. 15 on the singles' charts) and an upbeat medley of hits by Louis Prima and Al Jolson, "Just a Gigolo/I Ain't Got Nobody." With tensions over the band's conflicting offstage antics and Roth's budding solo career, it came as no shock to fans when, in late 1985, Roth announced he was leaving the group.

Roth's departure was followed soon after by the announcement that Sammy Hagar, formerly with the band Montrose, would join the group as Van Halen's new lead singer. Faced with considerable and ongoing fan resentment over the departure of Roth, Hagar became part of a continuing debate over which of the group's lead singers—Roth or Hagar—is/was better. In fact, Hagar proved to be part of the group's expansion during this period, which saw both its commercial success and its fan base grow. Clearly, the replacement of Roth with Hagar did not slow down Van Halen's ability to sell albums or be recognized for its musical artistry, even though die-hard Roth fans expressed displeasure at Hagar's softer, more commercial sound. Still, all four studio albums recorded with Hagar, including 1986's *5150*, 1988's *OU812*, and 1995's *Balance*, reached No. 1. And 1993's concert album *Van Halen Live: Right Here, Right Now* topped the charts at No. 5.

But it was 1991's No. 1 album *F.U.C.K. (For Unlawful Carnal Knowledge)* that secured the band's place in rock history. Nominated for two Grammy Awards, Van Halen won the "Best Hard Rock Performance with Vocal" for the album. In addition, some of their songs were used in commericals and movies in the 1990s, signifying yet another crossover for the increasingly mainstream heavy metal group. But even these critical and commercial successes would not spell stability for the band. Following another series of personality conflicts and artistic disagreements, Sammy Hagar left (or was ousted from) the band in 1996. The group continued to perform into the twenty-first century, adding, then dropping Gary Cherone from the band Extreme.

In March 2004, Van Halen and Sammy Hagar announced their reunion for an album release and concert tour. Meanwhile, Roth continued to pursue solo ventures. To many fans, it is clear that Van Halen's history and cultural contributions are still being written and that the story of its success is far from over.

Besides its musical contributions to rock 'n' roll, Van Halen has been a pioneer in other entertainment arenas. The band's use of the "concert technical contract rider," specifying their "wish list" (i.e., stage measurements, production standards, transportation arrangements, personal requirements, etc.), has become a standard in the music and entertainment industry. Perhaps the most memorable anecdote centers on the band's request that a bowl of M&M's—with all the brown ones removed—be available in their dressing room at every scheduled concert. To some, this rather bizarre request confirmed the self-indulgent pandering that was synonymous with being a rock star/celebrity. But, according to Roth (from his 1997 autobiography *Crazy from the Heat*), the M&M request served as a kind of checkpoint to the band's other, more practical rider requests (i.e., if the M&M's were not delivered according to specifications, other issues concerning size of the stage or sound quality might also be compromised).[8]

Whatever the group's rationale for the now-infamous M&M preference, its relevance in popular culture continues to be a topic of scholarly and popular discussion. Its lead singer replacement sagas, personal and outrageous lifestyles, notwithstanding, Van Halen has proven to be a band of considerable musical innovation and commercial appeal. Though fans still bristle at the mention of Van Halen being a "heavy metal" band, many rock historians[9] still use that term to describe the unfailingly edgy consistency—not disregarding its sometimes groundbreaking musicality—that is part of the band's imprimatur. Again, the problem may not be so much the descriptor but the connotation of the description itself.

Despite the controversy and chaos that have surrounded the band for thirty years, Van Halen's ongoing importance in American popular culture cannot be overlooked. One—and maybe the quintessential—example of its enduring importance came on October 21, 1996, as David Letterman read one of his Top

As one of the early "hair" metal bands of the 1980s, Def Leppard made its way toward mainstream rock superstardom. Courtesy of Photofest.

10 lists. On that evening, he sardonically implied that then presidential candidate Bob Dole could gain popular support of the American people if he "would just convince the members of Van Halen to stop fighting so they could 'start crankin' out some more bitchin 'tunes.'"[10] Almost a decade after Letterman's droll advice, Van Halen's story and its music continue.

DEF LEPPARD

If fans and critics continue to debate whether or not Van Halen's musical style can be classified as "heavy metal," few would argue Def Leppard's status as perhaps the most definitive hard-rock band of the 1980s. With its founding members hailing from Sheffield in the United Kingdom, Def Leppard's first rehearsal—and official name change from "Deaf Leopard"— reportedly took place at a local British spoon factory sometime in November 1977. Part of the new wave British heavy metal movement of the late 1970s, Def Leppard was really a fusion of the glam-rock and metal movements from earlier in that decade, a curious combination of Queen with its energized musical prog-rock theatrics and Led Zeppelin's heavy guitar sound.

To many fans, Def Leppard is more than the name for one of rock 'n' roll's most dangerous-sounding metal bands. It is also a name that became synonymous with being "jinxed" or "cursed." Lead singer Joe Elliott (born Joseph Thomas Elliott on August 8, 1959) had persuaded founders Rick Savage (born Richard Savage on December 2, 1960) and Pete Willis (born Pete Willis on February 16, 1960), who had previously co-founded the band Atomic Mass, to name their new group Def Leppard after Elliott envisioned it in a dream. But after drummer Rick Allen lost his arm in an automobile accident in 1984 and "Riffmaster" Steve Clark died of complications related to alcoholism in 1991, the group's name often elicited more images of horrific nightmares than visions of rock 'n' roll sugarplums.

Still, Def Leppard's contributions to the metal sound of the 1980s merits some discussion. In January 1978, original band members Elliot, Savage, Willis, and drummer Tony Kenning were joined by guitarist Steve Clark (born Stephen Maynard Clark on April 23, 1960). Between February and July of that year, the band practiced "interminably" until Clark threatened to quit if they did not find a gig. On July 18, 1978—and paid approximately $10.00 out of one of their teacher's pockets—the band played its first public concert at Westfield School in Sheffield. By November, Kenning had been fired and replaced by then fifteen-year-old drummer Rick Allen (born Richard John Cyril Allen on November 1, 1963).

From 1979 to 1980, Def Leppard's reputation as an exciting live band was recognized in England and across the Atlantic. While other band members quit their day jobs, Allen dropped out of school, and in September 1979, the band opened for Sammy Hagar at London's "rock mecca," the Hammersmith Odeon.[11] With the help of AC/DC manager Peter Mensch, the band signed recording contracts with Phonogram (UK) and Mercury (USA) Records. During that same time, the group's first single, "Wasted," was released, followed by their debut album *On Through the Night*, in March 1980. Later that spring, a contract with the prestigious Leber-Krebs management company booked them for an American tour opening for several different artists, including Pat Travers, Judas Priest, Ted Nugent, and AC/DC. When the band returned to England in August, British fans, who had viewed their U.S. tour as a crass acquiescence to American capitalism, pelted them with tomatoes and beer cans.

Def Leppard followed the success of *On Through the Night* with 1981's *High N' Dry*, which became the group's first platinum album in the United States. Still barely out of their teens, the group's youthful energy and good looks and MTV's strong airplay for "Bringin' on the Heartbreak" would be vital to their staying power here and in their native England. As the group prepared to record its third album in January 1982, guitarist and co-founder Pete Willis quit the group, to be replaced by Phil Collen (born Philip Kenneth Collen on December 8, 1957, in London). A year later, the band's third—and most critically acclaimed—album, *Pyromania*, with its mega-single "Photograph," was released to huge sales. In the United States alone, *Pyromania* sold 100,000 a week for most of the year and ended up selling over 7 million copies. Yet even with a bona fide American audience, global success continued to elude them. It was not until April 1983 that Def Leppard's first U.S. headline tour began.

Pyromania, which emphasized melody and minimized their previously heavy guitar riffs, seemed to position the band for imminent crossover success. The group, whose MTV videos exuded both boyish good looks and a mischievous sexuality, hoped to solidify rock stardom with a quick follow-up to *Pyromania* when tragedy struck the first time. Late in 1984, drummer Rick Allen lost his left arm in a car accident, the first of many problems that plagued the group's career.

Undaunted, Allen recovered to return as the group's drummer, this time with the assistance of an electronic "drumkit," which assisted him in experimenting with various rhythm ideas. Even lead singer Elliott has said of Allen's post-accident contributions: "[He] became a better drummer than he was with two arms."[12] Indeed, Def Leppard managed to pull through such tragedies and even expanded its large audience. During its summer 1986 Monsters of Rock tour, which took the band to Ireland, England, and Germany, fans seemed to have forgotten the pelting that took place a few years earlier. This time audiences cheered the group's triumphant return, taking them to their hearts and embracing them as their own. In typically eerie Def Leppard style, the band's final concert in Mannheim, Germany, was marked by a thunderstorm lasting exactly the duration of the band's set.[13]

The release of 1987's blockbuster *Hysteria* signaled another world tour, this one beginning in the United Kingdom in August. Seven of the album's twelve songs were released as singles, and *Hysteria* wound up selling 16 million copies worldwide; 12 million were sold in the United States alone. The band began work on what would be its fifth and, in some countries, most popular album, *Adrenalize*, in 1989. Also that year, the band performed "Tear It Down" live on the MTV Video Awards, a gig that would turn out to be Steve Clark's last appearance with the band. The band relocated its recording studio to Dublin and continued to work on *Adrenalize* for over a year. On January 8, 1991, after combining pain medication for a broken rib injury with alcohol, Steve Clark died from a lethal overdose.

In April 1992, Def Leppard revealed its newest incarnation at Wembley stadium during a memorial concert for Queen's Freddie Mercury, adding Irish guitarist Vivian "Viv" Campbell (born Vivian Patrick Campbell on August 25, 1962) to the group. *Adrenalize* entered the U.S. charts at No. 1 and went on to sell 6 million copies here. In countries like Japan and Mexico, *Adrenalize* became the group's biggest-selling album. Their record 241 concert dates to promote the album also became a milestone for the group.

As the 1990s began, mainstream hard rock shifted away from Def Leppard's signature pop-metal sound and toward edgier (read: louder) bands. Even so, the group maintained a sizable audience into the late 1990s and remained one of only a handful of '80s metal groups to survive the '90s more or less intact.[14] By the end of the millennium, the group was preparing to release its tenth album, *X*, and to embark on another global tour. No matter how rock historians may quibble about the nature and characteristics of "heavy metal," Def Leppard did more than pour a little sugar on the style. The band molded and synthesized it to create its own unique, dangerously heavy, but never ponderously dull, sound.

BON JOVI

"Like a cowboy, Jon Bon Jovi rode in on a steel horse to sell . . . millions of records and set the standard in the art of the power ballad. Only this cowpoke was a New Jersey boy named John Bongiovi."[15] Blurring the line

With their signature power ballads, Richie Sambora's expert guitar, and lead singer Jon Bon Jovi's classic American look, Bon Jovi brought credibility and acclaim to glam-metal rock. Courtesy of Photofest.

between heavy metal and mainstream rock even further was Bon Jovi, another New Jersey–based band that has been described as mixing the "working-class sensibilities" of Bruce Springsteeen with the loud, tuneful metal of Def Leppard.[16] Fronted by lead singer Jon (born John Francis Bongiovi Jr. on March 2, 1962, in Perth Amboy, New Jersey), Bon Jovi included guitarist Richie Sambora (born July 11, 1959), keyboardist David Bryan (born David Rashbaum on February 7, 1962), drummer Tico Torres (born October 7, 1953), and bassist Alec John Such (born November 14, 1956).

A typically restless student at Sayreville High School, John scored high marks in theater[17] but mostly dreamt of rock stardom. He and Rashbaum eventually joined eight other musicians to form the R&B cover band Atlantic City Expressway. But when Rashbaum moved to New York to study at the Juilliard School of Music, John Bongiovi followed, eager to break into the recording industry. After convincing his cousin Tony, who owned the famous Power Station recording studios in New York, to give him any kind of work (he was hired as a janitor), John hung around the studio for two years, recording demos with members of the E Street Band and Aldo Nova.[18] Finally, Billy Squier agreed to produce John's own demo tape. The resultant track called "Runaway" was played on local radio stations and earned him a post on a local talent compilation CD (one that included such novelty songs as "R2D2, We Wish You a Merry Christmas").[19]

John then reunited with Rashbaum and acquired the services of already established studio musicians David Sabo, Torres, and Such to back up his first release. By July 1983, the group had secured a recording contract with Polygram/Mercury Records, though stories still persist about whether the band was signed or just John, who, along with Rashbaum, changed his name at the time of the signing to deemphasize its ethnicity. Before entering the studio, the band replaced guitarist Sabo with Richie Sambora, and Bon Jovi was born. During summer 1983, Bon Jovi garnered support slots touring with Eddie Money and ZZ Top and seemed to be on its way. Almost.

Prior to signing the contract with Polygram, Jon had been offered the Kevin Bacon role in the movie *Footloose*, which he had turned down to focus on his music. Jon's attractive, boyishly photogenic face, which became the mainstay of the group's videos, became a sort of albatross that hung around Bon Jovi's musical neck for some time. The same stereotype that plagued other handsome rockers, like Rick Springfield, also hurt Jon—and the band's—musical credibility early in their career. The idea that real rock 'n' roll artists had to "ugly up," or at least appear to affect a grungy, edgy look in order to be taken seriously as musicians, remained an unwritten criterion for excellence, at least in the minds of some critics. Interestingly, even Dylanesque folkies like Bruce Springsteen changed their appearance during the MTV-driven 1980s. One look at Springsteen's buff physique and rolled-up shirtsleeves in his "Dancing in the Dark" video is an indication that even the Boss' visual image had moved from gaunt outsider to hip, working-class cowboy.

Bon Jovi's self-titled debut album was released in 1984, with "Runaway" earning a spot in the Top 40. Angered at being excluded from their initial success, Jon's cousin Tony Bongiovi sued the band, claiming he was responsible for developing their successful sound. The case was settled out of court. The following year, a second album, *7800 Fahrenheit*, was released and went gold. Yet despite the respectable returns from the first two albums, Bon Jovi still had not achieved the kind of rock superstardom for which it had hoped.

Going into the studio for what would be their third album, they changed their approach to designing the album's concept and songs. In doing so, Bon Jovi forever changed the pop/metal sound in rock. To prepare for 1986's *Slippery When Wet*, the band hired professional songwriter Desmond Child as a collaborator. The group then auditioned almost thirty songs before local New Jersey and New York teenagers, ultimately basing the album's running order on their opinions. Finally, they rejected the album's raunchy cover photo that focused on a large-breasted woman wearing a wet T-shirt. Instead, Jon suggested the title be spelled out in water across a plastic garbage bag. *Slippery When Wet*, which was released in mid-August 1986, sold 9 million copies in the United States and over 14 million copies worldwide. The album also produced three hit singles: "You Give Love a Bad Name" and "Livin' on a Prayer," both of which reached No. 1, and "Wanted: Dead or Alive," which made the Top 10. Bon Jovi biographer Laura Jackson has called the release of *Slippery When Wet*

Bon Jovi's defining moment, even though some reviewers remained decidedly uncomplimentary about the band:

> *Rolling Stone* delivered a put-down that Bon Jovi were "a third generation smudgy Xerox of Quiet Riot." David Bryan was so affected by the swipe that he kept the review and framed it, confident that one day the influential magazine would have to change its mind about the band. In fact, nine months later, Jon Bon Jovi in full rock star pose dominated the front cover of its 500th edition.[20]

Early in 1987, the award season saw Bon Jovi receiving more accolades, winning trophies at the American Music Awards for "Favorite Pop/Rock Band," the People's Choice Award for "Band of the Year," and MTV's "Best Performance Award" for "Livin' on a Prayer." But with these awards came increased pressure to maintain the momentum of its meteoric rise in popularity.

Then 1988's *New Jersey* further enhanced the group's commercial success and finally established them as superstars. But, to some critics, *New Jersey* was no more than a formulaic replica of *Slippery When Wet*, including the "You Give Love a Bad Name" sound-alike hit "Bad Medicine." *New Jersey*, which shot to No. 1 upon its release, sold 5 million copies in the United States and was only slightly less successful than its *Slippery* predecessor. In addition to "Bad Medicine," the power ballad "I'll Be There for You" reached No. 1, and "Born to Be My Baby," "Lay Your Hands on Me," and "Living in Sin" landed in the Top 10. In 1989, the band extended its support to other artists including Loverboy and Cher, who was then dating Sambora. Playing on her *Heart of Stone* album as well as the hit single "We All Sleep Alone," the band shuttled back and forth between recording studio and international tour dates.

Upon completing the eighteen-month tour, the band went on hiatus. Jon Bon Jovi ended the decade alone artistically, soloing on the sound track for the film *Young Guns II*, which earned him Oscar and Grammy nominations for the song "Blaze of Glory" (1990). He also married his high school sweetheart, karate black belt Dorothea Hurley. The following year, Bon Jovi reunited to record their fifth album, *Keep the Faith*, which was released in the fall of 1992. The album did not match the blockbuster status of its predecessors, largely because musical tastes had shifted in the four years between it and *New Jersey*. In 1994, the band released its first hits collection, the fourteen-track *Crossroad*, and rumors of a permanent split were imminent.

Simultaneously, Jon reportedly commented that it was time to "Ride my bike into the hills, learn how to garden, anything except do another Bon Jovi record."[21] Jon decided to pursue an acting career and appeared (to good reviews) in several films during the late 1990s: *Moonlight and Valentino* (1996), *The Leading Man* (1997), *Little City* (1999), *Pay It Forward* (2001), and *U-571* (2002) and guest stints on popular television comedies *Ally McBeal* and *Sex and the City*. He also released his first official solo album, *Destination Anywhere*, in the summer of 1997. The band later reunited in 2000. *Crush*, the group's first release of new material in over five years, spawned the commandingly energetic megahit "It's My Life" as well as another ballad, "Thank You for Loving Me."

The band that was once ridiculed for its slick, commercial pop/metal sound and manicured designer look is now praised for its contribution to a musical style imitated since by countless others and has secured a popularity that is rivaled by few.

GUNS N' ROSES

They came from as far away as Stoke-on-Trent, England, and as close as Cleveland, Ohio. The real bad boys of heavy metal—noted for their late (or canceled) concerts, fistfights, racist comments, and romantic dramas (i.e., Axl Rose married Erin Everly, daughter of Don Everly in 1990; the marriage lasted three weeks)—were a Los Angeles–based quintet known as Guns N' Roses. The band's big breakthrough came in 1987 with the release of the album *Appetite for Destruction*. But their story began earlier and was characterized by a series of musical mishaps, personal setbacks, serendipitous reunions, and professional insults. Highly derivative of heavy metal and hard-rock bands from an earlier era (not atypical for 1980s heavy metal artists), Guns N' Roses laced its music with strains of Led Zeppelin, Frank Zappa, and Chuck Berry, and, like

Guns N' Roses became one of the most successful metal acts of the 1980s. Courtesy of Photofest.

Van Halen and Bon Jovi, both defy and redefine its sense (and ours) of heavy metal.[22]

Guns N' Roses was first billed for a show at The Troubadour in Los Angeles on March 26, 1985. The flyer read: "L.A. Guns and Hollywood Rose presents the band Guns N' Roses."[23] The lineup: Axl Rose (born William Bailey on February 6, 1962, in Lafayette, Indiana), Izzy Stradlin (born Jeff Isbell on April 8, 1962, also in Lafayette), Traci Guns, Ole Beich, and Rob Gardner. By June 6, 1985, the lineup had changed: Axl and Izzy remained but were joined by Duff McKagan (born Michael McKagan on February 5, 1964, in Seattle), Slash (born Saul Hudson on July 23, 1965, in Stoke-on-Trent, England), and Steven Adler (born on January 22, 1965, in Cleveland, Ohio). After rehearsing only a couple of days, and with no manager, recording contract, or scheduled bookings, the band embarked on "The Hell Tour."

Its first gig on the tour was at Seattle's Omni Room. Only thirteen people reportedly saw the show. Returning to Los Angeles, the band lived on Sunset Boulevard in a place they called "The Hell House." They had not much, if any, money, so they reportedly lived on cheap wine and biscuits or stole money from the groupies who sometimes visited them at their makeshift home. Playing covers of other artists, including "Heartbreak Hotel," "Jumping Jack Flash," and Aerosmith's "Mama Kin," Guns N' Roses eventually worked its own original songs like "Welcome to the Jungle," "Reckless Life," "It's So Easy," and "Don't Cry" into sets at the Troubador, the Whiskey A Go-Go, the Roxy, the Water Club, and Scream.

 WELCOME TO THE JUNGLE— GUNS N' ROSES (1987)

Gun N' Roses' debut single "Welcome to the Jungle" established the group as one of glam metal's most popular and musically influential bands of the late 1980s. Playing off metal's bad-boy image was lead singer Axl Rose, whose excessive behavior and controversial comments only contributed to the success of the single's record sales and subsequent video play. What separates this video from many other of its genre is the way the song plays off and up the angry, tattooed, big-haired glam-metal look and sound that typified many post-1985 groups.

In March 1986, the band signed a recording contract with Geffen Records but did not release an album until July 1987. *Appetite for Destruction*, which was released during the band's first European tour, rose to No. 1 and stayed there five weeks. In addition, the album produced three Top 10 singles, including the No. 1 "Sweet Child o' Mine." The band's follow-up album, *GN'R Lies* (live) was an extension of their 1986 four-song album titled *Live Like a Suicide*. The additional four tracks gave this 1986 sophomore effort a total of only eight tracks, yet the album still peaked at No. 2 and boasted a No. 4 single, "Patience."

Because it includes songs recorded before and after their rise to fame, *Lies* has been the subject of considerable study among rock historians. For example, some critics have noted the "surprising variety of styles" represented on the album, especially considering that only two years passed between the original album and its extended version. In many ways, *GN'R Lies* makes a clearer, though still fine, aural distinction between late 1980s hard rock and heavy metal:

> The first two songs (both from 1986) are typically heavy metal, complete with screaming vocal, fast, pounding rhythm, steady duple subdivision of the beat, distorted "power" guitar accompaniment, and defiant lyrics. . . . [I]n [the third track] "Move to the City," notice that lead singer Axl Rose lowers his voice range from the high scream of the first two songs. Also notice that the beat is no longer a steady duple subdivision (straight eighth notes), but a more rocking long-short pattern. This difference is also evident on the last of the 1986 songs, "Mama Kin." Here the guitar accompaniment is almost Chuck Berry–like at times.[24]

The 1986 cuts, including the hit "Patience," boast even more variety, including acoustic guitars and whistling. Similar to the opening musical foreplay found in Led Zeppelin's "Stairway to Heaven," "Patience" never builds to "Stairway"'s climactic power conclusion. Instead, its emphasis on Rose's vocals is more reminiscent of 1970s singer-songwriter ballads. "Used to Love Her" finds Rose moving from heavy metal scream to quirky Zappa-esque vocals, and "One in a Million" harkens again to the songwriter styles associated with artists from an earlier decade.[25]

Not without controversy, Guns N' Roses has taken its share of the kind of criticism commonly associated with heavy metal groups: vulgarity and sexism. "Used to Love Her," for instance, contains the violently misogynist lyrics, "Used to love her, but I had to kill her." In addition, some of their lyrics have drawn accusations of racism. "One in a Million" refers to "police and niggers" and complains that "immigrants and faggots" are spreading diseases and speaking unintelligible languages.[26] In the AIDS awareness/homophobic climate of the late 1980s, such lyrics served as much to inflame as to endear Guns N' Roses to heavy metal audiences.

The bad-boy behavior of the band did not help or hurt its image, either. During their October 1987 Amsterdam concert, Rose took the opportunity to respond to accusations that Guns N' Roses' musical style was merely derivative of other, older heavy metal groups: "Paul Stanley from KISS can suck my dick! And some of these old guys, that say we're ripping them off, maybe they should listen to some of their earlier albums and remember how to play them."[27] Unfortunately, Rose's spontaneous comments were not the exception to the band's rude behavior. His words more often represented the group's standard difficulty getting along with other bands and musicians.

In May 1988, while the band was on tour with Iron Maiden, Rose developed throat problems that forced Guns N' Roses to cancel the last part of the tour. Rumors that the band really canceled because they were upset over not headlining the tour gained some momentum when, after their cancellation, some of the band's members stepped onstage to jam with LA Guns, who had been hired as their replacement. Later that summer, after returning to the concert circuit as the opening act for Aerosmith, their crude behavior, coupled with their growing popularity, continued to cause professional problems. Tim Collins (Aerosmith's manager at the time) commented:

> By the end of the tour, Guns N' Roses were huge. They basically just exploded. We were all pissed that *Rolling Stone* showed up to do a story on Aerosmith, but Guns N' Roses actually ended up on the cover of the magazine. Suddenly, the opening act was bigger than we were. . . . But we felt sorry for them. One, they were so fucked up it was ridiculous. Two, their stupid manager had negotiated a bad deal for them and never bothered to renegotiate it or even complain. Three, they were traveling like Gypsies, their old suitcases held together by twine and gaffers tape. At the end of the tour, we bought them all new Halliburton cases, which their manager took as an insult.[28]

Continuing their 1988 summer tour at the Monsters of Rock series held at Castle Donnington, England, Guns N' Roses faced even more negative press when, despite stopping their set three times, two fans were crushed to death as the audience rushed the stage.

They returned to the United States that fall to perform "Welcome to the Jungle" at MTV's Video Music Awards and won in the "Best New Artist" category. Two weeks later at a Texas Jam concert headlined by rival metalers INXS, Rose told the crowd, "Apologize if, I sound like shit, but too many planes and too much cocaine, but you know where the fuck you are?"[29] Despite—or perhaps because of—such vulgarity, Guns N' Roses soon embarked on an international tour, playing Japan, New Zealand, and Australia in December.

The year 1989 brought more awards and more problems for band members. The controversy over racist lyrics in "One in a Million" did not stop the *LIVE* album from securing a No. 5 slot, making Guns N' Roses the first band in fifteen years to have two records in the U.S. Top 5 simultaneously. More concert sets and impromptu duets with other artists, including Great White and Tom Petty, occur. But so do increasingly irresponsible, destructive behavior patterns. On August 27, 1989, Izzy Stradlin was arrested at a Phoenix airport for public disturbance. Reports indicated he urinated on the floor, verbally abused a flight attendant, and smoked in a nonsmoking area. The following month, a Chicago work session for the next album never materialized when Rose and Stradlin did not show up.

Fed up with the group's unreliable behavior, Rose dramatically threatened to quit the band unless Slash, Stradlin, and Adler promised to clean up their respective acts. While opening for the Rolling Stones at the LA Coliseum in October 1989, Rose announced: "I hate to do this on stage. But I tried every other fucking way. And unless certain people in this band get their shit together, these will be the last Guns N' Roses shows you'll fucking ever see."[30] All three agreed to do better, but their pattern of crude and irreverent behavior continued.

In January 1990 Slash uttered several four-letter words during his acceptance speech at the American Music Awards. In April, Duff divorced his wife of two years, Mandy. In July, Steven Adler was fired from the band for failing to handle his drug abuse problem. His replacement was Matt Sorum (born November 19, 1960). Problems also arose with the release of their next album, *Use Your Illusion* (the title was taken from a painting by artist Mark Kostabi). Because they had recorded thirty-six songs, too many, said producer David Geffen, for one CD and too expensive to release a boxed set, two albums, *Use Your Illusion I* and *II*, were released simultaneously. In September 1991, Guns N' Roses became the first artists to hold the Top 2 album spots in the United Kingdom and the United States for *Use Your Illusion I* and *II*.

As the band moved into the 1990s, its successes continued but never came close to the meteoric popularity and stardom it experienced at the end of the 1980s. Its accomplishments, though sometimes dubious, continue to be acknowledgments of its fifteen minutes in the heavy metal spotlight, being ranked No. 43 on *Spin* Magazine's "50 Greatest Bands of All Time," No. 10 on *Rolling Stone's* "Twenty Greatest Live Acts in the World, as Named by *Rolling Stone* Readers," No. 9 on VH1's "100 Greatest Artists of Hard Rock," and No. 1 on MTV2's "Top 69 Epics" (for "November Rain"), as well as being named to other video-based lists.

QUIET RIOT

One of the first metal bands to experience crossover popularity during the 1980s was Quiet Riot. Originally founded in 1975 by singer Kevin DuBrow, Quiet Riot featured guitar impresario Randy Rhoads, bassist Kelli Garni, and drummer Drew Forsyth. After failing to break out of the LA metal scene with a recording contract, as Van Halen had done, Quiet Riot ultimately landed a deal with Columbia Records in Japan. Two album releases, *Quiet Riot* (1978) and *Quiet Riot II* (1979), failed to score with critics or audiences, and Rhoads left to help Ozzy Osbourne launch his solo career.

After the group disbanded, DuBrow ventured out on his own solo career, forming a backup band that included drummer Frankie Banali, bassist Rudy Sarzo (formerly with Osbourne's touring band), and guitarist Carlos Cavazo. Reborn as Quiet Riot, the band signed a deal with Pasha Records and recorded *Metal Health*, which was released in 1983. Two strong singles, the title track and "Cum on Feel the Noize" became major hits in the United States, and the album's success is considered a touchstone in helping initiate the glam-hair metal explosion of the 1980s. With over 6 million copies sold, the album holds a reputation as the biggest-selling rock debut album of its time.

By comparison, Quiet Riot's sophomore effort *Critical Condition* (1984), which sold only 2 million copies and was also panned critically, raised serious questions about the group's musical viability. Internal conflicts surfaced; DuBrow began making disparaging remarks about other metal bands in interviews, and Sarzo finally left the band (in 1985, later joining Whitesnake). Since then, band members have made several unsuccessful attempts to reunite and record new material, but none of these ventures have proven artistically or commercially successful, although rumors of a reunion surfaced as recently on October 2004.[31]

Quiet Riot's history is typical of many hair-metal bands who experienced initially enormous but ultimately fleeting popularity. Like Poison, Warrant, Whitesnake, Ratt, and other hair-metal bands, Quiet Riot paved the very short path that most hair-metal bands took: almost instant popularity with catchy pop/metal crossover hits that faded as soon as audiences grew tired of their banal lyrics and pedestrian melodies. It should not be surprising that many music critics hated glam rock and derided it as vapid, derivative, market-driven music that, as with teen idol promotion, focused as much, if not more, on the band members' hair, clothing, and makeup than on their music.

POISON

They came in like the wind—and left almost as quickly. Formerly known as Paris, the Harrisburg, Pennsylvania-based band Poison was formed in 1984 by singer Bret Michaels (born Bret Michael Sychak on March 15, 1963), bassist Bobby Dall (born Robert Kuykendall on November 2, 1963, in Miami), and drummer Rikki Rocket (born Richard Ream on August 8, 1961). Guitarist C. C. DeVille (born Bruce Anthony Johannsen on May 14, 1962, in Brooklyn, New York) was added to the group after they traveled from Pennsylvania to Los Angeles. Poison's meteoric rise to metal stardom and commercial popularity was equaled only to its rapid decline from the charts and fan loyalty. Poison vanished almost as soon as it arrived but still managed to leave a huge dent in the metal scene during its time in the spotlight.

Poison's first album, *Look What the Cat Dragged In*, was released by Enigma Records in 1986 and produced three Top 10 hits: "I Want Action," "Talk Dirty to Me," and "I Won't Forget You." Within a year of its release, *Look What the Cat Dragged In* sold over 2 million copies. Despite some critics' catty observation that there was a perverse connection between the album title, the band members' peroxide-processed hair, and the album's overall "painfully amateurish"[32] production and musical value, Poison went on to record a second album, 1988's *Open Up and Say . . . Ahh!* which climbed to No. 2 on the charts.

Considered the band's commercial breakthrough, *Open Up* contained three more massive hits: "Fallen Angel," "Nothin' But a Good Time," and the power ballad "Every Rose Has Its Thorn."[33] A successful tour with former Van Halen

Similar to Guns N' Roses, Poison recaptured the bad-boy sound of the power ballad. Courtesy of Photofest.

lead singer David Lee Roth followed, as did a third album, 1990's *Flesh & Blood*. This third studio effort produced two more singles, "Unskinny Bop" and "Something to Believe In." The band's mainstream sound, perfunctory and derivative at best, was popular with many pop/metal fans but often derided as "annoying and pointless" by heavy metal devotees.[34]

Internal problems surfaced shortly after the Roth-paired tour and the release of *Flesh & Blood*. During an appearance on MTV, guitarist DeVille reportedly played nearly half the song with his guitar unplugged, and a backstage brawl among band members erupted after the disastrous performance. DeVille had been battling increasingly serious problems with substance abuse and was fired from the band shortly after the release of the band's 1991 live album, *Swallow This Live*.

After DeVille's departure, the band tried to recapture its popularity with a new album (1993's *Native Tongue*) and concert tour. Both were commercial disappointments. The 1990s saw the group literally disappear from public view, although late in the decade several members resurfaced as part of a nostalgia tour. Poison's legacy to metal bands may be minimal, but its brief time at center stage gave fans several still recognizable power hits and perhaps gave the hair-metal genre its most memorable caricature.

WARRANT

Another 1980s metal band whose life in the spotlight was brief but shining was Warrant. Formed in Los Angeles in 1984, the group featured guitarists Joey Allen and Erik Turner, bassist Jerry Dixon, drummer Steven Sweet, and lead singer Jani Lane. Like Poison, Warrant's pop-metal sound could not sustain itself commercially, but while the band was together, it produced two double-platinum albums.

Their 1988 release *Dirty Rotten Filthy Stinking Rich* climbed into the Top 10, launching three hit singles: "Down Boys," "Sometimes She Cries," and "Heaven," which peaked at No. 2. A second album, 1990's *Cherry Pie*, fared even better, moving faster into the Top 10 and spawning singles "I Saw Red" and the title song. By the early 1990s, the alternative blitz eclipsed most metal bands, and Warrant was one of its many casualties. Though their third album, 1992's *Dog Eat Dog*, landed gold, a subsequent effort, 1995's *Ultraphobic*, failed to chart. Warrant continued to perform throughout the '90s, but their fan base dwindled and contributed to their early demise.[35] Recently, the band reunited and began touring again in 2005.

WHITESNAKE

Rivaling Warrant for its brief moment in the hair-metal spotlight was Whitesnake, a reincarnation of 1970s hard-rock band Deep Purple by its former lead singer David Coverdale (born September 22, 1949, in Saltburn-on-the-Sea, Yorkshire, England). Whitesnake formed in 1977 but failed to ignite any real musical sparks among fans or producers until 1984 when Coverdale reshuffled musicians yet again to produce the band's first platinum album: revitalized and energetic *Slide It In*. Relying on tried and true hooks reminiscent of Led Zeppelin and Deep Purple as well as Coverdale's trite but popular cock-of-the-walk sexism, *Slide It In* put Whitesnake on the charts, if only briefly.[36]

Another band member reorganization followed, as did the release of another album, *Whitesnake*, in 1987. This most commercial, if not critically acclaimed, effort pleased old fans and produced the group's only No. 1 hit, an "infectious" reworking of "Here I Go Again" (the original version can be found on 1982's *Saints and Sinners*) and another Top 10 Led Zeppelin-esque single called "Still of the Night." Before another album could be recorded, Coverdale reassembled the group yet again for 1989's *Slip of the Tongue*, this time featuring guitar virtuoso Steve Vai.[37] Although the album went platinum, Whitesnake's unstable chart track record and numerous member changes were a major disappointment to record distributors, and as the decade drew to a close, the group embarked on a permanent hiatus.

MÖTLEY CRÜE

The last of the big, big-haired bands included here was one of the first formed in the 1980s and is considered second only to Guns N' Roses for its gritty reputation and bad-boy antics. Mötley Crüe's nefarious roots can be traced back to 1981 when bassist Nikki Sixx (born Frank Ferranno on December 11, 1958, in San Jose, California) and drummer Tommy Lee (born Thomas Lee Bass on October 3, 1962, in Athens, Greece) left their respective bands to start a new project that would include guitarist Mick Mars (born Robert Deal on April 3, 1956, in Huntington, Indiana) and vocalist Vince Neil (born Vincent Neil Wharton on February 8, 1961, in Hollywood, California). It was Mars who ultimately suggested the band's name, a variation on the description of his former band, "a motley looking crew." During the 1980s, Mötley Crüe had a series of hit albums, culminating with 1989's *Dr. Feelgood* and an even bigger series of tabloid exploits.

After its debut album, *Too Fast for Love*, sold a respectable 20,000 copies, the band signed with Elektra Records. Their first Elektra release, *Shout at the Devil* (1983), which featured the video hit "Looks That Kill," went platinum. Mötley Crüe's initiation into stardom, unfortunately, was interrupted when Vince Neil was found guilty of vehicular homicide and, in 1985, served thirty days in jail in addition to performing community service and paying a large cash settlement for driving a car under the influence of alcohol, which led to the death of his friend, passenger Nicholas Dingley, and injured several others. While Neil underwent various legal and personal trials, the band recorded and released *Theatre of Pain*, which climbed the charts with a hit cover of Brownsville Station's "Smokin' in the Boys' Room."

Soon after *Theatre*'s release, the band regrouped with Neil to film a music video for "Home Sweet Home," an effort that became MTV's most requested video for four months straight. In 1986, *Uncensored*, a forty-five-minute video featuring rare live concert footage and interviews, was released. That same year, Tommy Lee married actress Heather Locklear, and the band released its fourth album, the controversial *Girls, Girls, Girls*. The title video, banned by MTV until a more appropriate version was released, provided only part of the controversy that would plague the band for the next two years. Ready to embark on their self-planned concert tour, Mötley Crüe canceled its European dates when Neil nearly died of a drug overdose. The rest of the band members spent the next two years in various drug rehabilitation programs before returning to the charts, clean and sober, with 1989's *Dr. Feelgood*.

Dr. Feelgood produced several hit singles, including "Kickstart My Heart," "Don't Go Away Mad (Just Go Away)," "Without You," and the No. 1 title track. The group embarked on another worldwide tour before releasing a "greatest hits" compilation CD, *Decade of Decadence*, in 1991. Resigning for Elektra Records for a reported $25 million, the band seemed ready to make more heavy metal history. But when its 1992 recording sessions for its much-hyped new album turned ugly, Vince Neil was fired and replaced by John Corabi, former leader singer for Scream. The album, 1994's *Mötley Crüe*, which peaked at No. 7 and eventually went gold, was a commercial disappointment, as was their 1997 effort, *Generation Swine* (even with Neil's return).

Personal issues continue to plague the group. Tommy Lee's divorce from Heather Locklear in early 1992 was followed by a much-publicized relationship and subsequent marriage to *Baywatch* actress Pamela Anderson in 1998. Accusations of spousal abuse added to Lee's already damaged rehabilitated bad-boy image, as did his involvement in the negligent swimming pool death of a neighbor's toddler in 2002. Lee left Mötley Crüe in 1999 to form the group Methods of Mayhem, only to be replaced by former Ozzy Osbourne drummer Randy Castillo.

Castillo died tragically of complications from an undisclosed illness in the spring of 2002. Neil has continued to pursue projects with Crüe as well as solo endeavors. Nikki Sixx has had several newspaper-related difficulties, including a public feud with Hole drummer Samantha Maloney (whose Web site reported a fight between her and Sixx's wife over reports of his infidelity during a 2000 concert tour) and being kicked off a nationally syndicated talk show for being "too drunk" to be interviewed.[38] Despite the success of the band's 2001 tell-all biography *The Dirt* (which includes input from Lee), Mötley Crüe's musical potential seems to have been buried consistently by the members' inability to work—or work together.

BIG-HAIR BANDS: MORE TO COME

The popularity of hair-metal bands reached new and astronomic proportions during the 1980s. Although still labeled "derivative" and static in their musical development, the bands included here represent more than huge record sales. From the creation of the power ballad to the fusion of heavy metal with other styles of music to the evolution of the concert performance, hair-metal bands of the 1980s demonstrated more than big hair and good looks. They helped move one brand of rock 'n' roll in new and innovative directions and, in the process, often solicited new (and loyal) pop and heavy metal fans.

NOTES

1. See, for example, "The History of Heavy Metal," included at http://myuselessinfo .com/uhistorymetal.html. This Web site is part of the *St. James Encyclopedia of Popular Culture*, 2002 Gale Group.

2. S. L. Duff, quoted on wysisyg://134http://launch.yahoo.com.st/artistFocus.asp? artistID=102807.

3. See ibid., also *Billboard* for album sales.

4. See, for example, http://enwikipedia.og/wiki/Van_Halen.

5. Joe Stuessy and Scott Lipscomb, *Rock and Roll: Its History and Stylistic Development*, 4th ed. (Upper Saddle River, NJ: Prentice Hall, 2003), 381.

6. "The 500 Songs That Shaped Rock and Roll," brochure, published by the Rock and Roll Hall of Fame and Museum, Cleveland, OH, 1996.

7. See *Rolling Stone* Biography Web site: http://www.rollingstone.com/artist.

8. David Lee Roth, *Crazy from the Heat* (New York: Hyperion, 1997).

9. Stuessy and Lipscomb, *Rock and Roll*, 381–382.

10. See, for example, Web site listed in note 4; also *David Letterman Show* (New York: CBS, October 21, 1996, episode).

11. See official Web site: http://www.defleppard.com.

12. Ibid.

13. Ibid.

14. Ibid.; also VH1 Web site: http://www.VH1.com/bio.

15. See, for example, *Spin Magazine* interview with Jon Bon Jovi, quoted in Laura Jackson, *Jon Bon Jovi* (New York: Citadel Press, 2003), back cover.

16. See, for example, Web site listed in note 14.

17. Jon Bon Jovi's report card from Sayreville High School was on exhibit at the Rock and Roll Hall of Fame and Museum. The report card showed high marks in theater and lower marks in math and other more traditional courses. On exhibit 2001–2002.

18. See Web site listed in note 14.

19. Evin Boyle, cited at http://www.CanEHdian.com (2002).

20. Jackson, *Jon Bon Jovi*, 71–72.

21. See, for example, http://www.hiponline.com/artist/music/b/bon_jovi.

22. Stuessy and Lipscomb, *Rock and Roll*, 379–380.

23. See, for example, http://www.heretodaygonetohell.com.

24. Stuessy and Lipscomb, *Rock and Roll*, 380.

25. Ibid.

26. See song lyrics; also ibid.

27. See Web site in note 23 for 1987.

28. Ibid.

29. Ibid., for 1988.

30. Ibid.

31. See, for example, Quiet Riot Web sites like the following: http://www.campusprogram.com/reference/en/wikipedia/q/qu/quiet_riot.html.

32. Martin C. Strong, *The Great Rock Discography*, 6th ed. (Edinburgh, UK: Canongate Books, 2002), 812.

33. Barry Weber, "Poison," *All Music Guide*, included at http://www.vh1.com; search Poison.

34. Strong, *Great Rock Discography*, 812.

35. Stephen Thomas Erlewine, "Warrant," *All Music Guide*, included at http://www.vh1.com; search Warrant.

36. See, for example, Stephen Thomas Erlewine and Greg Prato, "Whitesnake," *All Music Guide*, included at http://www.vh1.com; search Whitesnake.

37. Strong, *Great Rock Discography*, 1131–1132.

38. See, for example, liveDaily: Mötley Crüe Bio, Articles, Discography: http://www.livedaily.com/artists/bio/773.html.

8

THE CHANGING FACE OF TEEN IDOLS

Just like the long-held stereotype in academia that scholars and intellectuals could not be cool, hip, or good-looking, rock 'n' roll has long upheld the notion that rock stars needed to posses that sexy, dark, and dangerous testosterone-driven look worn by the likes of a Mick Jagger or an Elvis Presley in order to be credible. Clean-cut, cute, softly attractive men could never been taken seriously in the hardcore world of rock music. By the late 1960s and early 1970s, rock music found a new audience: the preteenaged girl, those who, at the time, were old enough to enjoy the pop/rock sound but too young to appreciate the musical paths taken by the later Beatles or Bob Dylan. As a result, the less-threatening, androgynous looks of Bobby Sherman, Davy Jones of the Monkees, David Cassidy, Donny Osmond, and Michael Jackson—and the softly suggestive prepubescent music they sang—soon became synonymous with the term "teen idol."

The concept of a "teen idol" was not new—Frank Sinatra had been called one when he appealed to the bobby soxers during the 1940s. Even Elvis Presley was considered a teen favorite when he began his career in the mid-1950s. Ricky Nelson used his parents' television sitcom *Ozzie and Harriet* to build a fan following in the early 1960s. But these artists were generally older and more mature and attracted an audience over the age of sixteen. The enormous popularity of the Beatles led some record producers to believe there was a younger, equally enthusiastic audience from which to market recording artists, an idea that subsequently became the impetus for *The Monkees* television show, which premiered in 1966. But even the show's popularity could not bring credibility to teen idols. The label still meant career death to any serious aspirations in adult rock venues.

The credibility problem aside, teen idols of the late 1960s and 1970s opened up a whole new audience of rock fans. Teen magazines like *16* and *Tiger Beat* capitalized on this phenomenon by filling their pages with glossy photos of popular artists (suitable for bedroom wall or locker door displays) and offering innocent interviews that suggested any adoring fan could win a kiss—or a romantic date—from a favorite singing star. By the 1980s, MTV, with its natural focus on physical image, provided yet another venue with which to market sweet, often syrupy "pop" music in an appealing visual context. More important, the presence and success of many teen idol artists, including Rick Springfield, Wham! and Duran Duran—and the music they created—moved the once negative rap against the handsome men into a new cultural sphere. While some artists only experienced fleeting (one- or two-hit wonder) celebrity, others grew their initial teen idol label into long, lucrative, and lasting careers that watched their fans grow and mature with them and their music. The 1980s saw a change in both the sound and image of rockers turned into teen idols. On both levels, MTV was a primary force in the creation, success, and revitalization of the teen idol image.

SHOCK/DENIAL/ANGER/ACCEPTANCE: RICK SPRINGFIELD

Though he hails from Sidney, Australia (born there Richard Lewis Springthorpe on August 23, 1949), Rick Springfield represents both a rock 'n' roll and an all-American success story. And though his recording career began with mixed success before the 1980s, it really is not until 1981 and the release of *Working Class Dog* (combined with his stint on ABC's long-running soap opera *General Hospital*) that he secures a place in rock history. An army brat (his father Norman was a colonel in the Australian army) who had spent much of his childhood learning to adjust to being the new kid in town, Springfield found music and books a natural escape from his difficulty in making friends.

He eventually dropped out of high school to pursue music, joining his first band, a '50s revival group called Rock House, in the mid-1960s. The band landed a tour in Vietnam at the height of the conflict there, and Springfield reportedly "found himself dodging bombs and throwing grenades."[1] Rock House disbanded shortly after its return to Australia, and Rick joined the very popular teen band Zoot in 1969.[2] His tenure with the band allowed him to polish songwriting and guitar-playing skills, and local record producers soon tapped him to try a solo career.

Springfield's tall (six-feet-two-inch), lanky frame, dark shag haircut, soulful brown eyes, and softly masculine features made him the perfect teen idol heir apparent to *The Partridge Family*'s already disenchanted star David Cassidy. Producers Steve Binder and Robie Porter, who assisted in the rerecording of Springfield's first pop single "Speak to the Sky" for Capitol Records, brought him to the United States, releasing his first album, *Beginnings*, there in 1972.

16 and *Tiger Beat* magazines quickly jumped on Springfield's boyish good looks and promoted him as a teen idol, though Springfield, at twenty-three, was already two years older than Cassidy and almost a decade older than Cassidy's biggest rival, Donny Osmond. A series of marketing mishaps and musical flops followed,[3] leaving Springfield's musical career in shambles until his reappearance early in 1981.

As cruelly as success seemed to have been snatched from him a decade earlier, fame now coincided with lightning speed to define his image. A contract with RCA Records and the release of the album *Working Class Dog*, with its classic pop teen angst single "Jessie's Girl," scored a bull's-eye with fans of all ages. Record stations played his music constantly, pushing the single "Jessie's Girl" to No. 1 in the summer of 1981. The role on *General Hospital* opened up a whole new contingent of fans, and magazines were eager to report on his newfound fame. "It was so fast," Springfield

Rick Springfield redefined the teen idol image to a whole new audience during the 1980s. Courtesy of Photofest.

remembers, "just a few weeks."[4] *Working Class Dog* spawned three Top 20 hits. The phenomenal No. 1 single "Jessie's Girl" captured almost perfectly the primal teen angst to which every preteen, teen, and adult can relate. With a memorable melody, good hooks, and playfully clever lyrics,[5] "Jessie's Girl" went on to win Springfield a Grammy Award for "Best Pop/Rock Male Vocal." Two other singles, the tougher, edgy "I've Done Everything for You" and the drivingly lyrical "Love Is Alright Tonight" peaked at No. 8 and 20, respectively. It was clear that Springfield's music had emerged as some of the "best-crafted 'power pop' of the decade,"[6] perhaps second only, if not equal, in the importance to Bon Jovi's "power ballad." *Working Class Dog*, which was released in January 1981, went gold in August, platinum in December, and reached a peak chart position of No. 7.

In spite of his sudden celebrity, Springfield could not shake the fact that many rock critics still could not trust a rocker with such a handsome face. With a new generation of teen fans, Springfield found the teen idol moniker continued to follow him, and his music was often dismissed as "vapid teen idol fare."[7] In 1982 *Success Hasn't Spoiled Me Yet*'s pop sound—a smoother, more polished studio formula than the more elemental rock 'n' roll, almost angrier feel of *Working Class Dog*—solidified, at least for some critics, that Springfield was just another pretty boy with little musical substance. His mismatched pink and purple Converse tennis shoes and matching concert suits did not persuade them differently. Riding on the crest of popularity from the previous year, *Success Hasn't Spoiled Me Yet* produced three Top 40 singles: "Don't Talk to Strangers," "What Kind of Fool Am I," and "I Get Excited," which peaked at Nos. 2, 21, and 32, respectively. *Success Hasn't Spoiled Me Yet* came out in March 1982, went platinum by May, and copped a chart position of No. 2.

Both *Working Class Dog* and *Success Hasn't Spoiled Me Yet* garnered ample radio and MTV play and increased Springfield's audience visibility. But, by 1983, the fans' demand for concerts began to conflict with his filming schedule on *General Hospital* (he had been cast in the supporting role of nurse station lothario Dr. Noah Drake just as RCA agreed to distribute *Working Class Dog*), and he asked to be released from his television contract. That same year, another chart-topping album, *Living in Oz*, was released. In addition to three more Top 40 hit singles, "Affair of the Heart" (No. 9), "Human Touch" (No. 18) and "Souls" (No. 23), platinum status, and a chart peak at No. 12, *Living in Oz* introduced a new Springfield image: tougher, edgier, darker. The songs mirrored this change in image—lyrics were more suggestive, subject matter ranged from passionate eroticism to forbidden love—as did Springfield's scruffily unshaven cover photo, accessorized with torn leather threads. Older fans embraced his new look, which complemented the hard-rock feel of the new album.

The year 1984 saw Springfield star in the big screen film *Hard to Hold*, a pedestrian love story disguised as an offbeat romantic comedy. The movie failed to turn him into a film star. In fact, it literally ruined any chance of a film career. In spite of the film's poor performance at the box office, the sound track soared, producing four Top 40 singles, including the driving rock ballad "Love Somebody" (No. 5), the plaintive "Don't Walk Away" (No. 26), and the funky "Bop 'Til You Drop" (No. 20), whose music video harkens back to Fritz Lang's 1926 silent movie masterpiece *Metropolis*. The platinum-selling sound track, which peaked at No. 16, offered Springfield the shocking realization that while his music was still hot, even his good looks could not save a movie that was once described by film critic Leonard Maltin as "hard to watch."[8]

Back in the recording studio, Springfield completed another album in 1985. *Tao* contained more sophisticated melodies and arrangements as well as more philosophical lyrics. The album's two charted singles, "Celebrate Youth" (No. 26) and "State of the Heart" (No. 22) are examples of Springfield's growth as a songwriter and lyricist. A two-year hiatus following *Tao*'s promotional tour, during which time Springfield entered psychoanalysis to find the source of the depression that had plagued him since his teens. He chronicled his two-year period of self-examination in his last album release during the 1980s, 1988's *Rock of Life*. With only the title track scoring in the Top 40 (No. 22), *Rock of Life*'s ten tracks speak of finding meaning in life, of not being ready for fatherhood, of dealing with the day-to-day difficulties of marriage.[9] Like *Living in Oz*, which contained songs about intimate sexual encounters and an affair with a married woman,[10] *Rock of Life* addressed issues far beyond the emotional maturity of some of Springfield's younger fans.

To some critics and fans, Springfield's career span seemed destined to stay in the 1980s. But as the title from his 2004 album *shock/denial/anger/acceptance* suggests, while Springfield's personal and professional journeys have often paralleled the psychological stages of grief, he remains committed to developing the hard-rock roots that originally fused his musical career. Springfield continues to write, record, and perform onstage. His concerts still draw consistently large numbers of dedicated fans. It should not be surprising that Springfield's fan club is known as "Rick's Loyal Supporters" nor that Springfield—despite many personal and professional setbacks—has retained boyishly playful good looks that now have transcended the "teen idol" label and settled in rock artist acceptability.

GEORGE MICHAEL AND WHAM!

Generally cited as the most commercially successful English pop group of the 1980s, Wham! sparked a kind of pop revival that lingered well into the 1990s. Some critics even singled out Wham! as musical stylists for the American boy band trend that dominated the 1990s. The dynamic duo, which consisted of George Michael (born Georgios Kyriacos Panayiotou on June 25, 1963, in London) and Andrew Ridgeley (born January 26, 1963, in Surrey, England), formed in 1982.

After making a series of impressive demos, Michael and Ridgeley were signed by Innervision, an independent recording label. Guided by music publisher Dick Leahy (assisted by Bryan Morrison), Wham! embarked on a series of personal appearances at local clubs while completing their debut single "Wham Rap!" Fan magazines quickly grabbed on to the duo's good looks and teen market appeal, even though the lyrics to their songs often spoke of hunger, unemployment, and deriding London's elitist rich.[11] A series of modest hit singles followed, with their debut album *Fantastic* (1983) scoring a notch on the UK album charts.

But conflicts over the group's bad-boy image and lyric content culminated in an acrimonious court case with Innervision that ultimately released the duo from their contract. The two immediately signed with

George Michael, shown left, with Andrew Ridgeley, had a sexy style and good looks that transcended the teen image and took him to pop/rock stardom after Wham! Courtesy of Photofest.

Sony's Epic label and celebrated their new artistic freedom with the monster international hit "Wake Me Up Before You Go Go" (1984), which peaked at No. 1 in both the United Kingdom and the United States, holding the No. 1 slot on *Billboard* 100 for three weeks. "Wake Me Up" was quickly followed by Michael's first solo effort, "Careless Whisper." The sexy love ballad, co-composed by Ridgeley, but credited to George Michael as an artist, shot to No. 1 and set the stage for Michael's subsequent solo career.[12]

Wham!'s second album, *Make It Big* (1984), reached No. 1, producing two Top 5 singles. In 1985 amid much publicity and growing rumors of a split, Wham! traveled to China, notable in that they were the first Western group to be invited to do so, and the United States. Both were very successful concert tours.[13] In 1986, Michael and Ridgeley fired their manager Simon Napier-Bell, whom they alleged sold a share of his management to a South African entertainment conglomerate. In response to the sale and as part of a stand against apartheid, George Michael immediately announced the group's breakup. On June 28, 1986, Wham! played its farewell concert before 72,000 fans at London's Wembley Stadium.[14] This act of "pop euthanasia"[15] signaled the end of Ridgeley's short-lived career but opened the door for Michael as pop heartthrob.

On his own, Michael rapidly ascended the pop/rock ladder by a method some critics derided: consistently gluing "his pretty, deliberately stubble-faced mug to nearly every television screen in the Free World. Helping considerably, of course, was the singer's noticeable growth as both singer and songwriter since his earliest days in the pop duo Wham!—which began as a nondescript pop/dance group and quickly metamorphosed into a huge international hit machine."[16] Having critics recognize his professional growth in spite of his sexy appearance is alone a statement about Michael's potential to become a credible solo rock act. That and his Live Aid duet with Elton John the summer before Wham!'s breakup seemed to position the singer to enter the pop/rock elite on his own.

In 1987, the year after he split with partner Andrew Ridgeley, George Michael's return to the spotlight remains, to some, his "most impressive achievement to date."[17] His megaselling album *Faith* came fully loaded with six Top 5 hits, four of which—"Faith," "Father Figure," "One More Try," and "Monkey"—went to No. 1. The album was No. 1 for twelve weeks and won the 1988 Grammy Award for Album of the Year. Michael's presence was an undeniable force in the pop/rock arena. But then he made a gutsy decision that could have spelled career anonymity. Instead of increasing his MTV presence, the singer made himself scarce.

After recording his follow-up album *Listen Without Prejudice*, Michael refused all interviews and made no videos to promote the album. As a result, the 1990 effort produced only two Top 10 hits, "Praying for Time" and "Freedom." Compared to *Faith*, which sold over 15 million copies worldwide and contained six hit singles, *Listen Without Prejudice*, with one-third the profits of its predecessor and only two hits, was considered a major commercial disappointment. In a 1989 interview, Michael commented on his decision to downplay his sex symbol image in recording and promoting the new album:

> I was trying to get rid of what I'd done with Faith. . . . I think stylistically, although the songs are really good, I'd wandered off my natural path. Also I was too concerned with criticisms of my earlier stuff and that led me to make an album that I thought maybe rock critics would have a more sympathetic view of. So in *Listen Without Prejudice* there were lots of acoustic guitars and much more natural instrumentation and I was trying to emulate certain things that were too white in origin for me to really be comfortable with. I can't truly express myself fully without some R&B influence and with it I drifted away from the black elements of my music.[18]

In spite of Michael's own critical assessment of *Faith*'s follow-up, many critics still commended Michael for his refusal to continue using his handsome face to sell records. His uneven musical choices eventually settled into a comfortably edgy musical image. In this way, trying to explain Michael's enduring popularity might seem tricky, although journalist Adrian DeVoy created a far simpler rationale: "Everybody's got a bit of George Michael in them."[19]

DURAN DURAN

If pop culture enjoys reinvention with each passing generation, Duran Duran is a testament to carrying that baton. Taking its name from a character in director Roger Vadim's 1968 psychedelic science-fiction film *Barbarella*, Duran Duran started out playing gigs without a drummer, using a drum machine to provide the rhythm for the keyboards. Claiming to have been inspired by artists like David Bowie and Roxy Music and post-punk and disco, childhood schoolmates Nick Rhodes (keyboards; born Nicholas James Rhodes on June 8, 1962) and John Taylor (guitar; born Nigel John Taylor on June 20, 1960) originally formed Duran Duran in 1978 with fellow classmates Simon Colley (bass, clarinet) and Stephen Duffy (vocals).

Duran Duran's first two years were unstable, plagued by musicians who came and went very quickly. Colley and Duffy exited the group within a year, replaced by drummer Roger Taylor (born Roger Andrew Taylor on April 26,

 I WANT YOUR SEX—GEORGE MICHAEL (1987)

Breaking away from his nonthreateningly soft, androgynous Wham! image, George Michael reinvented himself as a solo act in the late 1980s, culminating his transformation with the megahit album *Faith* and marching into the video world with tantalizingly teasing videos. Besides its salacious title, *I Want Your Sex* combined Michael's stubbly good looks with stylish quick-cut video bites to leave much of the song's lyrical meaning to the viewer. Together with Rick Springfield, George Michael integrated his rough good looks with appropriately suggestive, catchy tunes to change the face of the teen idol, literally and figuratively.

Combining picture-perfect good looks with style and panache, Duran Duran also produced music that struck a chord with audiences worldwide. Courtesy of Photofest.

1960) and vocalist Andrew Wickett, whose stay with the band only lasted a few months. Guitarist Taylor switched to bass, adding John Curtis on guitar, only to have Curtis quit the band within months after his arrival. An ad in *Melody Maker* caught the attention of Andy Taylor (born Andrew Taylor on February 16, 1961), who took over as the group's guitarist. By 1979, the group seemed almost complete but still lacked a vocalist. Two more singers would pass through before Simon Le Bon (vocalist; born Simon John Charles Le Bon on October 27, 1958), a drama student at Birmingham University and former member of the punk band Dog Days, joined the group early in 1980.

With five members intact, Duran Duran began playing the "new romantics"[20] circuit in England, gaining a popularity that would secure their first recording contract with EMI Records late in 1980. The group's first single "Planet Earth" rose to No. 12 during its spring 1981 release, moving the group to the top of the new romantics heap and drawing heavy media attention. That same year, the group's raunchy, racy music video for "Girls on Film" stirred more media hype when the BBC banned the video, which quickly moved to the Top 10 list in England. In May 1982, Duran Duran released its first album, *Rio*, which entered the charts at No. 3 and stayed on the charts for 118 weeks. By November 1981, Duran Duran members were superstars in England but had not made much of an impression on American audiences.

Enter MTV, which quickly inserted the group's stylish videos into its rotation. The network's constant playing of videos like *Hungry Like the Wolf* eventually landed *Rio* in America's Top 10, and by 1983, Duran Duran mania was in full swing in the United States.[21] The band followed its initial success with another Top 10 single, "Is There Something I Should Know," and a second album, *Seven and the Ragged Tiger* (strategically released in time for the 1983 holiday season). *Seven and the Ragged Tiger* peaked at No. 8 in the United States (it reached No. 1 in England) and produced two more hit singles, "Union of the Snake" and "The Reflex," the latter becoming the group's first No. 1 single in America. After completing an international tour in the spring of 1984, Duran Duran took an extended hiatus, reuniting only to record the title track for the 1985 James Bond film *A View to a Kill* (which opened the American portion of Live Aid that summer).

Andy and John Taylor formed a side group called Power Station, which included vocalist Robert Palmer and former Chic drummer Tony Thompson. The remaining members of Duran Duran—Nick Rhodes, Simon Le Bon, and Roger Taylor—released their own album, *So Red the Rose*, in the fall 1985. Early in 1986, Roger Taylor announced his plans to take a year's sabbatical from the group. He never returned. Andy Taylor officially left that same year. Duran Duran's next album, *Notorious*, released late in 1986, failed to generate much buzz, even though it went platinum in the United States and landed a Top 10 slot for the title track. As the decade came to a close, Duran Duran saw its popularity gently decline. During the 1990s, the group released three albums with the added support of former Missing Persons guitarist Warren Cuccurullo (born Warren Bruce Cucurrullo on December 8, 1956). But even with the success of 1993's comeback album *Duran Duran* and its two light, funky adult contemporary singles, "Ordinary World" and "Come Undone," the group has not regained the popularity it achieved during the 1980s with the help of MTV.

Duran Duran, with its mainstream new wave style, built its musical reputation through music videos. While other attractive rock artists, like Rick Springfield and George Michael, tried to downplay their obvious good looks, Duran Duran capitalized on their glamorous, runway model appearance in countless music videos. In addition to the controversy that followed *Girls on Film* and *The Chauffeur* for their explicit sexual content, the group also hit the mark making videos that were often based on popular, contemporary movies: *Hungry Like the Wolf* curiously echoed *Raiders of the Lost Ark* (1981); *Union of the Snake* and *The Wild Boys* conjured up images of *The Road Warrior*. Between 1983 and 1985, Duran Duran used MTV to turn its little-known British underground pop-funk style into an American pop teen idol sensation. Its short-lived time in the pop/rock spotlight is evidence that if it had not been for MTV, Duran Duran's sound alone, once described as "the Sex Pistols meets Chic,"[22] would have never brought the band international rock stardom.

 GIRLS ON FILM—DURAN DURAN (1981)

Early on in its history, MTV embraced controversy. No better example was there than Duran Duran's sexy bed romp to their single "Girls on Film," a pre-*Centerfold* brush" with the *Playboy* view of rock 'n' roll. Unlike its successors, *Girls on Film* was close to soft porn in its graphic, sometimes lewd depiction of women. For Duran Duran, the pretty boys whose photogenic good looks made them as much about clothes and style as music, the racy video seemed to run counter to their teen idol niche. Nonetheless, almost twenty-five years after its release, *Girls on Film* remains a provocative landmark music video.

THE TEEN IDOL PHENOMENON

The life span of teen idols can usually be clocked from the time a preteen reaches junior high school until she finds her first steady boyfriend. Teen idols who have not continued to grow and mature artistically are probably doomed to a celebrity life shorter than Andy Warhol's promised fifteen minutes. But artists like Rick Springfield, George Michael, and Duran Duran, who began their careers as teen idols yet came equipped with real talent and other artistic options, have survived—and at times *thrived*—in the entertainment and recording industry long after their faces faded from the covers of teen magazines.

Teen idols of the 1980s paved the way for many of the teen idol acts and images of the 1990s: from Britney Spears and Christina Aguilera to the Backstreet Boys and 'NSYNC. Wholesome—and now, not-so-wholesome—images of teenage artists continue to dominate music videos as expressions of other important issues facing teens today: sexuality, social acceptability, even future career success. If the ongoing popularity of teen idols tells us anything about rock 'n' roll, it suggests that the rebellious spirit of music that defined American culture a half-century ago still speaks—sometimes with new lyrics and a slightly different beat—to every teenage generation as it hopes and dreams and waits for life to happen.

NOTES

1. See fan site, for example, http://www.rickspringfield.net/biography.html.

2. See rock celebrity profiles by Steve Huey, "Rick Springfield," *All Music Guide*, included at http://www.mtv.com; search Rick Springfield.

3. "Rick Springfield, a Discography," included in fan club packet, Vivan Achinelli, president, *Rick's Loyal Supporters* (founded 1989).

4. See, for example, note 1.

5. Rick Springfield, "Jessie's Girl," song included on *Working Class Dog* (RCA Records, 1981); lyrics at http://www.geocities.com/SunsetStrip/Venue/97969/pop/j/jesses_girl.html.

6. See Huey, "Rick Springfield."

7. Ibid.

8. Leonard Maltin, *2000 Movie & Video Guide* (New York: Signet, 1999), 577.

9. See fan site, as listed in note 1.

10. Rick Springfield, "Allison," included on *Living in Oz* (RCA Records, 1983); the song tells the story of a fantasy relationship between a married woman and a single man (Springfield).

11. See, for example, http://www.music.lycos.com; search Wham!

12. See Ed Nimmervoll, "Wham!" *All Music Guide*, found at VH1 Web site: http://www.vh1.com; search Wham!

13. See, for example, Web site at note 11.

14. Nimmervoll, "Wham!"

15. Ibid.

16. Dave DeMartino, "Wham!" found at http://music.yahoo.com; search Wham!

17. Ibid.

18. Adrian DeVoy, "1989 Interview with George Michael," included at http://www.songmusic.co.uk/georgemichael.biog/.

19. Ibid.

20. The new romantics movement emerged in the United Kingdom during the 1980s as a backlash against the austerity of the punk movement and included such groups as Duran Duran, Spandau Ballet, and Flock of Seagulls.

21. Stephen Thomas Erlewine, "Duran Duran," *All Music Guide*, found at the MTV Web site: http://www.mtv.com; search Duran Duran.

22. Ibid.

9

WOMEN ROCKERS AND MTV

If we learned anything from Cyndi Lauper's 1984 video romp to her hit single "Girls Just Want to Have Fun," it might be that women in rock wanted to be taken as seriously as their male counterparts. At a time when MTV's blatant promotion of women (including rockers) as sex objects threatened to destroy any artistic credibility women had earned since the dawn of rock 'n' roll, Lauper's single (and video) seemed to take the never-ending argument about gender in rock music and push it back in the faces of critics, fans, and male artists.

But Lauper was not alone. Other 1980s female artists took Helen Reddy's 1973 anthem "I Am Woman, Hear Me Roar" and the feminist movement to heart, empowering themselves musically as never before. Although many women rock 'n' rollers never cited feminism as their cause—some, in fact, denied it—their connection to women's issues can be seen in their video images and heard through their music. This DIY (do it yourself) attitude about music, which sprang primarily from the late 1970s punk movement, opened doors for both male and female artists in terms of speaking their minds, and for women, having the courage to organize and front a band. Still, accusations of sexism and the treatment of women in the recording industry as second-class citizens continued throughout the 1980s, while simultaneously artists like Madonna, Joan Jett, Aimee Mann, the Go-Go's, and Michelle Shocked broke new ground in areas that including writing, producing, and controlling their own careers and images.

The 1980s became a watershed decade for women in rock 'n' roll, especially those who had imagination and a sense of humor. For them, the option of "appropriating the traditional images of femininity and, through blatant exaggeration, subverting them"[1] became a means of artistic empowerment. As a medium, music video offered women artists an excellent opportunity to explore, comment on, and question gender roles, with many female artists successfully taking advantage of this opportunity. Instead of passively allowing MTV to swallow up their artistry and turn it into eye candy, women in rock 'n' roll grabbed gender stereotypes by the balls and turned them back on audiences, broadening the scope of women's involvement in the artistic process and setting new standards for the status of women in rock music.

JOAN JETT

Playing elemental rock 'n' roll without specifically focusing on gender, Joan Jett became a role model for the tough, independent female rocker. Born Joan Larkin (September 22, 1960, in Philadelphia), Jett was raised in both Pennsylvania and Los Angeles (her family moved there when she was twelve). By the age of fifteen, she had formed her first band and began performing around the LA area. A chance meeting with record producer Kim Fowley in the late 1970s led to a recording contract with Mercury Records and the birth of her renamed all-girl group, the Runaways. Though the Runaways never found much commercial success, releasing three albums during their time together, Jett was already connecting with Los Angeles' punk and hard-rock crowd so that when the Runaways disbanded in early 1979, Jett seemed poised for a solo career.

But Jett took the Runaways' breakup hard, becoming despondent and leaving the American rock scene. After spending time in London, where she had worked with ex–Sex Pistols Steve Jones and Paul Cook, Jett returned to the United States and teamed up with producer/manager Kenny Laguna, who helped her release her self-titled debut album independently when no record labels would sign her. Jett's first solo effort was more traditional rock 'n' roll than the punk sound produced by the Runaways, yet it retained the kind of raw defiance that had been one of the group's distinct features. Industry interest in Jett's

Joan Jett, the new poster girl for tough chicks in rock, revitalized mid-1960s hard rock during the 1980s. Courtesy of Photofest.

album, which sold well for an independent release, led to a contract with Boardwalk Records. In 1981 Boardwalk remixed and reissued the album under the title *Bad Reputation*, adding the Blackhearts (guitarist Ricky Bird, bassist Gary Ryan, and drummer Lee Crystal) to give an end result that has been described as "a heady hoedown of post-glitter raunch-pop, cruising on a hefty dose of punk energy and a healthy, two-fingered attitude to music industry convention."[2] Jett's reissue quickly climbed up the charts, peaking at No. 51 in the United States.

Her breakthrough came in 1982 with the hit "I Love Rock 'n' Roll," the title track from her second album, which soared to the top of the charts early in 1982. The album itself landed a No. 2 spot and spawned two additional Top 20 hits, covers of "Crimson and Clover" and "Do You Wanna Touch Me (Oh Yeah)." Jett became one of the first—and only—female artists to play straight-on, kick-ass rock 'n' roll with no nod to prevailing music trends.

Although 1982 was Jett's biggest commercial year, she remained on the music scene, scoring hits again in 1987 with the title track from the film *Light of Day*. Directed by Paul Schrader, *Light of Day* paired Jett with popular television star Michael J. Fox as brother and sister struggling to break out of their blue-collar Cleveland existence. The song "Light of Day" made the Top 40. The following year, Jett released another album, *Up Your Alley*, which peaked at No. 8 and produced another Top 10 single, "I Hate Myself for Loving You." The album became Jett's second platinum record. By 1990, Jett's success had cooled a bit, as an all-covers album *The Hit* only reached No. 36 on the album charts. Hot on its heels, 1991's *Notorious* failed to chart.

By 1994, Jett and the Blackhearts' release *Pure and Simple* seemed outdated and antiquated compared to the material being released by harder, alternative female rockers who touted an even more minimalist style and riot grrrl punk rockers (those who openly, angrily rebelled against feminine stereotypes like the passive, docile woman) like Bikini Kill whose in-your-face defiance bore more bravado than Jett's own bad-girl image. Still, artists from Bikini Kill to L7 have credited Jett and The Runaways as seminal influences on their grunge and post-punk styles. In 1999, Jett reunited with the Blackhearts for an album release titled *Fetish*.[3]

Always a step or two ahead of her time, and adamantly refusing to kowtow to any faddish musical trends, Joan Jett never allowed herself to be pigeonholed musically. But, as a result, she also failed to find her artistic niche. Between her work with the Runaways and the Blackhearts, Jett bridged the gap between heavy metal and punk. Songs like "Bad Reputation" and "Cherry Bomb" integrated a kind of hard-nosed pop sensibility with "a certain punk rock scrappiness as well as a metallic edge."[4] Her gritty-edged vocals often beg comparison to AD/DC's Bon Scott. Unfortunately, her musical hybrid has made it difficult for her to find ongoing commercial success, although she has always been recognized for making consistently interesting music. To this day, Jett remains one of rock 'n' roll's most underrated successes.

"Miss Sweet Petite," Pat Benatar's big voice helped her rock status grow in the early part of the decade. Courtesy of Photofest.

PAT BENATAR

A native New Yorker with a trained operatic voice, Pat Benatar (born Patricia Andrzejewski on January 10, 1953, in Brooklyn) acquired her stage name from her first, short-lived teenage marriage to Dennis Benatar. A bank teller by day and aspiring rock singer at night, Benatar met future husband and musical partner/guitarist Neil Geraldo during her early cabaret singing days in the mid-1970s. After connecting with manager/mentor Rick Newman, who discovered her when she auditioned at his Catch a Rising Star nightclub, Benatar changed her previously safe, middle-of-the-road singing style to a tougher, harder-edged approach that landed her a deal with Chrysalis Records.

Her first album, *In the Heat of the Night*, released late in 1979, went platinum, establishing her tough-woman image as an obvious by-product of the power-pop movement and labeling her style new wave: "Her undeniable vocal prowess almost made up for the weakness of the original material.... [Benatar] transformed Smokie's 'If You Think You Know How to Love Me,' into a sultry mood piece, while John Mellencamp's 'I Need a Lover' benefited from her scuffed velvet tones."[5] Matching Benatar's soaring vocal tones were Geraldo's smoothly booming guitar riffs, a pairing that quickly became a formula for commercial success and one that would eventually move Benatar's style out of the "new wave" category.

Benatar's biggest hits came in 1980 with her second album release, *Crimes of Passion*. The album, which peaked at No. 2 on the album charts, produced several hits into the following year, including "Hit Me With Your Best Shot," which landed a No. 9 spot, and "Treat Me Right," which made the Top 20. The million-selling album also won Benatar her first of four consecutive Grammy Awards for Best Female Rock Vocal Performance. The timing of *Crimes of Passion* could not have been more auspicious, at least initially, with single videos complementing the early days of MTV.

Even so, Benatar's impressive vocal range and her hard-edged delivery were not enough to secure her place as a credible rock 'n' roller: "'Her musical and performing stance is original only in that she *is* female,'" proclaims *The Harmony Illustrated Encyclopedia of Rock*. "Whether the power-chord clichés and humorless posturing of heavy metal are rendered any more interesting when performed by a tiny, spandex-clad redhead (even with natural talent) rather than by the usual macho howlers is questionable."[6] The media focus on Benatar's sexuality included everything from nicknames like "Miss Sweet Petite" to promotional cutouts of her wearing her signature spandex tights. MTV only seemed to enhance her image rather than her music, again much to the detriment of her being viewed as a serious rock artist.

Benatar scored twice more in the American market with *Precious Time* (1981) and *Get Nervous* (1982), which charted in the United States at Nos. 1 and 4, respectively. *Precious Time* also produced Benatar's driving video anthem "Promises in the Dark," which peaked at No. 38. Her biggest single arrived in the form of the broody pop/rock "Love Is a Battlefield," released in 1983 and reaching No. 5 on the charts later that year. A year later, in what some critics describe as her best vocal effort, Benatar charted another hit single with the seductively lyrical "We Belong."

 PROMISES IN THE DARK—PAT BENATAR (1981)

"Miss Sweet Petite" emerged as a tough chick early in her career and MTV's lifetime. Today, some of her not-so-subtly-staged videos seem almost campy—the choreography a kind of poor girl's Michael Jackson; nonetheless, her operatic range paired with Neil Geraldo's driving guitar provided an appropriate backdrop for a new generation of women in rock, an era that often saw women in music videos move back and forth between images of masculinity and/or androgyny (à la Annie Lennox) and the coyly prefeminist vixen (Madonna, the Go-Go's). *Promises in the Dark* extended the deeply rooted feminism found in many of Benatar's songs, cutting through sugary romanticism and exposing the dark reality of women and relationships in a postmodern world.

Her hair cut short and tights discarded in defiance of the media's emphasis on her sexuality, Benatar continued to tour and record successfully into the mid-1980s. Two final rock-based album releases, 1984's *Tropico* and 1985's *Seven the Hard Way*, were only moderately successful, and by 1986, Benatar took an extended break to look after her first daughter with her second husband Geraldo. The two would eventually welcome a second daughter, but Benatar's sudden and prolonged absence from the music scene—along with Chrysalis's 1989 compilation disc *Best Shots*—made it appear, at least on the rock surface, that she had disappeared from the planet.

Not so. Instead, Benatar opted to shift gears musically, moving toward R&B with a collection of ill-received blues-based tracks titled *True Love* in 1991. Two years later, Benatar revisited her arena rock roots with the release of *Gravity's Rainbow*; four years later she followed with *Innamorata*, released in 1997, which was a rock-inspired but mostly acoustic set. Both albums received mixed reviews and were not commercially successful. By the middle of the 1990s, Benatar and Geraldo returned to touring, often co-headlining with other '80s acts like The Steve Miller Band and Styx. In 2003, Benatar released another MOR-rock (middle-of-the-road) album called *Go*, redefining her rock image and following it with an extensive tour.[7]

Fans responded to Cyndi Lauper's brand of kooky, feminine independence, shown here in 1986. Courtesy of Photofest.

A woman who was never comfortable with the recording industry's exploitation of feminine sexuality, Benatar has remained steadfast in her defense of the driving vocal style that became synonymous with her music. Seldom credited for her originality, Benatar penned such haunting pieces as "Hell Is for Children," a scathing attack on child abuse that predated Suzanne Vega's Top 5 folk/pop hit "Luka." Though she has never enjoyed significant cachet with the rock critics, Benatar's recordings, even the studio-glossiest, are great listening sessions, and often convey oddly "hip moments that belie their ostensibly mega-fi style."[8]

GIRLS JUST WANT TO HAVE FUN— CYNDI LAUPER (1984)

It was sometimes hard to tell who was laughing harder at this video: viewers or Cyndi Lauper in this *Bye Bye Birdie* meets *The Honeymooners* video. In a deliberately campy take-off on 1950s domesticity, Lauper romps through a myriad of family-related stereotypes, from a disenchanted stay-at-home mother to a crass, beer-bellied working-class father (memorably played by wrestler Lou Albano). As she leads a motley chorus of diverse blue-collar workers through her apartment and into the street of Brooklyn, Lauper evokes an infectious lightheartedness that powerfully underscores her free-spirited egalitarian anthem. Unlike Helen Reddy's militant 1973 hit "I Am Woman," *Girls Just Want to Have Fun* speaks directly to women of the post-Vietnam age, who often viewed sexual equality as more social than political and whose idea of empowerment assumed many different incarnations.

CYNDI LAUPER

She may have been too unusual to sustain her fans' interest and taste, but Cyndi Lauper (born June 22, 1953, in Queens, New York) remains one of the biggest stars of the early MTV era and a purveyor of the post-punk new wave sound of the early 1980s. Lauper, who dropped out of high school to sing with several local cover bands, entered the 1980s with a series of early recording flops under her belt, including the bankruptcy-producing duo (with keyboardist John Turi) the Blue Angel.

By 1983, after continuing to sing in local clubs, Lauper's manager/boyfriend David Wolff finessed a recording contract with Portrait Records, a deal that led to her debut album, *She's So Unusual*. Aided by MTV's heavy video play of the album's joyously feminist first single "Girls Just Want to Have Fun," *She's So Unusual* became a major hit in the spring of 1984, peaking at No. 4 on the U.S. album charts.[9] The album, with its "giddy mix of self-confidence, effervescent pop-craft, unabashed sentimentality, subversiveness and clever humor . . . [was] a multi-faceted portrait of a multi-faceted talent, an artist [who's] far more clever than her thin, deliberately girly voice would indicate."[10] *She's So Unusual* turned platinum five times and carried its popularity to the United Kingdom and Europe.

In addition to the now-iconic "Girls Just Want to Have Fun," which reached No. 2 on the U.S. singles chart, *She's So Unusual* produced three more Top 10 hits: the hauntingly ethereal ballad "Time after Time," which went to No. 1; plus, the funky rhythm "She Bop" and "All Through the Night." The success of *She's So Unusual* made Lauper a uniquely shining star, but it was that same one-of-a-kind quirkiness that kept her from sustaining her popularity. In spite of her direct—and often humorous—approach to girl talk, Lauper's campy image—embodied in everything from her clothes to her squeaky Betty Boop–sounding voice—gave her a wacky image that was hard to take seriously and, for Lauper, was almost impossible to shake.

Falling victim to the Grammy jinx as Best New Artist of 1984, Lauper's second album, *True Colors*, released in 1986, was dubbed much weaker than her debut effort by critics, in spite of its peak at No. 4 on the album charts and its netting two Top 5 singles, including the title track.[11] *True Colors'* softer, more adult sound also proved lethal to Lauper, as she lost some fans to its adult-contemporary sound. She waited three years before releasing another album, 1989's *A Night to Remember*, which only climbed to No. 37, even with the single "I Drove All Night" hitting the Top 10.

A woman who successfully used MTV to launch her career, Lauper is also an example of how powerfully television can ingrain an image in the minds of its viewers. Never able to escape the kooky camp image associated with her first video, Lauper's image remained frozen in an MTV-created time warp and was not able to move her music forward in a way that fans or critics would follow. Unlike Madonna, whose calculated reinventions helped keep audiences off base and her music fresh and inspired, Cyndi Lauper's directly feminist musical style seemed to keep hitting the same note, limiting her artistic growth and relegating her to a potently bright style and image that, unfortunately, has been perceived as kitschy and dated.

CHRISSIE HYNDE

Another female artist who experienced a commercial breakthrough in the early 1980s was Ohioan Chrissie Hynde (born September 7, 1951, in Akron). Growing up on a diet that consisted of "anything a kid in Ohio with a transistor radio could pick up on,"[12] Hynde first learned the ukulele before picking up a guitar. In 1973, after three years at Kent State University, Hynde left for London, where she met Hereford-based guitarist James Honeyman-Scott (born November 4, 1957, in Hereford, England), bassist Pete Farndon (born 1953, in Hereford), and drummer Gerry Mackleduff. Mackleduff, a session musician, was soon replaced by Martin Chambers (born September 4, 1951 in Hereford, England).

After a brief stint as an *NME* journalist, Hynde relocated in Paris, then returned to Ohio, briefly joining the R&B band Jack Rabbit before heading back to London, where her impressive self-penned songs attracted the attention of Dave Hill, then in the process of launching his own label, Real. Hynde cut a demo tape for Hill in August 1977, and he responded by asking her to form a group. The Pretenders were born in March 1978, with Hill serving as Hynde's manager.

The group's first single, a cover of the Kinks' "Stop Your Sobbing," garnered much critical acclaim for its fresh new wave/power pop sound, a welcome relief in the aftermath of punk overload. The single, released in January 1979, reached the UK Top 30. Mackleduff left the group after its initial success, replaced by Martin Chambers (born September 4, 1951, in Hereford). The Pretenders followed their first hit with two more: "Kid," released in June 1979, charted at No. 33 in the United Kingdom, and "Brass in Pocket," released in November that same year, peaked at No. 1: "A simmering, swaggering slice of white pop-funk . . . [in which] Hynde was fast gaining a reputation as one of the finest songwriters around with an evocatively sultry voice to match."[13]

Their self-titled debut album appeared in January 1980 (released on Real Records in the United Kingdom; Sire Records in the United States) and was welcomed with almost unanimous critical acclaim. The twelve-track set—all but two written by Hynde—boasted a stylishly diverse range of tempos and kick-ass rock intensity, with Hynde's compelling vocals and musical presence clearly leading the group, both commanding in its defiance (i.e., telling listeners to "fuck off" if they could not take it) and brilliant in its fresh departure from punk. Despite Hynde's powerful force as the band's leader, the Pretenders still functioned as one finely integrated unit, as *Rolling Stone* magazine noted in its review of their debut album: "[T]he rest of the Pretenders are neither subservient to Hynde nor condescending to her; the Pretenders are a group and unlike certain other bands that make that claim, there is never any doubt about it."[14] The *Pretenders* topped the UK charts at No. 1 and peaked at No. 9 in the United States, making the group a household name and launching its first stadium tour in the summer of 1980.

Back in the United States, Hynde met her idol Ray Davies (ex-Kinks), and the two embarked on a tempestuous love affair that resulted in the birth of daughter Natalie but not marriage. Updating the "tough chick" image by boldly demonstrating that motherhood and rock 'n' roll were not necessarily mutually exclusive, Hynde's unique blend of career and family served as an inspirational role model to fans and fellow artists alike. At a time when few women maintained the dual role of mother and rock star (or any other career choice), Hynde broke new feminist ground, although she was clear in her position that feminism was not one of her causes.

A second album, the much-anticipated *Pretenders II*, was released in August 1981 to mixed reviews. Lacking the energy of its predecessor, this sophomore effort still charted on both the UK and U.S. Top 10s, peaking at No. 7 in England. Tracks like "Message of Love," "Talk of the Town," and "The Adultress" were highlights, but by the following year internal struggles within the band created other challenges. On June 14, 1982, Farndon was fired from the band because of drug abuse. Sadly, only two days later, on June 16, 1982, guitarist Honeyman-Scott died of an overdose of heroin and cocaine. Farndon later died of a drug overdose in April 1983.

Faced with reconstructing her band, Hynde returned in February 1983 with former Manfred Mann Earth Band guitarist Robbie McIntosh (born October 25, 1957) and bassist Malcolm Foster (born January 13, 1956). The new Pretenders released a single, "2000 Miles," in time for Christmas and another album, *Learning to Crawl*, in January 1984. Although reviews were mixed, *Learning to Crawl* performed well in the United States, peaking at No. 5, and was only slightly less successful in the United Kingdom, cresting at No. 11. The now-classic single "Back on the Chain Gang" was one of the album's—and the group's—stellar achievements.

Hynde remained fairly low-key in 1985, following her May 1984 marriage to Simple Minds guitarist Jim Kerr, coming out only for a performance at Live Aid and a collaboration with UB40's cover of the Sonny and Cher gem "I Got You Babe." With yet another reassembled Pretenders lineup, Hynde released *Get Close* in 1986. Using McIntosh and mostly session musicians, Hynde's warmer, more middle-of-the-road album included the lovely "Hymn to Her"—sung to her new daughter (with Kerr) and the politically charged "How Much Did You Get for Your Soul." The year 1988 saw Hynde's global awareness reveal itself even more with a billing along with UB40 at a Nelson Mandela concert at Wembley Stadium. She also scored with another Top 10 UB40 cover collaboration of Dusty Springfield's "Breakfast in Bed."[15]

In 1990, Hynde released *Packed!* to little critical or commercial fanfare. That same year, her marriage to Kerr ended. Hynde returned in 1994 with *Last of the Independents*, which some critics termed a noteworthy comeback. But Hynde's importance extends beyond her critical acclaim and ongoing musical viability. Since 1980, her presence as a musician carried more weight than her views on feminism, yet she became an unintentional model for women in rock, redefining the tough chick image in ways that broadened gender roles for both men and women. Never one to be caught up in rock's cult of celebrity, Hynde retained a strong sense of independence, powerfully underscored by a streak of defiance and a soul filled with talent. In 2005, the Pretenders were inducted into the Rock and Roll Hall of Fame.

ANNIE LENNOX

As MTV's first major female star, Annie Lennox epitomized how visual images could be used to challenge traditional images of women in rock. Born in

Shown here with Dave Stewart, Annie Lennox's androgynous look and deep contralto underscored the *Eurythmics'* new wave sound and helped redefine the image of women in rock 'n' roll. Courtesy of Photofest.

Aberdeen, Scotland (December 25, 1954), Lennox began playing music as child, mastering both piano and flute before winning a scholarship to London's Royal Academy of Music in her late teens. Dropping out of the Academy just before taking her finals, Lennox performed various jobs around London by day, singing at night. In the late 1970s, she met guitarist Dave Stewart and, along with songwriter Peet Coombes, formed a group called the Tourists. As the Tourists, they released three albums between 1979 and 1980, scoring a No. 4 hit with a cover of Dusty Spring-field's "I Only Want to Be With You." In 1980, Lennox and Stewart, who had become lovers, left the Tourists to form the Eurythmics, named after the Greek word for a dance movement: "It [the Eurythmics] described what we wanted to be," said Stewart, "European and rhythmical."[16]

While they might have intended to express their European heritage, the Eurythmics clearly touched a responsive chord in America when their second album, *Sweet Dreams*, was released in the United States in 1983. The album's title track, "Sweet Dreams (Are Made of This)," quickly ran up the single's charts, topping them at No. 1, while the album settled in at No. 15. Accompanying their single smash was the Stewart-directed video, unleashing a new look for Lennox, complete with slicked hair and men's suits. Lennox's stark and shocking presence—she sported an orange crew cut and wielded a riding crop—coupled with the song's cynical commentary on the nature of motivation made for a memorably surreal video, one that was both teasing and threatening, sexual and androgynous.

The success of *Sweet Dreams* prompted the duo to reissue "Love Is a Stranger," which had previously been released in the United Kingdom without gaining much notice. This time, the song—and its accompanying video—received much attention and even more controversy. In the video, Lennox assumes three different personas: a glamorous long-haired blonde, a leather-clad brunette dominatrix, and a man in a suit. Initially, MTV blocked out the shots of Lennox changing from woman to man, having assumed Lennox was a male transvestite. It was only after she produced legal documentation proving her gender that MTV removed the ban on the video's gender-bending cuts. For Lennox, the Eurythmics' infectiously clever Euro-pop sound explored as much musically as her own visual transformations challenged traditional notions about women and women in rock.

The Eurythmics' next album, *Torch*, released in November 1983, continued to explore new techno-pop/rock rhythms, while Lennox's video appearances pushed notions of sexual ambiguity even farther. The album's chart at No. 7 in the United States made it the highest notch ever attained by the pair. Hit singles included the blockbuster "Here Comes the Rain Again," which peaked at No. 4, and video eye-openers like *Who's That Girl?* in which a lovelorn Lennox ultimately ends up with her male alter ego and kisses herself at the video's conclusion.

After a sound-track project for the movie *1984* was largely ignored in the United States (their music was not used in the final film version, and some U.S. radio stations refused to play the controversially titled "Sexcrime"), Lennox and Stewart returned to the recording studio, releasing *Be Yourself Tonight* in the spring of 1985. For many critics, *Be Yourself*'s lively collection of techno-rock featured Lennox's emergence as a powerful vocal force. Duets with Stevie Wonder on the Top 30 hit "There Must Be an Angel (Playing With My Heart)" and Aretha Franklin on the Top 20 climber "Sisters Are Doing It for Themselves" solidified Lennox's diva-aspirations and talent. It also foreshadowed a peak for the Lennox-Stewart pairing, as subsequent releases were often seen as clumsy attempts to capture a big-rock (read: stadium concert) audience.[17]

By 1989, the pair's final release *We Too Are One* seemed contradictory to the artistic directions they wanted to take. When the album failed to inspire much commercial interest, Lennox announced she was taking a two-year sabbatical to have a child. During this hiatus, Lennox and Stewart quietly dissolved their relationship, and Lennox returned as a solo artist in 1992 with her debut album *Diva*.[18]

Assessing her own evolution with gender issues that coincided with her own musical artistry, Lennox has said,

> "One of the main reasons I wear the clothes I do and have an androgynous image, is because I didn't want to be seen as a 'girlie' singer wearing pretty dresses. I don't want to change sexual labels—I want to sidestep them, and to confound people a little bit with something fresher and less clichéd."[19]

Instead of using music video to promote their music, the Eurythmics used the video medium as a form of artistic expression, which allowed them to manipulate their own image, rather than be manipulated by the image itself. That idea fits well with Lennox's own determination to be more than a girl singer, to have more involvement (read: control) over her career choices, and to—consciously and not—change the image of women in rock 'n' roll. Neither tough chick, man-hater, nor coy ingénue—and yet all of these—Lennox redefined the image of women in rock videos by seamlessly transforming her image along with the Euro-rock beat of her music.

AIMEE MANN

A graduate of the prestigious Berklee College of Music, Aimee Mann (born August 9, 1960, in Richmond, Virginia) began her professional career working with future industrial metal rocker Al Jourgensen. Their group the Young Snakes (one album from 1982 is still available) experimented with various musical styles until Mann formed her own band, 'Til Tuesday, around 1984. 'Til Tuesday's new wave, pop/rock sound included guitarist and backup singer Robert Holmes (born March 31, 1959, in Hampton, England), keyboardist Joey Pesce (born April 14, 1962, in Bronx, New York), and drummer Michael Hausman (born June 12, 1960, in Philadelphia, Pennsylvania).

The group's 1985 debut album *Voices Carry* contained much of Mann's material concerning her breakup with former lover Hausman. Its title track charted in the United States at No. 8, while the album hit the Top 20, peaking at No. 19. For Mann, much of her work would spring from personal relationships and experiences, although her sometimes intimate material combined with the band's eclectic new wave/post-punk style made it difficult to cultivate a large fan base. As such, the band's sophomore effort, 1987's *Welcome Home*, did not attract much critical or fan attention and stalled at No. 49 on the album charts.

It was the group's third (and final) album that garnered the most critical attention, even though it never charted—1989's *Everything's Different Now*, again inspired by one of Mann's romantic entanglements (this time with co-writer Jules Shear), provided her most introspective and compelling compositions to date. Unfortunately, behind-the-scenes gossip (à la Steve Nicks and Fleetwood Mac's couplings and uncouplings) and the album's poor sales led to the band's eventual breakup. Conversely, Mann's rich and provocatively thoughtful songs pushed her to pursue a solo career, which she launched in 1993.

More folk than punk-based in her reinvention, Mann still failed to capture the interest of many fans, although critics were impressed with her self-effacing rawness and deeply personal artistic self-examination. A modest hit from 1995, "That's Just What You Are," was included in the sound track for the popular television series *Melrose Place*. Mann remains elusive, although her acerbic lyrical style and crossover punk-folk fusion have sustained interest with rock critics and nonmainstream fans.[20]

MICHELLE SHOCKED

According to her own apparently semifictionalized autobiography, Michelle Shocked (born Karen Michelle Johnston, February 24, 1962, in Gilmer, East

Texas) had a vagabond childhood, moving from army base to army base with her fundamentalist Mormon mother and stepfather. A turbulent adolescence followed, one that included a time in a psychiatric hospital (where Shocked's mother had her committed) and a brief stint as an anarcho-punk squatter in San Francisco. Shocked also rekindled her relationship with her biological father, one that introduced her to many of the artists who influenced her own songwriting.

As each of these experiences became fodder for her post-folk-rock-based musical grist, Shocked moved to Amsterdam in 1984, returning two years later as a volunteer at Texas' Kerrville Folk Festival. There British producer Pete Lawrence heard her campfire-side improvisations and taped her on his Walkman. Later that year, amid some suspicions about the music industry in general, Shocked released her first album, *The Texas Campfire Tapes*, on Cooking Vinyl Records and became a hit in England, although the album failed to chart in the United States: "It holds the distinction of being the only major label LP that cost less to make than it does to buy,"[21] read a comic-tinged accompanying press release in the United States.

In 1988, Shocked's second release (this time for PolyGram Records in England) *Short Sharp Shocked* settled in at No. 73 in the United States but climbed higher to No. 33 in England. *Short Sharp Shocked* revealed more of Shocked's songwriting talent and musical style, "combining the informal, tradition-rooted folkiness of *The Texas Campfire Tapes* with a postmodern feminist perspective and punk attitude."[22] The album quickly solicited praise and respect from the indie/alternative community and critics. No less effective than its music was the album's controversial cover photo that showed Shocked in a police stranglehold. Among the album's politically charged protest songs was the affecting "Graffiti Limbo," an elegy for slain street artist Michael Stewart.

Not one to be stereotyped musically or otherwise, Shocked followed up her 1988 critical and commercial success with 1989's *Captain Swing*, a collection of '40s big band, swing-inspired songs that might have left her fans surprised but not her critics who cheered at her determination to explore new musical territory. Another step in a different direction was 1992's *Arkansas Traveler*, in which Shocked took her own musical pilgrimage, collaborating with American roots musicians Taj Mahal, Pops Staples, Doc Watson, and Uncle Tupelo. Although it failed to chart, *Arkansas Traveler* reestablished Shocked as a critical favorite, one who insisted she be reviewed on the merits of her art, not her looks or video image.

In this way, Shocked rejected the growing awareness of a "women in rock" image, saying,

> "[W]hen I start being compared not on the basis of music, but on the basis of image, I felt like they [the media] were winning the game. . . . [W]hen really pressed to it, beyond image and style, there weren't many musical similarities between myself and Tracey Chapman."[23]

As defiant in her defense of artistic integrity as she was adamant about controlling her music and her image, Michelle Shocked's unique combination of rock, punk, folk, and American roots music added new dimension and renewed opportunities for women in the rock industry. She continues to record, but spends much of her time working quietly for non-violence in the environmental and global justice movements.

MELISSA ETHERIDGE

Melissa Etheridge's instrument of choice has always been the acoustic guitar, but her folk-based roots have never overshadowed the fact that she is a rock 'n' roller. Born in Leavenworth, Kansas (May 29, 1961), Etheridge was a budding singer/songwriter by the time she reached her teens and traveled east to study at the Berklee College of Music. After graduation, she relocated to California, where Island Records executive Chris Blackwell signed her to a recording contract.

Etheridge's eponymous self-titled debut album was released in 1988, and it was her "raw and impassioned delivery [that] set her apart from other female singer-songwriters of the time as true rocker in the gutsy manner of Janis Joplin, whose songs she performed."[24] Singer Holly Near recalled her reaction to hearing Etheridge for the first time: "'At first I thought, *Oh, no, another girl with a guitar.* But she was tearing them up. She ended with a Janis Joplin classic and did it no discredit.'"[25] Fellow artists and record industry insiders must have agreed that Etheridge was, indeed, a new age rocker with deeply rooted blues-based traditions. Grammy nominated for Best Female Rock Vocal Performance for "Bring Me Some Water" (from her debut album), Etheridge ultimately lost the award to Tina Turner, but her live performance of the song at the awards show introduced her to a whole new audience. Her debut album eventually climbed to No. 22, as did her sophomore effort, 1989's *Brave and Crazy.*

In 1993, Etheridge's persistence finally paid off with her breakthrough single (and subsequent rock star status), "I'm the Only One," a track from her accompanying multiplatinum album *Yes I Am.* Since then Etheridge continues to rock in the genre's most basic, honest, and unaffected tradition, mixing personal insights with social issues in a style that defies age, ethnicity, or gender. A lesbian, she is the natural bridge between the "women in rock" video debate of the 1980s and the rise of more independent gender-liberated artists of the early 1990s, letting her art speak for her image and her music define her worth.

THE GO-GO'S

In addition to women as solo artists and women fronting mixed-gender groups (à la Chrissie Hynde), the 1980s witnessed a rebirth of sorts among girl groups. Leading the pack early in the decade was California-based the Go-Go's, the most popular all-female band to emerge from the punk/new wave rush of the late 1970s and early 1980s. Formed in 1978 as the Misfits, the quintet subsequently adopted the Go-Go's name in response to their association with Hollywood's new wave "Masque" club and the nearby "Canterbury Arms" apartment building crowd.

Original band members included vocalist Belinda Carlisle (born August 17, 1958), lead guitarist Charlotte Caffey (born October 21, 1953, in Santa Monica, California), rhythm guitarist Jane Wiedlin (born May 20, 1958), bassist Margot Olaverra, and drummer Elissa Bello. Before the group's first single release, Gina Schock (born August 31, 1957, in Baltimore, Maryland) replaced Bello and, shortly after

Led by the Go-Go's, girl groups enjoyed a renaissance during the early 1980s. Courtesy of Photofest.

their first UK concert tour in 1980, Kathy Valentine (born January 7, 1959, in Austin Texas) replaced Olaverra. Though they would later cultivate a more wholesome image for MTV audiences, the Go-Go's initially lived the hard-partying, drug-taking life associated with most rock bands, with one of their 1979 shows ending in a much-touted riot.

By the dawn of the 1980s, the Go-Go's had lost much of their early rawness, settling instead on a smoother pop sound that attracted the attention of British ska (a form of Jamaican music, which began in the late 1950s), revivalists Madness, who invited the group to join their 1980 UK tour. Their concert tour exposure led to a contract with Stiff Records, who released their first single, "We Got the Beat," in the spring of 1980. An imported copy of the single became an underground hit in the United States, suggesting their potential commercial marketability. Early the following year, Police manager Miles Copeland, looking for a stable of artists to support his IRS/Faulty label, signed the Go-Go's to a recording contract. They responded by landing their first single in the Top 20, the bubbly pink vinyl summer classic "Our Lips Are Sealed." The July-released single was followed the next month with the band's debut album, *Beauty and the Beat*, which became one of 1981's surprise summer hits, holding the No. 1 U.S. album position for six weeks and selling over 2 million copies. In addition to the success of "Our Lips Are Sealed," the band's rerecorded version of "We Got the Beat" spent three weeks at No. 2 on the singles' charts.

The beauty of *Beauty and the Beat* lay, in part, in the band's ability to harness some of their original raw garage punk style with the effervescence of California pop. Their second effort, 1982's *Vacation*, had a more commercial sound, and while it sold well (going gold and climbing to No. 8 on the U.S. album charts), it could not sustain the momentum generated by the first album. Further deflating the group's rising rock balloon was Caffey's broken wrist, which disabled her and the group's touring opportunities throughout much of 1983. When the girls returned with a third album in May 1984, their musical camaraderie seemed to have waned.

Talk Show (1984), perhaps the Go-Go's most ambitious album musically, performed well commercially, producing two Top 40 hits—"Head Over Heels," which peaked at No. 11, and "Turn to You"—but ultimately failed to go gold.[26] To some insiders, the group's fast lifestyle and clashing egos had finally reached a gridlock, so it was without much surprise when Wiedlin left the group at the end of the year. In May 1985, the Go-Go's officially disbanded, leaving Carlisle, with the most airbrush-friendly video clone potential, to pursue a solo career.

THE BANGLES

A second entry in the all-girl band movement was the Bangles, a California-based band that first called themselves Colours, Supersonic Bangs, and the Bangs before settling on the name that made them famous. The all-singing, all-performing all-female Bangles formed in 1981, having sprung from the male-dominated L.A. Paisley Underground scene. Led by Susanna Hoffs (born January 17, 1957, in Newport Beach, California), who had responded to an ad placed by Peterson sisters Debbi and Vicki, on vocals and bass, the original trio included lead guitarist Vicki Peterson (born January 11, 1958) and drummer Debbi Peterson (born August 22, 1961). Before their first album release, the girls added—briefly—bassist Annette Zilinskas, who was replaced by ex-Runaways bassist Michael Steele (born June 2, 1954) in 1982.

Initially, the group played original, 1960's-influenced guitar rock, self-releasing the single "Getting Out of Hand" in 1981. The song, which sounded a lot like an unreleased treasure from the Mamas and the Papas, pushed the girls to release a four-song garage pop album on IRS/Faulty Records before signing a contract with CBS/Columbia Records. With the Peterson sisters' harmonies reminiscent of the Grass Roots, the Byrds, and the Beatles, the Bangles released their debut album *All Over the Place* in March 1985. Unfortunately, the album's title was somewhat suggestive of its uneven tracks, which, having smoothed out the band's musical raw edges for a commercial audience, did not produce a hit single.

But help was on the way, in the form of Prince, who penned what would become the Bangles' breakthrough hit, "Manic Monday," a post–Dolly

Partonesque 9-to-5 tale about the workday frustrations. Recapturing their Mamas and Papas sound, the Bangles took "Manic Monday" to No. 2 and set the stage for what would be their best year. The year 1986 saw the March release of *Different Light*, a successful second effort that climbed to No. 2 on the U.S. album charts (No. 3 in the United Kingdom). *Different Light* included "Manic Monday," another tiny hit cover of Jules Spears' hauntingly melancholy "If She Knew What She Wants," and the monster No. 1 hit "Walk Like an Egyptian." In 1988, the Bangles returned with an impressively strong cover of Simon and Garfunkel's "Hazy Shade of Winter," recorded as part of the *Less Than Zero* sound track, which charted at No. 2 in the United States. That same year, another hit album titled *Everything* shot to No. 15 in the United States and No. 5 in the United Kingdom, spawning a U.S. Top 5 hit, "In Your Room."

With the Bangles' star seemingly limitless in its ascension, internal tensions again reared an ugly head. Like the Go-Go's, the Bangles had one member whose looks and sex appeal seemed to outshine the others. Lead singer Hoffs had become the group's pin-up darling, creating personal riffs among band members, especially the Peterson sisters whose harmonies were credited with giving the group its unique sound. The Bangles thus brought their own string of hit records to a halt in 1990 when they officially disbanded. Hoffs pursued a modest solo career, while the Petersons went underground, continuing to perform and record on various indie band projects.[27]

HEART

One of rock's most enduringly creative forces and one of the first female hard-rock success stories, Heart's beat seemed to have suffered cardiac arrest when Epic Records terminated its contract in 1983. But, by 1985, with the release of the self-titled *Heart*, California-born sisters Ann (born June 19, 1951, in San Diego) and Nancy (born March 16, 1954, in San Francisco) Wilson saw their career resuscitated. Aided by hit power ballads like "These Dreams" and "What About Love," the Wilson sisters used MTV to peddle a post–Stevie Nicks style of "leather-n-lace" soft rock and wound up cornering the market on what became their own brand of reinvented feminine muscle-pyrotechnics.[28]

Ann's powerful vocals and Nancy's accompanying guitar riffs continued with 1987's *Bad Animals*. They ended the decade with a No. 2 hit single, 1990's "All I Wanna Do Is Make Love to You," from the No. 3 album *Brigade*. Their live album *Rock the House* was released in 1991.

THE ROLE OF WOMEN IN ROCK MUSIC IN THE 1980s

The advent of MTV brought new challenges—and raised old arguments—about the role of women in rock music, including, but not limited to, the images they projected and the image the media wanted to create. The difference in artist reaction to and use of MTV was as diverse as the women themselves: from Madonna's blatant manipulation of music video as a career builder to Belinda Carlisle's failed attempt to use video as a substitution for artistic quality to Michelle Shocked's obvious disdain for the medium. In each case, the extent to which an artist could—and did—control her career was as important as how successful she was within the recording industry's male-dominated, often sexist milieu.

The other important point to remember about women in rock during the 1980s is the range of musical diversity that fell under the category of rock. This series focuses on rock 'n' roll artists, often at the exclusion of many successful and influential pop artists. If the genre were broadened, there would be many more women included here, from the powerful gospel pop of Whitney Houston to the R&B–pop-funk fusion of Janet Jackson to the folk-pop quirkiness of alternative duo the Indigo Girls or the post-folk relevance of Suzanne Vega. All of these women artists have merit, though not within the more exclusive ranks of rock 'n' roll.

To that end, female rock artists from earlier eras found renewed success during the 1980s. Tina Turner, who bested then-newcomer Melissa Etheridge for a Grammy Award at the end of the decade, proved that age and an entrepreneurial spouse did not define her rock artistry. Her renaissance without ex-husband Ike was as defiant and exciting as the hits she produced, from the angry anthem "What's Love Go to Do With It" to the seductively erotic "Private Dancer" and the almost campy, yet driving postapocalyptic "We Don't Need Another Hero," from the film *Mad Max: Beyond Thunderdome* (1985).

The same case might be made for Cher, who came into her prime as an actress and artist during this decade, improving on her once quaintly charming television star persona and embracing a darker, more brooding power pop style with singles like the wistful "If I Could Turn Back Time" and the bleakly prophetic "We All Sleep Alone." Like Turner, her musical roots and raspy vocal styles come from an earlier generation of rock artists but maintain a timeless quality throughout the decade. And, like Turner, both women entered the 1980s as survivors of both personal and professional setbacks. However we might try to define these women in rock during the 1980s, it is clear that they were determined to define themselves through their music, that the increasingly fragmented rock genre simultaneously opened up new opportunities for creative musical pairings and fusion, and that this transition decade—for good or for ill—set the stage for ongoing discussions about women, image, and music for sometime to come.

NOTES

1. Gillian G. Gaar, *She's a Rebel: The History of Women in Rock & Roll*, exp. 2nd ed. (New York: Seal Press, 2002), 260.

2. Martin C. Strong, *The Great Rock Discography*, 6th ed. (Edinburgh, UK: Canongate Books, 2002), 540.

3. Stephen Thomas Erlewine, "Joan Jett: Bio," *All Music Guide*, included at http://www.mtv.com; search Joan Jett.

4. Sandy Masuo, "Joan Jett Biography," included at http://music.yahoo.com; search Joan Jett.

5. Strong, *Great Rock Discography*, 83.

6. Gaar, *She's a Rebel*, 234.

7. Greg Prato and Stephen Thomas Erlewine, "Pat Benatar: Bio," *All Music Guide*, included at http://www.vh1.com/artists/az/benatar_pat/bio.jhtml.

8. Richard Riegel, "Pat Benatar," included at http://music.yahoo.com; search Pat Benatar.

9. Stephen Thomas Erlewine, "Cyndi Lauper: Bio," *All Music Guide*, included at http://www.mtv.com/bands/az/lauper_cyndi/bio.jhtml.

10. Stephen Thomas Erlewine, "She's So Unusual: Expert Review," *All Music Guide*, included at http://shopping.yahoo.com/p:She's%20So%20Unusual%20[Bonus%20Tracks]:192100936.

11. Gaar, *She's a Rebel*, 266.

12. Ibid., 231.

13. Strong, *Great Rock Discography*, 826.

14. Gaar, *She's a Rebel*, 232.

15. Strong, *Great Rock Discography*, 826; and Stephen Thomas Erlewine, "Pretenders: Bio," *All Music Guide*, included at http://www.mtv.com; search Pretenders.

16. Gaar, *She's a Rebel*, 266.

17. Strong, *Great Rock Discography*, 350–351.

18. Stephen Thomas Erlewine, "Annie Lennox: Bio," *All Music Guide*, included at http://www.mtv.com; search Annie Lennox.

19. Gaar, *She's a Rebel*, 264.

20. Strong, *Great Rock Discography*, 647; and Stephen Thomas Erlewine, "Aimee Mann: Bio," *All Music Guide*, included at http://www.mtv.com; search Aimee Mann.

21. Gaar, *She's a Rebel*, 306.

22. Chris Woodstra, "Michelle Shocked," included at http://www.vh1.com; search Michelle Shocked.

23. Gaar, *She's a Rebel*, 305.

24. Ibid., 302.

25. Ibid.

26. Strong, *Great Rock Discography*, 417–418; and Stephen Thomas Erlewine, "The Go-Go's: Bio," *All Music Guide*, included at http:www.mtv.com; search The Go-Go's.

27. Strong, *Great Rock Discography*, 59; and Denise Sullivan, "The Bangles: Bio," *All Music Guide*, included at http://www.mtv.com; search The Bangles.

28. Strong, *Great Rock Discography*, 470–471.

10

CONCERTS FOR HUMANITARIAN CAUSES

By the end of the 1970s, rock music's connection to social and political causes seemed all but vanished. The spontaneous gathering at Woodstock in August 1969 was slightly more than a decade past, but its youthful optimism and dedication to the cause of world peace had fallen out of fashion during the cynical '70s and the rise of the "Me" generation. Rock 'n' roll had gone commercial, with record producers eager to find another multiplatinum seller like *Frampton Comes Alive* (1976) or *Saturday Night Fever* (1977). By 1984, Michael Jackson's *Thriller* (1983) had clearly upped the album-selling ante, and it appeared that megabucks, megastars, and marketability had become the buzz words that defined rock music's new generation.

Yet in the midst of what many feared would be the commercial demise of rock 'n' roll music, an almost contradictory phenomenon emerged: the recurring trend of benefit concerts and songs written especially to build awareness about specific social and political causes. Unlike the Woodstock era, when fans began questioning the integrity of artists who espoused a peace/love philosophy but still lived comfortably in expensive mansions pampered by agents, managers, and their personal entourage, 1980s audiences saw rock artists become more consistent in their personal beliefs and public behavior. For the first time, rock musicians put their musical and monetary clout together in an attempt to raise awareness about serious global issues like poverty, hunger, disease, and political oppression. From Band Aid to Live Aid, Artists against Apartheid to Amnesty International, Farm Aid to USA for Africa, musicians appealed to their fans to make the world a better place.[1] And the results were as varied and awesome, as satisfying and problematic as the artists who designed, promoted, organized, and participated in them.

Rock 'n' roll showed its heart during the 1980s with a "no-egos" allowed "We Are the World" recording session led by Ray Charles, Michael Jackson, and producer Quincy Jones. Courtesy of Photofest.

USA FOR AFRICA/BAND AID

The enormous success Michael Jackson had experienced by early in 1984 with *Thriller*'s both record-breaking sales and his coronation as the "King of Pop" turned a different corner later that year when he and *Thriller* producer Quincy Jones teamed up with Lionel Ritchie to write a song that became a rock music event: USA for Africa's "We Are the World." Originally, singer Harry Belafonte had promoted the concept of a benefit concert for Africans by African American artists. Enter Ken Kragen, owner of a personal management and television company, who thought an American version of Band Aid would be a better idea.[2] From inception to production, the contrast between the two projects becomes a metaphor for the differences between American and British culture.

Band Aid, the foundation for Ethiopia and Africa, was a group of British recording artists gathered by Boomtown Rats' lead singer Bob Geldof, who released a straight-to-No. 1 single in England called "Do They Know It's Christmas?" in November 1984. Geldof, disillusioned with the frustrations of promoting another Boomtown Rats album, returned home after a series of tiresome interviews to see a horrifying television news report on the plight of famine victims in Ethiopia. Desperate to do something and fearing that as a punk-rock musician whose own music was not selling he would have little impact on making the rest of the world aware of Ethiopia's problems, Geldof (with the help of Midge Ure of Ultravox) called on rock artists like Bono, Sting, Paul Young, Paul McCartney, Boy George, George Michael, Simon Le Bon, David Bowie, Phil Collins, the Eurythmics, and others to join him in this unprecedented musical project,[3] which was truly a British pop/rock community effort.

The resulting hit single brought Geldof recognition for his efforts and showed that marketability and social awareness did have natural and appropriate links to rock stars and their music. Geldof's marketing strategy to buy "Do They Know It's Christmas?" was simple but powerful: It would help save lives. He said, "If you don't like the music, buy the record and throw it to rubbish. You don't need to like the music, but we need you to buy the records to save lives."[4] Reports of people buying fifty copies, keeping one, and giving the rest back to the record stores to sell again became part of Band Aid's legend, and it quickly became the all-time best-selling single in British history.

Geldof had promised to give every penny received by Band Aid to Africa. He did not want to follow the path of many foundations whose administrative causes and material fees often left less than 30 percent of their collected funds for distribution to their respective causes. "Do They Know It's Christmas?" sold over 3 million copies in Great Britain alone, and 50 million worldwide. On March 11, 1985, Band Aid co-producer Midge Ure personally accompanied over $70,000 worth of food and medical supplies to Ethiopia.[5]

Back in the States, Stevie Wonder had agreed to sing on Jackson and Richie's recording. Other artists quickly expressed an interest in participating, but Quincy Jones needed to find a way to get as many of them together as he could at one time. Unlike Geldof, who had organized every aspect of production and release for "Christmas," from securing studio time to convincing artists and engineers to donate their time, Jones found that many American artists expected recording schedules to conform to their own personal agendas. Frustrations ran high until Geldof was called in for assistance.

The recording solution eventually came about by booking it on January 28, 1985, the night of the American Music Awards and the perfect way to assure most artists would be available. Instrumental tracks had been recorded ahead of time and sent out to the interested musicians with a note to "check your ego at the door" during the recording session. At the studio, the artists stood in semicircular rows around six microphones, their places marked with masking tape on the floor. Watching the video of the recording session, it is clear that, at some level, Jones' ego-curbing directives were taken seriously by the artists who participated.

The recording session roster reads like a "Who's Who" of established and new rock artists and musicians: Dan Aykroyd, Harry Belafonte, Lindsey Buckingham, Kim Carnes, Ray Charles, Bob Dylan, Sheila E., Bob Geldof, Daryl Hall and John Oates, James Ingram, Jackie Jackson, LaToya Jackson, Marlon Jackson, Michael Jackson, Randy Jackson, Tito Jackson, Al Jarreau, Waylon

Jennings, Billy Joel, Cyndi Lauper, Huey Lewis and the News, Kenny Loggins, Bette Midler, Willie Nelson, Jeffery Osborne, Steve Perry, The Pointer Sisters, Lionel Richie, Smokey Robinson, Kenny Rogers, Diana Ross, Paul Simon, Bruce Springsteen, Tina Turner, Dionne Warwick, and Stevie Wonder. With several artists taking one-line solos and a few carrying the song's emotional message—most notably Jackson, Springsteen, Dylan, and Charles—"We Are the World" seemed to a capture a collective American spirit of human concern not seen before in rock 'n' roll. Still, Geldof remained critical of how American capitalism and individualism reared its ugly head during the project: "The contrast between British and American recordings could not have been more dramatic. Where in London everybody had just rolled up looking pretty much as they would look on most Sunday's at home, here in L.A. the whole affair was 'show-biz.' "[6]

On Tuesday, March 7, 1985, 800,000 copies of "We Are the World" arrived in record stores across America. They were sold out by the weekend. Two weeks later, on March 23, "We Are the World" entered the *Billboard* Hot 100 at No. 21, the highest debuting single since John Lennon's "Imagine" in 1971. Within three weeks, "We Are the World" reached No. 1, becoming the fastest-rising chart-topper since Elton John's 1975 hit "Island Girl." "We Are the World" went on to win Grammys for "Song of the Year" and "Record of the Year." The single also marked the eighth consecutive year Lionel Richie had written a No. 1 song.[7] Today "We Are the World" may seem outdated in the twenty-first century's terrorist-frenzied world, but its powerfully human message and beautiful melody might someday lend themselves to a rerecording with contemporary artists like Norah Jones, Alicia Keyes, Brian McKnight, and Justine Timberlake.

LIVE AID

The successes of "Do They Know It's Christmas?" and "We Are the World" were first steps in making the world aware of problems in Third World countries, particularly regions in Africa. For Geldof, monies earned from the single were not enough. He wanted to do more, to change the world attitude about Africa. Contacting all available artists on both sides of the Atlantic, Geldof decided to organize a charity concert designed to run simultaneously in England (at London's Wembley Stadium), and the United States (at Philadelphia's JFK Stadium) called Live Aid. Moved by a news story depicting famine in Ethiopia, Geldof became proactive in making the western world aware of the poverty, hunger, and economic deprivation found in many third world countries. Soliciting the partnership of promoter Harvey Goldsmith, who was responsible for the concerts for Kampuchea, Geldof's goals were ambitious: "We should try to have the most important rock artists of the last twenty-five years on stage. . . . It's going to be a global telethon. . . . Because people are

Bob Geldof took rock's social conscience to new levels with the highly acclaimed Live Aid concert, held simultaneously in London and Philadelphia in the summer of 1985. © Jacques Langevin/Corbis Sygma.

dying."[8] On July 13, 1985, 95 percent of all television sets in the world—and a projected audience of over 2 billion people—were tuned in to the concert. It has been estimated that more people watched Live Aid than Neil Armstrong's first step on the moon in 1969. This statistic is especially important when considering that satellite links between Great Britain and the United States were far less common and more difficult to establish in 1985 than they are today.

As much as Live Aid aspired to promote one audience, one cause, one world, audiences who watched the seventeen-hour broadcast had very different concert experiences, depending on the country, network channel availability, and selectivity. For example, in Europe, where the video feed was supplied by the BBC (a public, commercial-free channel), audiences could see lots of interviews and backstage chatter between the musicians' sets. As long as the concert was running, newscasters hosted various VIPs (very important persons) in the commentary booths. The television feed was mono but offered a stereo simulcast on BBC Radio 1. Overall, the BBC producers were able to broadcast the best choices (i.e., performance or interview at all moments), notably missing only the Crosby, Stills, Nash and Young reunion and, for the American audience, much of the Who reunion (due to transmission difficulties).

In the United States, the two main picture sources were ABC and the still fledgling cable MTV network. Both had established deals with commercial sponsors who had agreed to pay for almost all broadcast time and production

LIVE AID CONCERT—VARIOUS ARTISTS (1985)

Boasting the largest-scale satellite linkup and TV broadcast of all time, *Live Aid* became the mother of all music videos with an estimated 1.5 billion viewers in 100 countries watching the sixteen-hour concert extravaganza live from London and Philadelphia. No single concert before or since has brought together such legendary talent from rock 'n' roll's illustrious history: performers from Paul McCartney to Phil Collins, from U2 to Queen. The historical significance of Live Aid, beyond its technological groundbreaking and impressive artistic lineup, is perhaps the impact it has had on the music industry's involvement in a variety of social and global issues. As a video, the concert's primal, sometimes disorganized performances are outshone by individual artist energy and a communal dedication on the part of the musical participants to use music as a powerful proactive agent for social change.

costs while minimizing commercial interruptions. Still, in spite of its coup by offering perhaps the best mix of music and interview, MTV was plagued by a multitude of commercial interruptions, some occurring in midperformance or during an interview. MTV's supply of VJs provided the opportunity to insert some interviews later, offsetting the numerous unfortunate commercial interruptions during the concert. Finally, ABC, hoping to snag a huge commercial audience, found itself embroiled with disaster after disaster, as audiences heard the Led Zeppelin reunion while simultaneously watching Madonna onscreen.

The laundry list of acts ranged from Elvis Costello and Joan Baez to Adam Ant and Spandau Ballet, from the Four Tops and B. B. King to Black Sabbath and REO Speedwagon, from Rick Springfield and Run-D.M.C. to Sade and Judas Priest, from Bryan Adams and the Beach Boys to U2 and Queen, from Simple Minds and Santana to Elton John and George Thorogood and the Destroyers. David Bowie, the Pretenders, the Who, Madonna, Paul McCartney, Tom Petty and the Heartbreakers, and Eric Clapton were also among the concert participants.[9]

Besides the impressive list of artists, Live Aid boasted some equally powerful reunions and interesting artist pairings that yielded several rare and powerful performances. The aforementioned Crosby, Stills, Nash and Young reunion went off without a hitch, except for a transmission failure that blacked out their performance for most audiences outside the United States. The Who's on-again, off-again reunion plans were confirmed the morning of the concert, with Geldof later commenting that the whole experience of getting them back together was "rather like getting one man's four ex-wives together."[10] Transmission glitches surfaced again, this time with American audiences blacked out to most of their set.

Duran Duran, who had not played together in over a year, provided a set as tight and professional as when they played together, opening the ABC-TV broadcast with their single "A View to a Kill," which was the No. 1 single in America at the time. The proposed Rolling Stones reunion never came off, as Mick Jagger ended up doing a solo set and Ron Wood and Keith Richards joined Bob Dylan in Philadelphia. Jagger also paired with David Bowie to record a new version of the Motown classic "Dancing in the Streets" specifically for the concert. Members of Black Sabbath and Status Quo also reunited for the concert, and U2, just back from a nine-month tour, "played with more energy than anyone else. The day was a turning point for them. They proved to the whole world that they were the best live rock and roll band at that time. They captured the heart and soul of the world by performing with integrity."[11]

Perhaps the most anticipated reunion was Led Zeppelin, whose members had not performed together in five years (five years, one week since their last live performance). With Phil Collins replacing the late John "Bonzo" Bonham on drums, the band performed three classics, including "Stairway to Heaven." Philadelphia's audiences went wild for Led Zeppelin's appearance, singing along with Robert Plant and validating the band's choice to reunite there, since American audiences had been consistently supportive of the group. Collins' stint with Led Zeppelin culminated an exhaustive day for him, shuttling between the British and American concert sites and making him the most visible performer at Live Aid. He had started the day performing solo in London. After singing two duets there with Sting, Collins hopped on the Concorde to New York, where a helicopter flew him to Philadelphia. After accompanying Eric Clapton (on drums), he reprised the two solos he had performed in London earlier that day ("Against All Odds" and "In the Air Tonight"), before jamming with Led Zeppelin's reunion set.

With all the stellar performances, the day was not without its difficulties, outside of technical ones. The two finales were as different as the planning and recording of "We Are the World" and "Do They Know It's Christmas?" In London, Paul McCartney's poignant rendition of the Beatles' classic "Let It Be" became even more touching when a spontaneous chorus comprising David Bowie, Alison Moyet, Pete Townshend, and Bob Geldof joined him and the audience to carry the words. What McCartney did not realize was that his microphone was dead, and everyone at Wembley seemed to come to his aid and filled the air with his music. At the end of the song, McCartney and Townshend lifted Geldof on their shoulders as he sang "Do They Know It's Christmas?" Geldof later described his feelings during this memorable moment: "I nearly died of embarrassment. It was terrible. These people were pop greats. . . . [L]ooking back, I am still embarrassed but intensely proud that I was carried on Paul McCartney's and Pete Townsend's shoulders."[12]

In the United States, Bob Dylan put a damper on the finale as he ended his set commenting on the plight of American farmers and suggesting it would be nice if some of Live Aid's money went to them. Geldof responded to Dylan's comment in his autobiography, calling Dylan's comments "crass, stupid and nationalistic"[13] and accusing Dylan of a complete lack of understanding about Live Aid's purpose. The American finale continued what has been termed an "anti-climax" to the day when Lionel Richie led everyone in singing "We Are the World," a seemingly appropriate way to end the concert but one that clearly lacked the sincerity and sense of community displayed by artists coming to McCartney's rescue in London.

Besides the contrast in finales, other financial and artistic differences had surfaced. Initially, Geldof had difficulties securing caterers willing to participate for free and phones for viewers to call in pledges and donations. Needing literally thousands of telephones worldwide, Geldof finally convinced British Telecom to donate the phones, and caterers agreed to donate food for the event. Less visible, but certainly no less important, was the issue of racism. Three of the hottest stars of the day did not appear: Bruce Springsteen, Prince, and Michael Jackson. Springsteen begged off because he was in the middle of a European concert tour (performing in England just seven days before Live Aid) and had just gotten married. Prince had retired from performing and could not be coaxed out of retirement to perform, though he would return to the stage soon after the concert. Jackson "just didn't seem to want to do it,"[14] although rumors of a performance continued until the concert day.

Overall and partly because of Prince's and Jackson's absence, there seemed to be a lack of black talent. Geldof argued that given Live Aid's purpose was to raise money, he would take whatever artists would generate the most donations. In the end, the number of black participants did not entirely support claims of racism, as the Four Tops, B. B. King, Billy Ocean, Run-D.M.C., Bo Diddley, Albert Collins, Ashford and Simpson, Teddy Pendergrass, Patti LaBelle, Eddie Kendricks, David Ruffin, Lionel Richie, and Tina Turner all participated. Excluding Prince and Jackson, the lineup of black talent could not have been better.

Live Aid reportedly made over $100 million worldwide during its seventeen-hour run. More important, Geldof accomplished his mission to change the world perception about Africa. It is clear that after audiences saw a clip of famine in Africa—with images of a mother who was so weak she could not hold her dead baby in her arms—set to the music of "Drive" by the Cars,[15] their minds and hearts were forever changed. And rock music, under the auspices of Geldof, proved how powerful music can be as a proactive agent for social change:

> He had pulled off the greatest concert of all time. There is no disputing that point. He did it because he cared about humanity. He did not do it for the money, nor the fame or career advancement. Bob Geldof showed everyone that one man can make a difference in the world.[16]

FARM AID

Within two months of Live Aid's international success, another charitable venture emerged to help American farmers. Perhaps as a nod to Geldof's venture, or perhaps because of Dylan's impassioned, if inappropriate, plea during Live Aid to consider the plight of America's farmers, Farm Aid embarked on a series of concerts that would continue well into the 1990s and the new millennium. For

Following in the steps of Live Aid, Farm Aid was a series of concerts organized to help the American farmer. Shown here is Texas Stadium, site of the Farm Aid musical extravaganza on March 14, 1992. Courtesy of Photofest.

Geldof, there was a huge difference between losing a home and losing one's life. In that way, Live Aid's appeal for those suffering from the famine that plagued Ethiopia carried a more critical (read: life-threatening) cry for help than those who suffered from economic depravity. Still, many American artists saw an opportunity to use their celebrity to raise money for a different type of worthy cause.

The plight of the farmer in America was not new. Issues, both economic and political, involving agriculture had surfaced in cyclical patterns since the nineteenth century.[17] By the 1980s, American farmers faced a crisis more severe than any since the Great Depression when Franklin Roosevelt attempted to control agricultural prices through the New Deal's Agricultural Adjustment Act. During the 1930s, Folk singers like Woody Guthrie had expressed concerns about the farmers' plight in numerous songs about the Dust Bowl. In "Talking Dust Bowl Blues," Guthrie tells the tale of a farmer uprooting his family and relocation in desperation while the government does nothing to help him. Recalling the pre-Depression Era when many Americans owned small farms and were able to feed and clothe their families with the money they made from the sale of their crops, Guthrie laments that, after the Dust Bowl devastated much of America's Midwest, all he could do was trade the farm in for a new car and keep heading west in search of a new job. A typical theme in Guthrie's songs during this time identified a detached, insensitive government and an increasingly disenfranchised America, both struggling to survive, but not always working together to do so.[18] Guthrie's songs became part of a larger, Depression-era effort that brought awareness about the farmers' dilemma and provided temporary respite from what seemed to be a hopeless plight against an uncaring government.

Guthrie's message was heard again in the 1980s when Reagan-era farmers found their circumstances so troubling that many succumbed to financial ruin. Stories about the tragedies on the Great Plains and beyond abounded. An Iowa farmer killed his banker, his neighbor, his wife, and himself. On a farm near Ruthton, Minnesota, a farmer and his son murdered two bank officials. And in Union County, South Dakota, a Farmers Home Administration (FmHA) official could not hold up under the pressure of foreclosing on so many destitute farmers, so he killed his wife, two children, and the family dog before turning the gun on himself.[19]

Reasons for the agricultural plight began in the 1970s when lowered trade barriers, couple with record purchases of American grain by the former Soviet Union, pushed farm incomes, commodity prices, and land values up. Farmers took advantage of low interest rates, so that by the early 1980s high interest rates, "tight money," and record harvest leading to overproduction pushed commodity prices down. Between 1981 and 1985, farmland value fell by 60 percent. As they watched profits drop an average of 36 percent between 1980 and 1986, American farmers saw their financial aggressiveness from a decade earlier turn to financial disaster, a rippling effect crisis that affected not only farmers but the surrounding rural communities as well. To make matters worse, the Reagan administration took a hands-off approach to intervention.

As a result, a widespread grassroots protest rose up against the government's laissez-faire response to the farm problem, though most organized groups found their voices unheard and the problem worsening. Enter American celebrities. Just as Hollywood responded in the 1930s and 1940s with films like *The Grapes of Wrath* (1940) and Charlie Chaplin's *Modern Times* (1936), 1984 saw two film productions whose stories came from the heartland, *Country* and *The River*.[20]

Then, on September 22, 1985, musical artists including Bob Dylan, Tom Petty, Billy Joel, Van Halen, Bon Jovi, and Foreigner performed at the first Farm Aid concert in Champaign, Illinois. Some 80,000 people packed the outdoor stadium in spite of inclement weather. The event was televised by the Nashville Network, during which 112 artists including Alabama, The Beach Boys, Glen Campbell, John Denver, John Fogerty, Arlo Guthrie, Sammy Hagar, Merle Haggard, Emmylou Harris, B. B. King, Carole King, Kris Kristofferson, Huey Lewis, Joni Mitchell, Lou Reed, Brian Setzer, Eddie Van Halen, and Neil Young performed. Conceived by Farm Aid founders Willie Nelson, Neil Young, and John Mellencamp, Farm Aid's purpose, like Geldof's Live Aid, was to "heighten public awareness about the plight of the American farmer."[21] Proceeds were channeled via grants to support farm organizations and provide needy families with food and/or legal assistance.

Together with proceeds from *Country* and *The River*, and grassroots activism from groups like the American Agricultural Movement, Iowa's Farm Unity Coalition, and Women Involved in Farm Economics, Farm Aid concerts made an important mark toward securing public awareness about the plight of the farmer. A 1986 *New York Times*–CBS poll found that a majority of Americans were willing to pay more taxes to help farmers keep their land. The farm crisis became "a cultural crisis unique in our history" because public sentiment had clearly attached itself to "an idealized image of the family farm."[22]

Since 1985, public interest in agricultural issues has waxed and waned. Farm Aid concerts have reocurred sporadically in places like Indianapolis, New Orleans, Austin, Texas, Ames, Iowa, and Lincoln, Nebraska, raising over $13 million in grant-directed money. Recently, Farm Aid has moved farther west to locations like Seattle, Washington. Their artist roundup has grown to include Bryan Adams, Garth Brooks, Don Henley, the Grateful Dead, Elton John, and the Neville Brothers; their message and logo (a tractor with an America flag) remain constant.

Almost a half century after Guthrie's plaintive treatise on the farmer's demise, Mellencamp echoed his themes of a cold, unfeeling capitalistic government in "Rain on the Scarecrow."[23] Using even more graphic images to suggest that, in a post-modern world, violence might occur if the government failed to respond to the needs of the farmer. No longer a naive society trusting in the government's empty promises, Mellencamp's proactive assertion picked up where Guthrie's lament left off, bringing awareness about America's heartland to a new generation of listeners while, at the same time, reminding all Americans that the farmer's dilemma was not a new phenomenon, but an ongoing challenge. In Mellencamp's story, even small town bankers and entrepreneurs had become messengers of big government, shaking the farmer's hand one moment while simultaneously taking away his land as well as his dignity. This sort of metaphorical back stabbing paralleled Farm Aid's commitment to recognizing the farmer's desperate need for federal assistance.

In 1935, *Time* magazine reported that an Oklahoma farmer was said to have fainted when a drop of rain fell on his head, to have been revived "only when two buckets of sand were thrown in his face."[24] In 1985, world conditions threw more than two buckets of sand in rock 'n' roll's face. Live Aid and Farm Aid symbolize the enduring power of music in the face of global crisis and the artist's ability to inspire people to rally around viable, important causes. In an

 ART FOR AMNESTY—VARIOUS ARTISTS (1988)

Though difficult to find in a video or DVD format, the 1988 Human Rights Now! Tour took the Live Aid concept to a new level. Spearheaded by Bruce Springsteen, Sting, Peter Gabriel, Tracy Chapman, and Youssou N'Dour, the concert tour was touted as a campaign for freedom rather than a "caravan for charity." Human Rights Now! attempted to introduce the idea of basic human rights protection to millions of people worldwide through the power of electronic media. Hundreds of thousands of fans filled stadiums from London to Buenos Aires during the tour's six-week, 35,000-mile tour, generating new interest (and revenue) for Amnesty International and extending the role and visibility of musical artists toward global awareness and human understanding.

age when rock music seemed destined to wallow in its own corporate profits, artists turned to activism, making them and their music active agents for social change.

On the days that rock 'n' roll cared during the 1980s, everyone from the artists to the audience to the disenfranchised seemed to rise triumphant. The music that was often criticized for its cultural connection to drugs and promiscuity seemed to take on a new humanitarian life. As Bob Geldof rejoiced at the news that over $100 million was donated to the Band Aid Trust after Live Aid: "Remember on that day for once in our bloody lives WE WON."[25]

NOTES

1. Adam Stanley, "Live Aid" (©2001), found at http://www.echoes.com/rememberaday/liveaid.html.

2. See Web site, for example, http://www.inthe80s.com/weworld.shtml.

3. See Web site, for example, http://www.inthe80s.com/xmaslst.shtml.

4. See Web site, for example, http://www.herald.co.uk/local_info/live_aid.html.

5. Ibid.

6. Bob Geldof, *Is That It?* (New York: Weidenfeld & Nicholson, 1986), 258; included at Stanley, "Live Aid."

7. See Web site at note 3.

8. Geldof, *Is That It?* 264; also see Stanley, "Live Aid."

9. See Web site, for example, at note 4.

10. Peter Hillmore, *Live Aid* (Parsippany, NJ: Unicorn Publishing House, 1985), 132; included at Stanley, "Live Aid."

11. See Stanley, "Live Aid."

12. Geldof, *Is That It?* 310; also see Stanley, "Live Aid."

13. Geldof, *Is That It?* 312; Stanley, "Live Aid."

14. Geldof, *Is That It?* 272; Stanley, "Live Aid."

15. See Web site at note 4.

16. See Stanley, "Live Aid."

17. The plight of the American farmer can be chronicled as a reform movement during the late nineteenth century (Grange Movement), as part of a third-party platform in 1892 (Populist Party), and during the Great Depression of the 1930s.

18. See lyrics for Woody Guthrie's "Talking Dust Bowl Blues" at, for example, http://www.fortunecity.com/tinpan/parton/2/dust.html.

19. Jason Manning wrote a summary of Farm Aid that is found at http://www.eightiesclub.tripod.com/id300.htm.

20. Hollywood responded to the farm issues similarly in the 1930s and 1980s: Charlie Chaplin's *Modern Times* (1936; Charles Chaplin, director) depicted problems faced by workers during the Great Depression; *The Grapes of Wrath* (1940; John Ford, director; starring Henry Fonda) adapted John Steinbeck's novel about the Dust Bowl for the screen. In the 1980s, two films were produced by actresses whose personal experiences on a farm inspired them to make the general public more aware of contemporary agricultural issues: *Country* (1984; Richard Pearce, director; starring Jessica Lange and

Sam Shepard); *The River* (1984; Mark Rydell, director; starring Sissy Spacek and Mel Gibson).

21. See Manning at note 19.

22. Ibid.

23. For lyrics to John Mellencamp's "Rain on the Scarecrow," see, for example, http://www.lyricsfreak.com/j/john-mellencamp/74537.html.

24. *Time*, April 1, 1935, found at http://www.fortunecity.com/tinpan/parton/2/dust.html.

25. Hillmore, *Live Aid* 7; included at Stanley, "Live Aid."

RAP MEETS ROCK

"Hip hop is the only genre of music that allows us to talk about almost anything. Musically it allows us to sample and play and create poetry to the beat of music. It's highly controversial, but that's the way the game is."[1] These comments, made by hip-hop's founding father of scratching and quick mixing, Grandmaster Flash, are powerfully modest, for creating hip-hop was more than a game. It was a revolution. And revolutions—whether they are political, social, cultural, economic, or musical—do not occur in a vacuum. Rather, revolutions are usually the culmination of a series of conflicting yet connected issues, ideas, and events. In the late 1970s, rock 'n' roll in America was impacted by several critical factors and events that inspired a new musical explosion. Social malaise after Vietnam and Watergate, growing drug use including stimulants and narcotics, unemployment, inner-city disenfranchisement, and Richard Nixon's massive military conscription of urban black eighteen- to twenty-year-olds created, almost overnight, a community-disruptive matriarchy that threatened the order of America's urban black community.

Particularly hard hit was New York City's subborough of the South Bronx, where violence dominated a neighborhood of burned-out warehouses and deteriorating projects. Out of the dark bleakness of this, the infamous 41st Fort Apache Precinct, came the birth of the brilliant b-boy nation, a spontaneous youth movement of preteen boys (and girls). B-boys (and girls), which stood for, alternately, "beat, break and Bronx . . . [used the streets as stage for] endless hardcore funk spun and vibed up by the DJ's/MCs [emcees] of the original block, playground and house party sound systems."[2]

In *Vibe* magazine's *History of Hip Hop*, Tom Terrell explains the culminating events of the 1970s and their impact on rap and hip-hop in this way: "As the

'70s wanted, the burgeoning b-boy and graffiti crews staged a palace coup against the old disco-and-R&B guard, rallying behind the cutting and scratching skills of DJ's like Grand Wizard Theodore or Grandmaster Flash and his MC posse the Furious Five."[3] By 1980, the Sugarhill Gang's megahit "Rapper's Delight" became the biggest-selling twelve-inch record ever (over 2 million copies), establishing "hip-hop" (coined from the song's lyrics) as a new cultural art form and making fledgling label Sugar Hill Records overnight power brokers in this new musical revolution. Using rhythms from a variety of resources, including gospel, jazz, James Brown/Motown soul, funk, disco, and drum machines—and remixing them in a process known as "sampling," hip-hop had formed its essential musical core.[4] And every day, it seemed that new artists were emerging from the streets of the South Bronx.

HIP-HOP, ROCK, AND MTV, 1981–1990

In July 1981, the Clash traveled to the United States for a now-famous seventeen-night gig at Time Square's International Casino. Eager to honor the hip-hop artists who had influenced and inspired them, the band invited Flash and the Treacherous Three to open the shows and hired graffiti artist Futura 2000 to spray stage backdrops and banners. This well-intentioned effort turned ugly when its mostly white punk audience jeered and booed the rappers, spat, and shouted offensive epithets that ultimately abbreviated their performances.

 ROCK THE CASBAH—THE CLASH (1982)

A mockingly catchy treatise on the energy crisis of the late 1970s, *Rock the Casbah*'s infectious tune and satiric lyrics gave the Clash a genuine hit, while the video's plethora of armadillos, oil rigs, and mohawks made it an instant classic. *Rock the Casbah* is a good example of early MTV at its best: videos that were jam-packed with conflicting, audacious, rapid-fire images that may or may not have had anything to do with the melody or lyrics. MTV's early ventures were aimed at getting the audience's attention—and holding it over repeated viewing. The fleeting multitude of images quickly became a mainstay of music video, performing the same visual hooks as catchy melodies did on the radio a generation earlier.

The Clash's efforts were not a total failure, however. Later that year, German synth-beat pioneers Kraftwerk included a scratched vocal/beat track on their album *Computer World* called "Numbers," which became a major influence on break beat DJs, as well as a break dancer anthem. New wave's Blondie scored a hit with what would become known as the first hip-hop–rock single to top both the U.S. and UK charts—"Rapture," an exciting fusion of rock guitar, new wave keyboards, hip-hop bass, and droll rap references to Flash, Fab 5 Freddy, and punk rock. "Rapture" influenced numerous pop recordings, including Billy Joel's "We Didn't Start the Fire" (1989) and Cake's "Going the Distance" (1996).

In 1982, Grandmaster Flash offered a demo to a group known as The Furious Five. The group of five MCs, including

Melle Mel, Cowboy, Rahiem, Mr. Ness, and Kid Creole, were not sure the demo was worth recording but did it anyway. A little over a month later, "The Message" sold over a million copies. "The Message" was the first rap record to address the hopelessness of African American ghettos, shifting from more typically arrogant rap lyrics that alluded to being the "biggest" and "baddest."

The following year, Grandmaster Flash and The Furious Five's Melle Mel recorded a powerful anti-cocaine single, "White Lines (Don't Don't Do It)," which became a classic rap anthem as well as an international hit. "White Lines" also unofficially signaled rap's foray from underground art form to mainstream acceptability. Further solidifying rap's entry into the mainstream and its connection to rock 'n' roll was Afrika Bambaataa, whose style was clearly influenced by Kraftwerk's synch-beat electronics. Inspired by their single "Trans-Europe Express," Bambaataa teamed up with Soul Sonic and created a new synthesized electro rap sound. The resulting hit, "Planet Rock," sold over 620,000 in the United States alone. Hip-hop "crews" now included graffiti artists and break dancers, shifting dance music in a different direction and establishing a whole new dance culture in the process.

Hip-hop continued to break new ground throughout the 1980s. In 1984, Run-D.M.C. burst onto the rap scene with a new rap style that included gold chains and sportswear. Establishing a new street style of dress, the group even dedicated a song to their shoes. "My Adidas" was so popular that Adidas paid the band a reported six-figure sum to wear their clothing, making Run-D.M.C. the first rap group sponsored by a clothing company. The following year, Miami rappers 2 Live Crew took rap in a different direction with their controversial album *As Nasty as They Wanna Be*, which U.S. courts labeled obscene. 2 Live Crew appealed the decision on grounds of free speech but made headlines that would forever connect rap lyrics to issues of obscenity, violence, and misogyny.

In 1986, Run-D.M.C. made positive strides for both rap and rock. Its debut album *Raising Hell* was released by Def Jam, selling 3 million copies in the United States alone. One of the album's tracks, "Walk This Way," paired the group with perennial rock bad boys Aerosmith, making them the first rap band to cross with rock. "Walk This Way" with complementary music video, became a huge crossover hit. Later that year, Run-D.M.C. appeared on the cover of *Rolling Stone* magazine, setting another "first" for rap in being the first rap group to grace the magazine's cover.

The year 1986 also saw white rap introduced to audiences by the Beastie Boys, whose "Fight for Your Right to Party" became an anthem for rebellious youth everywhere. Making Volkswagon pendants their symbol, the Beastie Boys, who began their career as an opening act for Madonna, went on to become one of hip-hop's biggest-selling acts. Their debut album *Licensed to Ill* sold over 4 million copies and stayed at No. 1 on the U.S. album charts for seven weeks. The Beastie Boys were also responsible for discovering another of rap's megastars, LL Cool J, whose handle stands for "The ladies love cool James." LL added yet another element to rap's repertoire, the sexy love ballad. "I Need Love" (1987) became the first rap love ballad, scoring on both American and European charts and helping LL earn his place as one of rap's most enduring artists.

The year 1988 was a kind of watershed year in rap, as new artists, styles, and controversies were introduced. MCs Eric B. and Rakim were credited for developing a more relaxed and refined style of rap, epitomized by the use of strings, flutes, and bass on their release *Follow the Leader*. Engaging in a more politically charged style of rap was Public Enemy, who relied on ongoing themes of alienation and rage with the African American community. Responding to media criticism for sending forth a message that spoke to violence, anti-Semitism, and sexism, Public Enemy released the single "Don't Believe the Hype." Later in the year, Public Enemy released its second, now-iconic album, *It Takes a Nation of Millions to Hold Us Back*. The album went platinum, securing the group's place among rap's breakthrough artists.

Following Public Enemy's lead of using a direct, almost confrontational political rap style was N.W.A. (Niggaz with Attitude), whose members included Dr. Dre, DJ Yella, MC Ren, Easy E, and founding rapper Ice Cube. N.W.A. based much of its poetry on violence, drugs, and guns, thus soliciting almost instantaneous media attention. With increasingly foreboding statistics verifying the rising death toll among young black males as a result of gang- and drug-related violence, N.W.A. raised awareness about America's inner-city ghettos. Claiming to be "reporters" on what was happening in the streets, N.W.A. eschewed criticism leveled at it for singles like "Fuck the Police," becoming one of the world's best-known gangsta rap groups, a title that remained long after the group broke up.

Women also entered rap's mainstream in a profound way in 1988. Backed by DJ Spinderella, rap duo Salt-N-Pepa released the single "Push It," which had an immediate impact on the New York rap scene. Following the single was their debut album *Hot, Cool and Vicious*, which stayed on the charts for over a year, while "Push It" sold over a million copies. A year later, the Grammy Awards announced a new category, Best Rap Act, for which Salt-N-Pepa was nominated. Learning that this particular award would not be televised during the awards show, Salt-N-Pepa upheld rap's already established rebellious tradition and refused to attend the Grammy ceremony.

Finally, 1987 welcomed another new and formidable rapper, Fresh Prince Will Smith. Part of the DJ Jazzy Jeff and Fresh Prince duo, Smith helped spin a new brand of hip-hop, devoid of politics and exclusionary rhetoric. Instead, DJ Jazzy Jeff and the Fresh Prince's debut album offered more playful lyrics and a variation on scratching called "transforming." *Rock the House* garnered much critical and media attention. DJ Jazzy Jeff and the Fresh Prince were awarded the Grammy for Best Rap Performance for the single "Parents Just Don't Understand." In 1989, the duo was nominated for "I Think I Can Beat Mike Tyson," from the album *And In This Corner*.

As the decade drew to a close, Public Enemy pushed the political envelope even farther by beginning to emulate the Black Panthers. Dressed in berets, camouflage fatigues, and onstage military maneuvers, the group drew increasingly negative media attention. "Fight the Power," which director Spike Lee used to open his 1989 film *Do the Right Thing*, became another rap anthem, this one instigating a Federal Bureau of Investigation report examining rap's impact on national security.

Beyond Public Enemy's ongoing political controversies, rap became more sophisticated in 1989 with Young MC's emergence as the maestro of "articulate" rap. Born in London, raised in New York, and educated at the University of California, Young MC's single "Bust a Move" was a Top 10 smash, while his debut album *Brainstorm* earned him a Grammy for Best Rap Record. Complementing Young MC's arrival on the rap scene was female rapper Queen Latifah. Although her name means "delicate and sensitive" in Arabic, Latifah's assertive style directly responded to some male rappers' sexist lyrics, allowing her to break through

 BUST A MOVE—YOUNG MC (1989)

One of the first rap singles to cross over to the pop charts, *Bust a Move* continued rap's integration into the pop/rock mainstream. The video's theme is fairly standard fare: Loser goes to party, sees an attractive woman whom he would like to "sex," and nothing happens. Same loser tries to pick up women in various other social settings, only to be rejected because he does not have a car or money. Moral of the video: If you have no money and no car, you have no woman. There you are. The single's—and video's—run up the charts produced almost excessive airplay until both the song and its artist (Young Marvin Young) became one-hit wonders. Still, the single remains remarkable in its marketing of rap to a broader, adult audience and its fresh depiction of how, in a capitalist society, money and love are inherently connected.

the male-dominated rap scene to become "Rap's First Lady." Her tracks became synonymous with promoting unity and collaboration, especially among black women.

Rounding out rap's auspicious decade was the launching of Ice Cube's solo career. Joining forces with former Public Enemy Chuck D, Ice Cube released the album *AmeriKKKa's Most Wanted* in 1990; the album went gold in ten days and wound up selling over a million copies. Ice Cube's outspoken attacks on white America outraged some right-wing extremist organizations that targeted him for assassination. Police discovered the plot later in 1993.[5]

Hip-hop's apparent mainstreaming during the 1980s—as well as its fusion with rock 'n' roll—almost seems like an effortless progression in the anti-disco, post-punk age. Yet, throughout the 1980s—and for most of its history—hip-hop has been the victim of an interesting paradox: "You can't get on MTV until hip hop becomes a major industry, and you can't compete as a major industry until you get on MTV."[6] This conundrum clearly had a history and some validity. For one thing, it had taken awhile for MTV to warm up to a black audience, beginning with its reluctant airing of Michael Jackson's *Billie Jean* video in 1983 (rumored to have been considered "inappropriate" in sound and content for MTV's demographic). Then, in 1984, Prince's five video entries for the *Purple Rain* film and sound track chipped away at MTV's seeming disinterest in cultivating an R&B audience.

So it was not until 1986 when Run-D.M.C. joined Aerosmith for the rap cover collaboration of the latter's hit "Walk This Way" that MTV opened the door for what would become hip-hop's first video classic. At the same time, the Beastie Boys' "(You Gotta) Fight for Your Right to Party" and the Fat Boys' "Wipeout" (with the Beach Boys) were also vying for airplay with the often seen "Walk This Way." All three singles had a common denominator of white people. Beyond that, the videos each contained striking visuals to which audiences responded: "Run-D.M.C wore black leather, the Fat Boys were fat, and the Beastie Boys shot Silly String out of their noses. The songs were light, the visual identities instant, and they became MTV's first rap staples."[7]

Run-D.M.C. paved the way for other rap artists to utilize the music video medium as a marketing tool. Still, many of the rap videos approved by MTV had more to do with persistent managers who massaged reluctant advertisers than it did MTV acting as a promoter of black urban American music or recognizing rap/hip-hop as both a cultural and musical force. In a 1987 *Adweek* article, one advertising executive commented, "Rap is identified by some as revolutionary, and the music can be threatening to clients. The biggest job we have is convincing the client that it's not race music and that the artists aren't necessarily angry."[8] For their part, rappers also became conspicuous conspirators in embracing crass consumerism. Besides Run-D.M.C.'s contract with and paean to Adidas, the Fat Boys rapped rhapsodic about their favorite foods, while LL Cool J dropped more commercial products' names on his albums than any American could find in the equivalent time span on television. Different from rock artists who had, until that time, rejected any identifiable connection with a product, rap artists raised consumer marketing as record promotion to a new level. By the end of the decade, Kool Moe Dee and Fresh Prince pitched Mountain Dew, while Kurtis Blow shilled for Coke. In what was perhaps the most regrettable commercial refusal, the Fat Boys declined offers from both Coke and Burger King.

With more artists and advertisers on board, MTV launched *Yo! MTV Raps* in August 1988. The first episodes aired on Saturday night with rap pioneer Fab 5 Freddy Braithwaite. Within a few months, *Yo!*'s popularity resulted in a week-night edition hosted by Ed Lover and Dr. Dre. In its prime, *Yo!* proved to be one of the best video shows ever aired on MTV. Rap artists previously shunned by the channel now showed up in videos and dropped by the studio for live interviews. There were also live performances by LL Cool J, EPMD, Public Enemy, Grandmaster Flash, and Eric B. and Rakim. For fans and critics alike, *Yo!* was about rap culture; it *was* rap culture. But even with its success, *Yo!* could not sustain itself against the changing face of rap music. As soon as N.W.A.'s seminal version of gangsta rap emerged, MTV backed away from its obvious politically charged message, offering less offensive rap acts in what many termed a watered-down version of what was really happening in the streets and with rap culture.[9] Nonetheless, rap and hip-hop made significant inroads in mainstreaming their art and their message during the 1980s. Just as indie rock bands gained a broader fan base and more airplay, so did the underground subculture from the South Bronx emerge as a viable expression of postmodern American urban culture. The nuances in rap and hip-hop might not have been found on MTV, but individual artists had greater visibility and more venues from which to promote their art as well as their political and social commentary.

RUN-D.M.C.

Straight up and moving forward, Run-D.M.C. broke into hip-hop and, in the process, paved the way for everyone else. No other hip-hop act had gained a mass audience or received significant video airplay until Run-D.M.C. made the scene. First forming in 1982 out of middle-class Hollis (Queens), New York, Run-D.M.C. consisted of childhood friends Run (born Joseph Simmons, November 14, 1964), MC D (a.k.a. DMC, born Darryl McDaniels, May 31, 1964), and DJ Jam Master Jay (born Jason Mizell, January 21, 1965). Simmons' brother Russell had already formed a hip-hop management company called Rush Productions in the early '80s and later teamed with Rick Rubin to form the seminal rap record label Def Jam. It was Russell who encouraged his brother Joe to form a rap duo; then Joe persuaded Russell to let him, D.M.C., and Jam Master Jay make a record.

Rap went mainstream during the 1980s, led by the urban rhythms of Run-D.M.C. Courtesy of Photofest.

The result was the seminal 1983 single "It's Like That" (b-side, "Sucker M.C.'s"), often referred to as the record that kick-started modern hip-hop. With Run and D.M.C. on vocals and Jam Master Jay scratching turntables, "It's Like That" had a sound unique to rap at that time: a sparsely blunt musical arrangement punctuated by hard beats and powerfully literate vocals. "It's Like That" became a Top 20 hit (R&B). "Sucker M.C.'s," the b-side single, substituted the usual live backing beat for a rhythm machine, giving the trio a smooth yet edgy appeal that complemented their black leather clothes and Adidas sneakers. A second single, "Hard Times" (b-side, "Jam-Master Jay"), also scored on the Top 20 R&B charts. With continued assistance from brother Russell, Run-D.M.C. signed a contract with Profile Records and released their self-titled debut album in 1984.

What really set Run-D.M.C. apart from other rappers was their third single, "Rock Box," "which laid a blistering guitar riff over a bass groove, thus adding a human quality to hip-hop that people quickly ate up."[10] It's successful marriage of metal and rap easily foreshadowed the group's subsequent pairing with metal favorites Aerosmith for 1986's blistering cover of "Walk This Way." Before that joint effort, Run-D.M.C. released a second album, *King of Rock*, in 1985. By the time of *King*'s release, the group had become the most popular and one of the most influential rap acts in the United States. With the album's title clearly suggesting a fusion of rock and rap, the tracks highlighted Run and D.M.C. rapping over heavy metal records with thickly dense drum beats in the background. The group's popularity also led to an appearance in the 1985 film *Krush Groove*, based loosely on the life of Run's brother Russell that featured fellow rappers Kurtis Blow, the Beastie Boys, and Fat Boys.[11]

By 1986, Run-D.M.C.'s mix of rock and rap peaked with the release of *Raising Hell*, their third album and the one that contained their genius collaboration with Aerosmith. "Walk This Way" charted in the Top 5 in the United Kingdom and made the Top 10 in the United States. Additional tracks like the style-frenzied "My Adidas" and the wordsmithed wonder "Peter Piper" pushed the album to the height of mid-1980s hip-hop popularity, becoming the first rap album to go platinum.[12] *Raising*

WALK THIS WAY—RUN-D.M.C. WITH AEROSMITH (1986)

Rock meets rap in this quasi-staged concert video or, more specifically, rock and rap face-off in a mock musical competition. The juxtaposition of Run-D.M.C.'s urban contemporary rap with Aerosmith's classic hard-rock bad-boy behavior makes for an effective and telling video image. Impacting society like no other musical form since the beginning of rock, rap/hip-hop had, by the mid-1980s, clearly migrated to mainstream acceptability. As members of the two bands break down an ersatz wall that divides them, so, too, did rap break down social barriers and cultural divisions the same way rock had democratized American society thirty years earlier. The video easily depicts two generations of pop/rock artists, placing them in simulated dissonance but ultimately bringing the two most powerful, popular, and transforming music forms of the twentieth century together, syncopating Run-D.M.C.'s funky poetic rhythms with Aerosmith's edgy, hard-rock machinations.

Hell also became the first rap album to hit No. 1 on the R&B charts, while *Walk This Way* received constant MTV airplay.

Run-D.M.C. spent most of 1987 recording their fourth album, *Tougher Than Leather*, which was released in 1988. The album was followed by a movie of the same name, a gentle send-up of 1970s blaxploitation films starring the group's leather-clad trio. Unfortunately, by the time the album and film were released, the rap world had changed. Run-D.M.C., who had begun both projects at the top of the rap world, found themselves competing with hardcore acts like Public Enemy. During their year of recording and filming, Run-D.M.C.'s crossover brand of hip-hop, like their designer brand of tennis shoes, had fallen out of favor with rap audiences. The movie bombed at the box office; the album only went platinum, failing to produce any major hit singles and signaling the group's unfortunate fall from hip-hop grace.

Two years after the release of *Tougher Than Leather*, Run-D.M.C. returned with *Back From Hell*, their first album that did not go platinum. Personal problems plagued Run, who was accused of raping a fan (the charges were later dismissed), and D.M.C., who battled alcoholism. In 1993, after their religious conversion as born-again Christians, Run-D.M.C. returned with *Down With the King*. No longer innovators in rap, *Down With the King* proved the group to be survivors in the recording industry and respected pioneers in the world of rap and hip-hop. Their continued attempts to update their sound have taken away some of the raw excitement of their early career, when dual microphones and turntables changed the sound of hip-hop and the place of rock 'n' roll in American culture. On October 30, 2002, Jam Master Jay was shot and killed inside a recording studio in Queens, New York. The murder remains unsolved.

THE BEASTIE BOYS

Often called the "smartest dumb band in the land," the Beastie Boys' brand of white rap served as an appropriate complement to Run-D.M.C.'s black urban middle-class mix of rock and rap. Organized in Greenwich Village, New York, in 1981 by "MCA" Adam Yauch (born August 5, 1965, in Brooklyn, New York) and "Mike D" Mike Diamond (born November 20, 1966, in New York), the Beastie Boys were initially a quartet. After drummer Kate Schellenbach and guitarist John Berry's quick departure, Yauch and Diamond recruited Adam Horovitz (born October 31, 1976, in New York) as their replacement. After two indie single releases, the trio was signed to Def Jam records with friend and co-Def Jam founder Rick Rubin taking a spin as the group's DJ/scratcher.

The band's debut album, *Licensed to Ill*, was released in November 1986 to international acclaim, becoming the fasting-selling debut in Columbia Records' history. Depending on one's musical taste and sense of humor, the band's attempt to create a "white, rock-centric take" on Afro-American hip-hop was

White boys met rap in controversial and commercially successful ways during the 1980s with the Beastie Boys, shown here in 1987. Darlene Hammond/Getty Images.

 FIGHT FOR YOUR RIGHT (TO PARTY)—BEASTIE BOYS (1986)

No other video can lay claim to being a generation's party anthem, which revels in the joys and discoveries of youth. Establishing that white boys could rap with the best of America's black urban culture, the Beastie Boys transcended race, gender, and social economic divisions with their tough but exuberant call to party on. Modeled after a scene from 1963's sophisticated *Breakfast at Tiffany's*, band members crash a party of geeks and nerds, trashing their place and escaping with beer and a stash of gorgeous girls. A near-perfect mixture of humor, satire, and kick-ass lyrics, *Fight for Your Right (to Party)* enhanced record sales of the band's album *Licensed to Ill* and quickly became the classic party video of the 1980s and beyond.

both audacious and silly.[13] That many of their best licks are stolen, or "sampled" as the group would suggest, from other artists and musical genres is second to their shameless pandering to "moshpit anthems" and fan-induced shoutalongs. The now-iconic mantra "Fight for Your Right (To Party)" has elements that suggest a kind of insistent funkiness, while the trio's stage antics make them come off "simultaneously as super-dunces and world-class dance machines."[14]

Licensed to Ill's chart success led to an equally successful headlining tour in 1987. As band members courted controversy whenever they played, Def Jam intervened, turning the uproar over songs like "Cookie Puss" (which pays homage to phone pranks) into a call to action for parental advisory labels on any questionable albums. The Beastie Boys, the first rappers to produce a No. 1 album, looked more like Brat Pack Rockers turned wannabe hip-hoppers. By the time the smoke cleared and the Beastie Boys teamed up with the ultra-hip Dust Brothers for their second album, *Paul's Boutique*, released in 1989, the group's popularity was negligible, and the album was more or less passed over by fans and critics. The tragedy here, in the minds of some reviewers, is that *Paul's Boutique* was one of hip-hop's lost gems, "a widescreen sampladelic collage"[15] that might have changed the course of the Beastie Boys' future as well as the landscape of hip-hop. Instead, this rarely heard funky tour de force pushed the boys out of hip-hop favor.

A long break from recording followed *Boutique*'s release, and the band returned in 1992 with a new album titled *Check Your Head*. Despite some critical affirmation for their continued pursuit of cutting-edge funk/rap, the group never quite returned to the same visceral or commercial hipness that once defined their image. With their "sonic collages," the Beasties Boys made high art of cultural plagiarism where no sound or style—from the Beatles to Curtis Mayfield or Pink Floyd—was ever too absurd or obscure to remove or exclude it from their unique sampled style of musical creation.[16] Fiercely energetic in concert and arrogantly sophomoric in their public demeanor, the Beastie Boys gave new meaning to the kind of primal immaturity that spoke to a generation of white—and black—hip-hop fans.

PUBLIC ENEMY

Taking rap to more politically charged levels of urban awareness, Public Enemy became one of the decade's most successful, edgy, hip-hop groups. Courtesy of Photofest.

Following Run-D.M.C.'s and the Beastie Boys' successful mid-1980s rap-rock fusion, Public Enemy emerged late in the decade with a whole new brand of rap, rewriting the rules of hip-hop to become perhaps the most influential and controversial rap group of that era. To many fans, Public Enemy is the definitive rap group of their time or any other. Building on Run-D.M.C.'s street-smart rhythms and early gangsta rap style, Public Enemy initiated a kind of hardcore rap that was musically rebellious and politically revolutionary. Formed in New York City in 1982 when Chuck D (born Carlton Ridenhour, August 1, 1960), then a graphic design student (and side-DJ) at Adelphi University on Long Island, met Spectrum City's main DJ Hank Shocklee, who would become Public Enemy's co-producer. The two subsequently paired up for Bill Stephney's rap show on WBAU radio.

While Chuck D practiced what would become his hard-hitting lyrical style, Shocklee experimented in creating funky noise collages. Their imaginative collaborations peaked the interested of Flavor Flav (born William Drayton, March 16, 1959), one of the show's most enthusiastic listeners and notable DJ in his own right. Flavor Flav eventually joined the show as a co-host, setting the stage for what would become Public Enemy. Enter Rick Rubin, Def Jam impresario, who charged Chuck D and Shocklee with combining Run-D.M.C.'s scathing rap lyricism with the Clash's melodic radicalism. With Shocklee as chief producer and Stephney as publicist, Chuck D assembled a crew that consisted of DJ Terminator X (born Norman Rodgers, August 25, 1966) and Professor Griff (born Richard Griffin, no birth date available), the "Minister of Information" and choreographer for the backup dancers, a militaristic group called Security of the First World (S1W).[17]

Taking its name from an early demo tape, Public Enemy unleashed its first album on an unassuming public in 1987. Produced by Def Jam records, *Yo! Bum Rush the Show* elicited a powerful sound of spare beats and awesome lyrical rhetoric that was praised by rap critics and aficionados. The public, however, mostly ignored the album, as did the R&B mainstream. Undaunted, Public Enemy returned the following year with *It Takes a Nation of Millions to Hold Us Back*, "a chaotic mix that relied as much on found sounds and avant-garde noise as it did on old-school funk."[18] Unlike the *Yo!* album, *It Takes a Nation* could not be ignored. Hailed by both rap and rock critics as a hip-hop tour de force, *It Takes a Nation* also established hip-hop as an active agent for social change. Under Shocklee's direction and the Bomb Squad's (Public Enemy's production team) guidance, Chuck D's lyrics were forceful and focused, while Flavor Flav's raps were wildly energized and frequently funny.

As Public Enemy's popularity increased, so did the controversy that often surrounds a breakthrough artist. In a now-infamous statement, Chuck D asserted that hip-hop was "the black CNN" and suggested that the mainstream media could not understand or televise the real crisis in America's inner cities. Compounding the controversy was a well-intentioned but uncomfortably damning endorsement by black Muslim leader Louis Farrakhan for "Bring the Noise." Then Spike Lee selected "Fight the Power"—with its criticism of Elvis Presley and John Wayne—as the opening track for his own controversial inner-city cinematic polemic *Do the Right Thing* (1989). Suddenly, Public Enemy's celebrity had turned into the notorious center of a treatise on black/white relations. At the same time, an interview given by Professor Griff to the *Washington Post*, which contained his belief that Jews were responsible for "the majority of the wickedness that goes on across the globe,"[19] fanned the flames of outrage among America's white community, even those white critics who had previously applauded the group. Griff's loaded comments also created dissension among the group, as an angry Chuck D first fired him, then brought him back, then broke up the group entirely. A final interview in which Griff openly attacked Chuck D (and all Public Enemy band members) led to his final departure from the group.

Public Enemy spent the rest of 1989 working on their third album, *Fear of a Black Planet*, which was released in the spring of 1990 to mostly enthusiastic reviews and a niche in the pop Top 10. Top 40 R&B singles included "911 Is a Joke," "Brothers Gonna Work It Out," and "Can't Do Nuttin' for Ya Man." Considered one of the loudest and most potent voices in hip-hop, Chuck D reestablished himself as a rapper who meant business. He continued to cultivate that tough image with the group's next release, *Apocalypse 91 . . . The Enemy Strikes Back*. One of the most striking tracks on this fourth effort was the rerecording of 1989's "Bring the Noise," this time as part of a partnership with metal band Anthrax. To some, Public Enemy's first crossover venture appeared as an olive branch to the white community; to others, the gesture signaled an end to Public Enemy's signature attacks on society. *Apocalypse 91* debuted at No. 4 on the pop charts but lost ground soon after. Public Enemy joined U2 for the second half of its Zoo TV tour, and Flavor Flav found himself repeatedly in trouble with the law.

By the early 1990s, Public Enemy's vicious iron-hand fist was no longer in the face of rap audiences or the media. Revolutionary and confrontational, while at the same time focused and articulate, Public Enemy packed far more of a musical wallop than its oft-compared counterparts, the Sex Pistols. In revising and rewriting the rules of hip-hop as both art form and social activist, Public Enemy's musical influence extended far beyond the realm of rap and into the heart of American inner-city culture.

WOMEN RAPPERS

In the first thirty years of its history, rock 'n' roll—and the recording industry—had been accused of cultivating a male-dominated art form. By the late 1980s, hip-hop was threatening to follow suit, making the emergence—and success—of women in hip-hop even more eventful. Since most early hip-hop fans were male, they became hip-hop's biggest consumers and wanted to hear other males. Female rappers, like the rock 'n' roll sisters, still lagged behind in popular and record sales. Still, early artists like Little Lee, Sweet & Sour, and Lady B were determined to break through the gender barrier, refusing to be relegated to the *other* minority.

In 1985, the infamous "dis" (or response) to a popular rap song gave the first woman rapper some notoriety when a trio of male rappers called U.T.F.O. recorded a song called "Roxanne, Roxanne." The single told the story of a stuck-up girl who boldly resisted their charms and proved to be a chart success. Then, seemingly out of nowhere, a record featuring "a 14-year-old with a high voice and debilitating wit slammed U.T.F.O."[20] Her name was Roxanne

Shante, from Queensbridge, New York. Shante pretended to be the Roxanne U.T.F.O. was rapping about and, with a deliciously nasty response, blasted onto the rap scene, immediately claiming the title "Mistress of the Dis." Other female rappers responded to the song, which solicited an estimated 100 responses to "Roxanne, Roxanne," including Joan Martinez, the New York waitress about whom the song was allegedly written.[21]

Salt-N-Pepa

It was another response record that launched the career of rap's first all-female crew, Salt-N-Pepa. Cheryl "Salt" James (born March 8, 1964, in Brooklyn, New York) and Sandy "Pepa" Denton (born November 9, 1961, in Kingston, Jamaica) were employed at a Sears department store in Queens when co-worker (and Salt's boyfriend) Hurby "Luv Bug" Azor asked them to rap on a song he was producing for an audio production class at New York City's Center for Media Arts. The threesome wrote a dis to Doug E. Fresh and Slick Rick's hit "The Show," calling it "The Show Stopper." Credited to Super Nature, the single was released in summer 1985 and became a minor underground hit, hitting No. 46 on the R&B charts. Taking a line from "The Show Stopper," Super Nature changed its name to Salt-N-Pepa and, in 1986, signed a contract with the independent New Plateau label. Adding DJ Pamela Green, the trio released its debut album, *Hot, Cool & Vicious*, in 1987.

Hot, Cool & Vicious spawned three moderate hits: "My Mic Sounds Nice," "Tramp," and "Chick on the Side." "Tramp," an ingenious update of an Otis Redding–Carla Thomas duet, saw Salt and Pepa trading "sassy lines with sly humor."[22] Then Cameron Paul, a San Francisco DJ, remixed the b-side of "Tramp" and turned it into a local hit. Soon after, the hip-grindingly sexy "Push It" was released nationally and became a huge hit, pop charting at No. 19. A remixed version released the following year hit No. 2 in the United Kingdom, and "Push It" became one of the first rap records nominated for a Grammy.

Late in 1987, Salt-N-Pepa replaced DJ Green with rapper/DJ Spinderella (born Deidre "Dee Dee" Roper), and released their second album, *A Salt with a Deadly Pepa*, in July 1988. Featuring the Top 10 hit "Shake Your Thang" (recorded with go-go band E.U.), the album received only tepid reviews and did not achieve its anticipated commercial success. In 1989, a remix album of Salt-N-Pepa's hits, *A Blitz of Salt-N-Pepa Hits*, was released while the group recorded its third album, *Blacks' Magic*.

This third album effort, released in spring 1990, met with both strong reviews and sales. Most important, *Blacks' Magic* was embraced by the hip-hop community, some of whose more outspoken members had initially attacked the group for trying to cross over into the pop market. A single from the album titled "Expression" spent eight weeks at No. 1 on the rap charts before even entering the pop charts, where it crested at No. 26. A second single, "Let's Talk about Sex," became their biggest pop hit to date, peaking at No. 13. (The group later rerecorded "Let's Talk about Sex," as a safe-sex rap retitled "Let's Talk about AIDS.")

After the success of *Blacks' Magic* success, Salt-N-Pepa separated from producer/manager Azor, who had been taking most of the songwriting credit, although group members insisted they were responsible for most of the lyrics. Signing a new contract with London/Polygram, Salt-N-Pepa went on to win a Grammy for Best Rap Performance in 1995. Since then, group members have gone on to tackle individual artistic projects.[23] Even though their career spanned a decade, the success of Salt-N-Pepa set standards as crossover artists in pop music and as designers of the newly hip feminine rap style. They also paved the way for other female rap artists of the 1990s, including soul artists TLC, hip-hop soul artist Mary J. Blige, and Lauryn Hill.

Queen Latifah

Queen Latifah (born Dana Owens on March 18, 1970, in Newark, New Jersey) certainly was not the first female rap artist, but she was the first real rap star. Possessing more charisma that many of her predecessors and projecting a direct, no-nonsense persona, one could argue that her style of rap was undoubtedly feminist. In 1978, Owens was given the nickname by one of her cousins, a Muslim whose choice of "Latifah"—which means "delicate" or "sensitive" in Arabic—seemed appropriate for the eight-year-old. Latifah, who had

worked in school theater productions, including *The Wiz*, began rapping in high school with a group called Ladies Fresh. In college, she adopted the name Queen Latifah and joined Afrika Bambaataa's Native Tongues collective, which aspired to bring a more positive, Afrocentric awareness to hip-hop.[24]

In 1988, Latifah released her first single, "Wrath of My Madness," for Tommy Boy records and followed it with "Dance for Me." In 1989, her debut album *All Hail the Queen* received solid favorable reviews, while her single "Ladies First" introduced her to a hip-hop audience. The album, which featured Latifah's own brand of tough-minded feminist hiphop, also saw the artist experimenting in R&B and reggae, dueting with KrS-One and De La Soul. *All Hail the*

Queen Latifah led the women's scene in rap and hip-hop in the late 1980s. Courtesy of Photofest.

Queen climbed into the Top 10 on the R&B album charts, leading Latifah to start her own management company, Flavor Unit Entertainment. A less-than-stellar sophomore effort forced Tommy Boy records to drop Latifah from its stable of artists. Soon thereafter, she was the victim of a carjacking and mourned the death of her brother Lance in a motorcycle accident.

Queen Latifah reemerged in the early 1990s with a new recording contract at Motown Records, and her album *Black Reign* (1993) became the first rap album by a female MC to go gold. Her third—and most popular—release, *Black Reign* produced her biggest hit single, "U.N.I.T.Y," which charted on R&B's Top 10 and won her a Grammy for Best Solo Rap Performance. By this time, Latifah had already begun acting, a career move that would find success on both television and in film, with Latifah receiving an Oscar nomination in 2002 as Best Supporting Actress in *Chicago*.

RAP IN ROCK CULTURE

Sometimes viewed as the only other dominant music form besides rock 'n' roll in the post-1945 age, rap can also be included as part of rock's culture. More than a rival for recording industry business, rap's evolution to hip-hop in the early 1980s opened the door to viable, creative partnerships with established rockers, artistic crossovers, and the acquisition of a whole new audience whose demographics transcended race or gender. The impact of rap and hip-hop has yet to be calculated,[25] but its hip, urban sound and revolutionary—sometimes defiant—political message have pushed it beyond its African American roots and into the heart of America's social and emotional consciousness.

NOTES

1. Grandmaster Flash, Foreword to *The Vibe History of Hip Hop*, edited by Alan Light (New York: Three Rivers Press, 1999), vii.

2. Tom Terrell, "The Second Wave: 1980–1983," in Light, *Vibe History*, 44.

3. Ibid., 44–45.

4. See, for example, the following Web site: http://www.rapworld.com/history.

5. Ibid.

6. Josh Tyrangiel, "Hip-Hop Video," in Light, *Vibe History*, 141.

7. Ibid., 138.

8. Ibid.

9. Ibid.

10. Courtney Holt, "Run-D.M.C. Biography," included at http://launch.yahoo.com/artist/artistFocus.asp?artistID=1023227.

11. Stephen Thomas Erlewine, "Run-D.M.C. Bio," *All Music Guide*, included at http://www.mtv.com; search Run-D.M.C.

12. Martin C. Strong, *The Great Rock Discography*, 6th ed. (Edinburgh, UK: Canongate Books, 2002), 896–897.

13. Ibid., 70.

14. Tristan Lozaw, "Beastie Boys Biography," included at http://music.yahoo.com; search Beastie Boys.

15. Strong, *Great Rock Discography*, 70.

16. See, for example, Web site at note 14.

17. See Strong, *Great Rock Discography*, 838–839; also Web sites that include biographical information, for example, http://www.tiscali.co.uk/music/biography/public_enemy_biography.html.

18. Stephen Thomas Erlewine, "Public Enemy: Bio," *All Music Guide*, included at http://www.mtv.com; search Public Enemy.

19. Ibid.

20. Laura Jamison, "Ladies First," in Light, *Vibe History*, 179.

21. Ibid., 180.

22. Strong, *Great Rock Discography*, 904.

23. Stephen Thomas Erlewine, "Salt-N-Pepa: Bio," *All Music Guide*, included at http://www.mtv.com; search Salt-N-Pepa.

24. Steve Huey, "Queen Latifah: Bio," *All Music Guide*, included at http://www.mtv.com; search Queen Latifah.

25. Zechariah Decker, "The Political Influence of Rap/Hip-hop" (unpublished undergraduate paper, Oakton Community College, November 2004), Decker's undergraduate study begins to explore statistical analysis of the impact of Russell Simmons' hip-hop activism on voter turnout among hip-hop fans between the ages of eighteen and twenty-nine.

ROCK AND FILM IN THE 1980s

Music and film have always gone together. During the silent film era, grand theater pipe organs, played live as the audience watched the film, set the mood for movies. Film scores were often created spontaneously, as able organists sat at the majestic keyboards and responded musically to whatever was happening on-screen. Later, sound allowed a more natural integration of music with film, again using it to underscore themes, heighten drama, or tell the film's story. The subsequent popularity of musicals during the 1930s, 1940s, and 1950s offered yet another way for audiences to visualize songs and place them within the context of a narrative. In each of these examples, music was created specifically (or, in the case of some musicals, translated from stage versions) for the film. Early rock 'n' roll artists sometimes used the film medium to promote a hit song (e.g., *Jailhouse Rock* [1957]), but it was not until the late 1970s that filmmakers began to see the artistic (and marketing) value of using previously recorded music as movie sound tracks. This combination not only helped boost record sales but, in many cases, often increased box-office receipts as well.

Dennis Hopper's 1969 motorcycle odyssey *Easy Rider* marked the first time contemporary music was used to underscore and integrate themes in the screenplay with plot and characters. Crafting a seemingly random selection of previously recorded songs from a variety of artists, Hopper subtly designed an arrangement of music that would define and emphasize his notions about freedom and democracy.[1] For fans already in tune with the ideals of the counterculture and its questioning of America's foreign and domestic policies during a time of social and political upheaval, Hopper's antiestablishmentarian masterpiece suggested that the hip rebelliousness of rock might really be a kind of patriotic oxymoron that expresses the true meaning of independence.

Easy Rider also established the new film sound track: a sometimes quirky, often compelling mosaic of musical selections that gives directors another way to connect with audiences as they tell their cinematic stories. By the 1970s, directors like Martin Scorsese followed Hopper's lead, lifting songs from their youth and juxtaposing them against contemporary events. In 1973's *Mean Streets*, the audience is jolted shotgunlike into the world of petty thievery to the strains of the Ronettes singing their 1962 hit "Be My Baby." The song plays prominently in the background as the opening credits roll and small-time hood Charlie Cappa (Harvey Keitel) prepares for the day. Later in the film, Scorsese choreographs a pool hall fight to The Marvelettes' plaintive 1961 doo-wop hit "Please Mr. Postman."[2] Using sexy, upbeat songs performed by girl groups to create a backdrop to male gang violence is both unsettling and effective as it emphasizes the way pop music is an integral, if sometimes incongruous, part of our culture and behavior.

For Scorsese, using songs from his childhood was his way of layering the inconsistent, often idiosyncratic place popular songs held in the everyday lives of New Yorkers—and of people everywhere. This technique is one way of suggesting that pop culture, whether it is related to music, film, television, or sports, lives in the hearts of each of us. It is what drives us, inspires us, connects us to other people, other places, other ages, and suggests why we often associate important moments in our lives with specific songs, movies, or other popular events. Scorsese's childhood memories during the 1950s, of walking through New York City's working-class ethnic neighborhoods, observing the daily street fights while doo-wop songs blared from a nearby store, serves as one reason why, twenty years later, he underscored cinematic violence with seemingly incongruous bubblegum pop songs.

Scorsese's creative borrowing from Hopper's use of previously recorded music to emphasize his movies' themes brought him critical attention, but it was not until 1977's disco-driven *Saturday Night Fever* that a sound track consisting of previously recorded rock 'n' roll and popular music from a variety of artists signaled a change in how films are scored and experienced. The amazing popularity of the *Saturday Night Fever* sound track (selling over 28 million copies)[3] not only rejuvenated the Bee Gees' career and ignited John Travolta's but signified a new and lasting connection between popular music and film, one that would come into its own during the 1980s.

In this chapter, three general types of films where pop/rock sound tracks were often effectively used during the 1980s will be discussed: teen angst, yuppie reunions, and rock idol dreams. Several examples of each of the three film types are included, which explain why these films represent some of the most innovative, provocative and financially successful integrations of film and music.

TEEN ANGST

Movies focusing on the teen experience appeared as early as 1955's Cold War–influenced drama *Rebel without a Cause*. Yet in spite of its hip, young twenty-something cast, including James Dean, Natalie Wood, and Sal Mineo—and its box-office appeal to older teenagers—*Rebel* is still more adult themed in its exploration of family life and its future in a postmodern world.[4] By the 1960s, former Mouseketeer Annette Funicello and teen idol Frankie Avalon defined the carefree nature of late adolescence in a series of beach blanket movies where "boy meets girl" plots were as simplistic as "She loves you, yea, yea, yea," but actors still looked at least ten years older than their high school years. Early attempts to capture the teen experience while retaining broader box-office support from adults permeated cinema throughout the 1960s and into the 1970s with few exceptions. Even *Easy Rider*'s and *Woodstock*'s audiences were college age or older, with themes, issues (Vietnam, psychedelia, democracy), and an "R"-rating directed at those more socially and politically sophisticated.

In the 1980s, the concept of a teen movie changed. Far from earlier beach romps or the darker, existential *Rebel*, teen flicks made during the 1980s—even and often presented as lighthearted fare like *Fast Times at Ridgemont High* (1982)—began to examine more substantive issues directly related to teen life. Situations involving date rape, academic performance, social acceptance, drug use, and teenage suicide were captured using of-the-moment actors, music, and dialogue. And the movies were marketed specifically to high school–aged teens. What is important to remember in these and many of the films discussed in this chapter is that the music was as important as—if not *more* important than—the film itself. It is thus easy to see why audiences still associate some of the actors in these films with the music played during pivotal scenes and why hearing some of these sound tracks twenty years later still produces a lasting connection with the film—and our own personal lives.

Fast Times at Ridgemont High

The movie's title has not even appeared on the screen, but the audience has already gotten the beat. Kicking off the 1980s teen angst genre films is first-time director Amy Heckerling's funny and refreshingly honest 1982 feature *Fast Times at Ridgemont High*. To introduce her vision of Cameron Crowe's similarly titled book, Heckerling uses the Go-Go's infectiously snappy 1980 hit "We've Got the Beat." This enormously popular film that boasted a memorable performance by Sean Penn and debuted Nicolas Cage (billed as Nicolas Coppola), Anthony Edwards, Forest Whitaker, and Eric Stoltz, *Fast Times* showed how to learn, live, and know the influence of pop/rock music in teen films.

Music is heard almost nonstop throughout the film, creating a kind of headphone experience for both the characters and the audience. It is as if pop

Musical sound tracks emerged as powerful expressions of teen angst in the early 1980s. Sean Penn's iconic performance in *Fast Times at Ridgemont High*, helped define an age and a genera-tion. Courtesy of Photofest.

music is continuously playing in our heads, underscoring our daily experiences, articulating our thoughts and feelings. Just as the ubiquitous boom boxes became synonymous with 1980s teens, *Fast Times at Ridgemont High*[5] offered visual images to complement its music. The social and sexual awkwardness associated with adolescence escapes no one in the film. Even totally cool stoner dude Jeff Spicoli (Sean Penn), whose dreams of surfer fame are mostly confined to his own rock 'n' roll fantasy, and whose ongoing feud with American history teacher Mr. Hand (Ray Walston) serves as one of the film's comic centerpieces, is really just a confused kid masking a self-conscious fear of failure. While Penn's Spicoli, who became the film's immediate pop culture icon, serves as a kind of extreme metaphor for the recklessness of adolescence, it really is the supporting ensemble that exemplifies Heckerling's connection of music with teenage issues.[6]

Fast Times at Ridgemont High paved the way for a plethora of other popular teen angst dramedies, including 1983's *Risky Business*; 1984's *Footloose*; and John Hughes' quintet—1984's *Sixteen Candles*, 1985's *Weird Science* and *The Breakfast Club*, and 1986's frothy *Pretty in Pink* and the irreverent *Ferris Bueller's Day Off*. Collectively, they represent a new genre of teen film and the success-ful merger of a pop/rock sound track to improve an otherwise trite or corny plot. Individually, this collection of teen movies also helps to identify important social and musical trends identified with this decade.

Risky Business and Footloose

When Tom Cruise's character Joel Goodsen slid across the hardwood floor of his parents' North suburban Chicago center hall colonial, clad in Oxford shirt, socks, and underwear, and danced with unabashed Midwestern teenage abandon to Bob Seger and the Silver Bullet Band's "Old Time Rock 'n' Roll," he gave Seger's 1978 hit a renewed shot of popularity and himself newfound movie stardom. Director Paul Brickman uses Seger's primal rebel rock anthem as catalyst that signals Cruise's Joel Goodsen's rite of passage into manhood. And while Cruise's mock-rock masturbation dance solo lasts little more than a minute, he single-handedly expressed the secret rock idol dreams shared by many. It is a scene that has been replayed, reinterpreted, and reiterated in many subsequent films, sometimes offering a wry realism (in

Tom Cruise's impromptu dance to Bob Seger's "Old Time Rock and Roll" made him a star in 1983's *Risky Business*. The film opened new doors to explore the teenage experience. Courtesy of Photofest.

1988's *Working Girl*, Joan Cusack tells fellow secretary Melanie Griffith, "Ya know, just cuz sometimes I dance around the apartment in my underwear, don't make me Madonna"); other times parodying an actor's own self-image (Hugh Grant as Britain's prime minister dancing solo at Number 10 Downing Street while the Pointer Sisters blare in the background in 2004's *Love Actually*).

Risky Business does not offer wall-to-wall sound. Instead, pivotal scenes, like Cruise's dance, are punctuated with appropriate music, from Muddy Waters' "Mannish Boy" (1955) to The Police and "Every Breath You Take" (1983). When Joel sneaks out for a drive in his father's treasured Porsche, we hear Jeff Beck's "The Pump" from his 1980 *There and Back* album. Later, as Joel scrambles to keep the vehicle from rolling into a lake, it is the Talking Heads singing "Swamp" (1983).

Ultimately, Brickman's use of Tangerine Dream's "Love on a Real Train" (1983) creates the hauntingly romantic eroticism of Joel's ultimate sexual experience with teen hooker Lana (Rebecca De Mornay). In a scene that takes place long after midnight, Joel and Lana board one of Chicago's famous L-trains to the sounds of Phil Collins' "In the Air Tonight" (1981). As the other passengers disappear into the night, Collins' music fades into the techno-pop rhythms of Tangerine Dream. The syncopated instrumental pulsates perfectly to Joel and Lana's lovemaking, backlit suggestively and filmed in quasi-slow motion. Like *Fast Times*, *Risky Business* integrates music that underscores the plot, theme, and action, as it simultaneously plays in the heads of the characters as well as the audience.

Risky Business, with its suggestive poster depicting Cruise's Joel in sexy half-pulled-down sunglasses, was contrasted the following year with *Footloose* (1984), an appealing, if hackneyed, story about a small town that has outlawed dancing. If we can forgive Dean Pitchford's corny script, it is mostly because of Kevin Bacon's energetic performance, director Herbert Ross' fast-paced choreography, and a sound track that scored several Top 10 hits, including Kenny Loggins' title song. The film's easy charm comes from an inspired combination of new songs and previously recorded ones that fit its more traditionally inspired Broadway musical roots. Like *Risky Business*, *Footloose* boasts attractive actors (Sarah Jessica Parker and Lori Singer complement Bacon's character Ren) and accessible teen dilemmas (kids versus parents, individualism versus authority).

Unlike *Risky Business*, *Footloose* never really addresses the subtle edginess of Reagan-era teens. Bacon's Ren is all fire and raw emotion. Cruise's Joel is mostly confused earnestness, but it is masked by the darker, more Machiavellian aspirations of upper-middle-class white young Republicans who want to be part of the system while they use it to get ahead. In both films, the music artistically addresses each theme, with Loggins' unabashedly enthusiastic melodies contrasting Tangerine Dreams' veiled eroticism, Collins' faux romanticism, and Seger's in-your-face rock 'n' roll. *Risky Business*'s diverse sound track parallels the film's layered, sometimes darkly conflicted message about growing up and getting what you want. *Footloose*'s sound track—like the film—is all about the boy. No hidden messages. Still, the musical differences found in each sound track represent the growing fragmentation in pop/rock music that continued throughout the decade.

John Hughes Quintet

Hughes' teenage films have been characterized as usually uneven, often vulgar, but generally entertaining. The box-office success of his screwball teen quintet continues to be validated by fans who, two decades later, still connect these films with their high school years, the songs with movie as well as personal moments. Hughes' films also introduced many of the actors who would later be included in Hollywood's "Brat Pack":[7] Molly Ringwald, Andrew McCarthy, Judd Nelson, Ally Sheedy, Emilio Estevez, Robert Downey Jr., and Anthony Michael Hall.

Of the five films, only *Sixteen Candles* (1984), *The Breakfast Club* (1985), and *Pretty in Pink* (1986) merit discussion here. *Weird Science*'s (1985) sound track (written especially for the film), although filled with a mix of everyone from Oingo Boingo singing the title song to Los Lobos ("Don't Worry Baby" [1984]), Lords of the New Church ("Method to My Madness" [1984]), The Del Fuegos ("Nervous and Shakey" [1984]), and Mike Oldfield ("Tubular Bells"), never really took off in terms of sales or fan identification. Most audiences remember the stunning Kelly LeBrock more than the plot or the music. And *Ferris Bueller's Day Off*, which boasted perhaps the most unusual array of music in the quintet, never produced a sound track, mostly because Hughes did not think anyone would buy so eclectic a collection.

Sixteen Candles (1984) is a Cinderella story about an awkward teenager (Molly Ringwald) longing to find Mr. Right and crushed that no one seems to remember her upcoming landmark birthday. While the plot and performances are fairly pedestrian (save Ringwald's charming misfit and Anthony Michael Hall's engaging, aspiring hustler), the film did include a nifty new wave sound track, assembled and partly composed by Jimmy Iovine. Iovine and director Hughes also create a movie-music first: scoring scenes with themes from television shows, including *Dragnet*, *Peter Gunn*, and *The Twilight Zone*. Hughes used the same idea two years later in *Ferris Bueller's Day Off*, inserting themes from *I Dream of Jeannie* and *Star Wars*.

Perhaps Hughes' boldest experiment was *The Breakfast Club*, depicting teens in a Saturday detention room talking about themselves. Structured almost theatrically like a group therapy session without a therapist, *The Breakfast Club* allows the audience to eavesdrop on five teenagers serving Saturday detention at Shermer High School. Each student represents a different teenage archetype: the princess, the jock, the bohemian Goth head case, the brain, and the punk. By film's end, having completed an essay on who they think they are, the five teenagers have exposed their respective fears and discovered they are not so different after all.[8]

The film's final not-so-shocking revelation is not new, but its journey there is. In teen flicks, such revelations normally come at a major high school event, like the prom, a party, or some other event where "the moment can be presided over by an applauding group of onlookers. *The Breakfast Club* keeps everything under a tight lid, taking these five kids and letting the outside world recede until all that matters is each other."[9] When the kids leave school after completing their detention, claiming to take their newfound discovery to the outside world, we do not know if they will. But it does not matter.

What does matter is that—for one day—they have connected with someone outside their own narrow world. In this way, *The Breakfast Club* is distinctive from any other teen film before or since, and the raw intimacy experienced by the kids is extended to the audience. It should be no surprise that the film's sound track, a not-so-standard collection of eighties tunes, ranging from Wang Chung's "Fire in the Twilight" (1984) to Karla DeVito's "We Are Not Alone" (1984) still resonates among fans and gave Simple Minds its greatest hit in 1984's "Don't You (Forget about Me)," written for the film. *The Breakfast Club*'s sound track might not be the most innovative, popular, or hit producing, but it struck a personally responsive chord with anyone who went to high school before 1990. Perhaps that is why it is still considered the "most meaningful" of Hughes's quintet.

The perennial girls' favorite from the Brat Pack era is clearly *Pretty in Pink* (1986), another updated Cinderella story with Molly Ringwald as Andie, a poor girl who makes excellent grades and her own clothes. Pursued by no less than three suitors, Andie's dilemma turns the film into more of a "treatise on economic strata than a romance."[10] Still, the dialogue, plot (including Andie's caretaker role with her alcoholic father), and emotions are real, the sound track an outstanding, almost edgy assortment of not-so-famous artists: Jesse Johnson ("Get to Know Ya" [1986]), Orchestral Manoeuvres in the Dark ("If You Leave" [1986]), New Order ("Shell Shock"), and a pre-"Luka" Suzanne Vega singing with Joe Jackson ("Left of Center" [1986]). Like *The Breakfast Club*, *Pretty in Pink*'s sound track works because it allows the audience to feel the emotions of the characters and to revisit them again and again long after the credits role.

The success of Hughes' quintet garnered him much acclaim as the writer-producer-director who best understood teenage angst, although, arguably, Amy Heckerling and Cameron Crowe have made equally significant contributions to this genre. One way that Hughes' impact can be gauged is by examining how subsequent teen movies have borrowed from or embellished on some of his themes and techniques. The year 1987's follow-up gender reversal to *Pretty in Pink* was the even more poignant, critically acclaimed, though less commercially successful *Some Kind of Wonderful*.[11] Hughes reunited as producer to Howard Deutch's director (they formed this same tandem for *Pretty in Pink*), to revisit a class conflict–driven love triangle, this one showcasing Mary Stuart Masterson as an adorable tomboy drummer who pines for Eric Stoltz, a poor, shyly sensitive painter who is Masterson's best friend but longs to be noticed by rich, pretty redhead Lea Thompson. Though understated in both performance and sound track—the music is definitely directed at teens whose taste is outside the mainstream (i.e., The Jesus and Mary Chain, Blue Room, Lick the Tins, and March Violets)—*Some Kind of Wonderful* still delivers a sweetly heartfelt exploration of how class differences affect the social development of teenagers, retaining the Hughes/Deutch trademark where a talented cast and interestingly idiosyncratic music often overshadowed a weak plot or, more frequently, offensive scenarios.

Bill & Ted's Excellent Adventure and Say Anything

Two very different films in tone, message, and music start to bring the decade to a close. Stephen Herek's outrageously witty comedy *Bill & Ted's Excellent Adventure* (1989) does for air guitars what *Fast Times at Ridgemont High* did for malls and surfer dudes. Keanu Reeves's (Ted) and Alex Winter's (Bill) characters could not have existed without their air guitar fantasies. The penultimate film about teen apathy in the 1980s (save, perhaps, 1986's chilling *River's Edge*),[12] *Bill & Ted's Excellent Adventure* follows two modern-day southern California misfits who learn that a future society will base all of its culture on the music of Bill and Ted's band, Wyld Stallyns. But that might never happen if the two slackers do not get their history report done.

Using mostly heavy metal to underscore the plot, and titles that speak to adolescent notions about sex (i.e., Extreme's "Play with Me," Robbie Rob's "In Time," and Power Tool's "Two Heads Are Better Than One," all written for the film in 1989, are a few examples), director Herek weaves a winning tale about time travel, dreams of rock stardom, and how the importance of music drives it all. Not since Sean Penn made words like "dude" and "gnarly" part of teenage—and American—vocabulary have burnouts had such an impressive grasp uttering polysyllabic adjectives like "triumphant," "awesome," and of course, "excellent."

That the film again addresses the sometimes silly but very real rock star fantasies shared by many teenagers (and held onto by adults) suggests yet again the enduring power of music in our lives and in our everyday experiences. And Bill and Ted's memorable phrase "Be excellent to each other"[13] becomes the 1980s equivalent of the counterculture's one-word salutation "Peace" or Spock's blessing "Live Long and Prosper." Ultimately, *Bill & Ted's Excellent Adventure* becomes a suitable companion to *Fast Times at Ridgemont High* (and forerunner to *Wayne's World* [1993]) for its benign ignorance, its world of living-with-your-headphones-on, its slyly savvy examination of what it really important in our culture.

At the opposite end of *Bill & Ted's* excessiveness is Cameron Crowe's understated and touching drama *Say Anything* (1989), starring John Cusack (Lloyd) and Ione Skye (Diane) in another tale of students separated by social and intellectual status. This time it is Cusack's average student longing for Skye's straight-A scholar. A great

Hollywood took on the sweet side of smartness in *Say Anything* starring John Cusack, an adolescent love story punctuated by rock songs of the moment. Courtesy of Photofest.

sound track, including Nancy Wilson's "All for Love" (1989, written for film), Cheap Trick's "You Want It" (1989, written for film), and The Red Hot Chili Peppers' "Taste the Pain" (1990), what makes this film worth watching is Lloyd's inspired boom box serenade to Diane. Using Peter Gabriel's haunting "In Your Eyes" to speak for him, Cusack's Lloyd puts a postmodern spin on every variation of unrequited love since Romeo and Juliet's balcony scene. No self-proclaimed troubador or rock star hopeful, Lloyd stands alone beneath Diane's window waiting for the music to bring her to him. It is a powerful, poignant moment that speaks not only to teen angst but to the hopeful romantic in all of us.

Hailed as a post–John Hughes innovator of teen films, Crowe scores here using music to speak for him through his characters. For every teenage boy who is ever longed to serenade a girl, and for every teenage girl who is hoped to be serenaded, Crowe shows us that anyone—even nonmusicians—can use music to express love and create romance. For that reason (and the touching performances by Cusack and Skye), *Say Anything* hauntingly echoes the tender aching of adolescent love.

Heathers and Pump Up the Volume

A sharp, if uneven, look at the high school social strata that pushed *Some Kind of Wonderful's* class-based themes even farther,[14] *Heathers* (1989) is named for the three catty character friends who share the name. The film's deeply troubled heroine, Veronica (Wynona Ryder), who tries to understand and unravel the social snobbishness of her peers as she copes with the unhappy realities of her own life, is, in many ways, a twisted postmodern version of her comic book alter ego.[15] Like Archie's duplicitous girlfriend, Veronica uses her intelligence in dark, manipulative ways (i.e., at one point, she feigns her own suicide to irk her parents). *Heathers* deviates from other teen movies in its use of black humor and satire, suggesting that as the decade drew to a close, teen movies and audiences wanted something alternative: edgier and less optimistic about the future.

Ultimately, *Heathers* is the antithesis of 1980s teen movies, especially with its lack of pop music on the sound track. Using only three songs throughout the film, director Michael

Adolescence looked darker and its music was heavier by the end of the decade, characterized beautifully in the film *Heathers*. Courtesy of Photofest.

Lehmann creates a kind of counter-teen flick. He bookends the film with different versions of the Doris Day corny, sentimental, prefeminist hit "Que Sera Sera" (first, a bluesy recording by Syd Straw, then a funky rendition by Sly and the Family Stone) to suggest effectively the movie's perverse notion about teen suicide, social acceptance, and class conflict. The other two songs, Big Fun's "Teenage Suicide Don't Do It" and Stewart Levin's ballad "You're the Only One for Me," serve as satirical commentaries on teenage immaturity, rebelliousness, and emotional dysfunction. In today's post-Columbine era, *Heathers* is even more chilling.

Heathers' antiheroic leading man Christian Slater is terrific again as another high school misfit who runs a pirate radio station at night in *Pump Up the Volume*, made one year later in 1990. As late-night teen shock-jock Happy Harry Hard-on (a sarcastic variation on the initials of the movie's fictitious Hubert H. Humphrey High School), Harry suggestively encourages his nocturnal teenage audience to "talk hard." Personifying a kind of Superman split personality (Harry's real name is Mark, a quietly intelligent, bespectacled bookworm/aspiring writer at school, a teasingly taunting DJ at night), Harry nightly engages in self-help conversation with classmates who do not know his real identity, except for the lovestruck Nora (Samantha Mathis), who matches Harry's hard talk syllable for syllable and figures out who he really is.

Harry's anthem, played over and over throughout the film with mockingly authoritative tones, is Concrete Blonde's 1990 version of Leonard Cohen's "Everybody Knows" (1988). And everyone listening knows that "sometimes being young is worse than being dead."[16] Tragically, Harry's chillingly tough mantra becomes reality when one of his listeners acts on this adolescent mantra and kills himself. That suicide sets up a chain of events that ultimately forces Harry to reveal his identity but not to give up his sense of independent antiestablishmentarianism that is part of the film's theme. As the movie fades to black and the credits roll, Harry and Nora are led handcuffed to a police van, his high school classmates cheering him on as if he were a rock 'n' roll hero.

Like Captain America and Billy in *Easy Rider* two decades earlier, Happy Harry Hard-on reminds us that rock 'n' roll is all about rebellion,[17] that the purpose of adolescence is to survive it. Director Allan Moyle pumps up this theme using a combination of rap, punk, and rock artists, from Liquid Jesus to Soundgarden, from Sonic Youth to the Cowboy Junkies, from the Pixies to Above the Law. If nothing else, the movie—and its sound track—talked hardest about teenage angst than any other teen film from this decade.

What teen movies in the 1980s did for rock 'n' roll—and vice versa—was to emphasize visual interpretations of music. Integrally tied to MTV (many MTV videos were—and continue to be—montages of the films in which they appeared), rock 'n' roll dominated teen movies, illuminating teen versions of themes from a decade earlier: alienation, social or academic acceptance, fear of failure, and disillusionment. In each of these movies—and countless others not mentioned here—music serves a variety of functions: highlighting themes, expressing emotions, serving as narrator. Like the boom boxes that define this decade, the music seemed to emanate from the souls of the characters themselves and straight to the hearts and minds of the audience. From Huey Lewis and the News' "The Power of Love" (*Back to the Future*, 1985) and Simple Minds' "Don't you Forget About Me" (*The Breakfast Club*, 1984) to songs written specifically for various films, rocks' artists found a new venue upon which to market their waves through movies.

YUPPIE REUNIONS

As much as teen movies targeted a younger, contemporary audience that wanted to hear its favorite music surrounding popular cinematic idols, movies about baby boomers coming of age in the 1980s similarly integrated rock 'n' roll from an earlier time to underscore themes of lost idealism, failed relationships, and redefining family.[18] In a decade where status was judged almost exclusively in terms of box-office receipts, producers needed to develop viable, commercial vehicles to capture both twelve- to twenty-four-year-olds, who purchased two-thirds of movie tickets,[19] and the over-twenty-four-year-olds swept up in the ruthless competitiveness fostered by Reaganomics.[20]

In *The Films of the Eighties: A Social History*, William J. Palmer explains how yuppies envisioned themselves in terms of American values and how those ideas were expressed on film:

> Yuppies saw themselves as a uniformed cavalry circling the wagons around what was left of the American dream, that dream's material icons: the job with a chance for advancement, the house (in its new condo form), the car; the status goods, perhaps even a controlled and economically justified family. The films of the eighties were acutely aware not only of the stereotypes and accoutrements of the yuppie lifestyle but also of the insecurity of the dying American dream.[21]

In many yuppie-centered films, including *Diner*, *The Big Chill*, *Dirty Dancing*, *Back to the Future*, *Bull Durham*, *Hannah and Her Sisters*, *Wall Street*, *Crimes and Misdemeanors*, and *Field of Dreams*, nostalgic music is the link for both characters and audience as they revisit fond memories, old resentments, and new problems.

Diner

"Who's the better singer to play when making out, Johnny Mathis or Frank Sinatra?"[22] This now-enduring question, part of an amusing argument about records, is debated by a group of college friends reunited during Christmas week 1959 in *Diner* (1982). The first of director Barry Levinson's quartet of

Diner's retro look at teenagers in the 1950s set musical and cinematic standards for teen flicks of the decade. Courtesy of Photofest.

movies about Baltimore, *Diner* followed the nostalgia found in John Sayles' critically acclaimed independent film from 1980, *Return of the Secaucus 7*, relying on an ensemble reunion as the springboard to examine deeper issues about yuppie lifestyles and culture. Sayles' breakthrough film about counterculture survivors, made for a reported $60,000 in 1980,[23] eschewed a cool commercial sound track in favor of a single ukulele and barroom trio (probably because securing rights to such music would have been cost prohibitive, given the film's limited budget). Nonetheless, its post-Vietnam examination of the counterculture coming of age became a cinematic lightning rod for other movies of its kind.

Diner picks up where *Secaucus* leaves off, using what critic David Abrams called "overlapping conversation[s] full of cocky male bravado"[24] to assess issues involving alcoholism, unsatisfying marriages, and destructive behavior. The film might take place in the precounterculture 1950s, but its plot, characters, and issues reveal a strong thematic link to the contemporary concerns of its target yuppie audience. The sound track, a Who's Who of late '50s rock 'n' rollers (Jerry Lee Lewis, Dion and the Belmonts, Carl Perkins, The Fleetwoods, Bobby Darin, Fats Domino, and Elvis Presley), provides the ambiance as songs play almost endlessly from the diner's tabletop juke boxes as Eddie (Steve Guttenberg), Boogie (Mickey Rourke), Shrevie (Daniel Stern), Fenwick (Kevin Bacon), and Modell (Paul Reisen) muse about life's essential questions.

Nostalgia is the key component here as Levinson uses its music to connect pre- and postcounterculture generations to the ongoing social issues of the decade.

That disillusioned marriages, the fragility of relationships, and proclivities toward unhealthy behavior surfaced after the 1960s is erased here, as notions about personal choices and life's challenges transcend age, gender, geography, and music. Levinson's use of 1950s music to identify and interpret ongoing social themes almost three decades later is a technique Robert Zemeckis would later borrow in *Back to the Future* (1985), as perennial teen actor Michael J. Fox plays a 1980s adolescent who must travel back to the 1950s to ensure his parents meet. Replete with kitschy throwbacks to another era, including Fox "introducing" Chuck Berry's duck walk at a high school prom, it is another example of effectively using nostalgia to express ongoing social and culture themes and linking generations together. The film's sound track, too, consists mostly of 1950s music, including "Earth Angel" and "Johnny B. Goode," while the only nod to the 1980s is Huey Lewis and the News' hit single "The Power of Love" (1985).[25]

Back to the Future is not nearly as thoughtful as *Diner* in its re-creation of a bygone era. It is all flash and show, mostly special effects designed to hold the interest of a younger audience. The film also appeals to their yuppie parents with themes about lost idealism and misplaced dreams. *Diner* is, as Abrams wrote, "like watching a filmed memory,"[26] a reverie with psychological layers that connect songs with philosophy, characters with real-life dilemmas. It also becomes the transitional yuppie reunion film, taking audiences from the austere art house feel of *Secaucus* to the bigger, grander, more commercial *The Big Chill* in less than three years.

The Big Chill and Other Reunion Films

Bookended by the Hoyt Axton–penned "Joy to the World," performed as the movie opens by director Lawrence Kasdan's toddler son Jon and Kevin Kline and as the credits roll by the song's original recording artists Three Dog Night,[27] *The Big Chill* catches up with a group of college friends fifteen years after graduation. Unexpectedly reunited to mourn the suicide of their friend Alex (an uncredited role by the unseen Kevin Costner), the friends reflect on their postcollege lives: dreams unrealized, roads not taken, and the disappointing frostiness of working in the real world.

Using rock 'n' roll from the late 1960s and early 1970s to recall their college days, director Kasdan uses music in three powerfully effective ways: to underscore the movie's contrasting themes of alienation and hopefulness, to express characters' emotions during several of the film's montages, and perhaps most important, to serve as narrative, replacing dialogue in sequences so as to speak for the characters.

News of Alex's death is never articulated with words. In the film's opening sequences, played out to Marvin Gaye's "I Heard It Through the Grapevine," the audience watches as the seven friends gather at Alex's funeral. No dialogue is necessary: The faces of each character express a range of emotions, from shock and confusion to resignation and despair, Gaye's funky Motown sound an almost mocking resignation of disbelief (irreverently complemented at the end of the service when Karen [JoBeth Williams] stoically plays the Stones' "You Can't Always Get What You Want" on the pipe organ).

Boasting an all-star yuppie cast including Glenn Close, Kevin Kline, William Hurt, Tom Berenger, Mary Kay Place, Jeff Goldblum and the never-seen Kevin Costner as the suicidal Alex, *The Big Chill* epitomized the cold, harsh reality facing early baby boomers who had spent most of their college years swept up in a passionate, counterculture haze. "I'd hate to think it was all just fashion," muses Close's character Sarah when the friends share some of the disillusionment they have faced since graduation.

The impromptu weekend that emerges post-mortem typifies the existential angst and youthful humanistic optimism that dominated a generation of Americans during the late 1960s. The spontaneity of the weekend gathering almost seems predestined by Alex's choice to end his life and forces his surviving friends to reassess their lives, their values and their choices as well. Throughout the many and varied conversations that take place, rock 'n' roll is clearly the link that connects these friends to another time, another place, and a yearning for the revolutionary ideas that shaped them. Place's Meg, a former public defender turned real estate lawyer, explains her career shift, "I didn't think they [the pimps, drug dealers and rapists she had defended] would be so *guilty*." Now representing a different group of clients whose "offices were very clean" and who were "only raping the land," Meg reflects on her own uneasiness at selling out for white collar legal respectability. During her confession, director Kasdan astutely eases Proctol Harem's "Whiter Shade of Pale" in as background.

By the end of the weekend, each character has unburdened him/herself from unresolved emotions and pent-up frustration, appropriately underscored by the Band's bluesy "The Weight." Re-nourished by their friendship and fortified to face the real world yet again, Alex's mourners promise to keep in touch, to never break the bond once forged by shared idealism and rock 'n' roll. As the credits roll, Three Dog Night's "Joy to the World," is reprised (it was originally sung at the beginning of the film by Kevin Kline as he gave a bath to his son), this time as a paean to an earlier time and an invitation to post-boomers to share in the joy and revelation of the music.

From the Pointer Sisters doing the "Neutron Dance" (1984) and Patti La-Belle establishing a "New Attitude" (1984) for transplanted Detroit police detective Axel Foley (Eddie Murphy) in 1984's action comedy *Beverly Hills Cop* to composer David Foster's pop/jazz instrumentals in *St. Elmo's Fire* (1985), yuppie reunion films provided the same aural trigger for their audiences as teen angst movies did for adolescents. Here, the blend of old and new music from pre-, early, and contemporary rock 'n' roll artists allowed yuppie audiences to face their fears of disillusionment and failure by returning them to the musical origins of their idealism, then returning them to a new rock 'n' roll reality. Too, both the ability and creativity of the directors to select music that not only enhanced but expressed the stories they were telling more fully are critical to the artistic and commercial success of these films. It would be just as easy to cite the many movie sound tracks that were a commercial flop (e.g., 1983's *Staying Alive*) or that produced one hit song (e.g., 1984's *Against All Odds*, which promoted Phil Collins's penned title song "Take a Look at Me Now"). Instead, like their teen angst counterparts, successful yuppie reunion films combined relevant social themes with musical links that reached the hearts and minds of the audience, producing, in many cases, both artistically complex and provocative movies that enjoyed varying degrees of box-office and *Billboard* success.

ROCK IDOL DREAMS

One thing that teen angst and yuppie reunion audiences had in common was an enduring fantasy to be a rock 'n' roll star. Whether that desire came from adolescent rebellion or middle-age frustration did not matter. Harold and Nick (*The Big Chill*) were as comfortable playing air guitar as Bill and Ted on their excellent adventure. The 1980s brought to the screen countless stories of men and women aching for fame. However, unlike other films that wove creative sound tracks with an interesting narrative, films about rock stardom and fame were often more about the sound track than the script, often starring rock stars promoting their own music.

The year 1984 was a banner year for movies about rock stars. From the hilarious mockumentary *This Is Spinal Tap*, perhaps most successful for the cult following it generated, to Prince's self-proclaimed *un*-autobiographical *Purple Rain*, to Rick Springfield's attempt to move from small-screen soap-throb (*General Hospital*) to romantic leading man in *Hard to Hold*, rock 'n' roll stardom was in everyone's face on the silver screen.

Spinal Tap is a parody of rock documentaries, following a faux British metal group of the same name on tour. Co-writers-composers Christopher Guest, Michael McKean, and Harry Shearer (director Rob Reiner also collaborated on the script) use clever performances and silly send-ups of rock songs to make the film's point about the absurd excessiveness that often defines rock stardom. Songs include the sexily redundant "(Tonight I'm Gonna) Rock You Tonight" as well as the more primal sounds of "Gimme Some Money," "Hell Hole," "Cups and Cakes," and "Rock and Roll Creation."

While *Spinal Tap* does not ever re-create rock 'n' roll, it certainly turns any idyllic notions about rock stardom on its ear, or as one character aptly suggests, "In the topsy-turvy world of heavy rock, having a solid piece of wood in your hand is often useful." *Spinal Tap* scores in its ability to poke fun at the way society has beatified rock stars, in this case, a group of crude, uneducated losers,

The quintessential "mockumentary," *This Is Spinal Tap* explored rock's excessive backstage indulgence. Courtesy of Photofest.

and craved their destructive lifestyles. In contrast, *Purple Rain* and *Hard to Hold* take themselves so seriously that, in the end, only the music and concert performances survive.

Prince has always claimed his film debut, "about a young Minneapolis black struggling to gain acceptance for his own brand of futuristic (and sexy) rock music,"[28] *was not* autobiographical, but it does not matter. His dynamic concert scenes and phenomenal original score, including the film's dance-infused opener "Let's Go Crazy," the lyrical "Take Me With U," and the hauntingly memorable "When Doves Cry," as well as the title song, make the sound track worth the investment. Unfortunately, when he is offstage, Prince's character remains a thoroughly unlikable punk who, among his many annoying habits and flaws, uses his own celebrity-thwarted frustrations as justification for physically abusing his girlfriend. It is unclear if Prince saw *Purple Rain* as a vehicle for telling his own story, but clearly the sound track stands as solid evidence in favor of his recent induction into the Rock and Roll Hall of Fame and Museum.

Rick Springfield already had his acting chops whetted before his stint as heartthrob Dr. Noah Drake on the ABC soap hit begun in the spring of 1981, *General Hospital*. He had done a variety of television guest spots, including a supporting role on the space fantasy *Battlestar Galactica*. But Springfield's post-"Jessie's Girl" (1981) leap to romantic film stardom in 1983, unfortunately, was a misstep. Like *Purple Rain*, the best scenes in *Hard to Hold* are the concert performances. The best-selling sound track, which produced the hit "Love Somebody," as well as touching ballads like "Don't Walk Away" and "The Great Lost Art of Conversation" or the dance-hopped "Bop 'Til You Drop" and "Stand Up," also included compositions by Peter Gabriel, Graham Parker, and Nona Hendryx.

Still, this tiresome romance about a self-indulged rock star who falls in love with a classical music fan psychologist falls short as both star vehicle and love story. For Springfield, a film flop like *Hard to Hold* had serious repercussions for his rock career, even if the musical quality of the sound track far surpassed the plot and performances. Some critics snidely drubbed the film "Hard to Watch."[29] Today, locating a copy of the movie and its sound track might best be described as "hard to find."

A final film from 1984 worth noting here is Milos Forman's exquisitely over-the-top rock-inspired pseudobiography *Amadeus*. While some critics objected to the liberal interpretation of factual data about Mozart's life and Forman's hedonistic depiction of the young composer, the film's frenzied urgency is underscored by Tom Hulce's portrayal of Mozart as a narcissistic rebel boar to rival composer Salieri (F. Murray Abraham in an Oscar-winning performance), the less talented, establishmentarian "patron saint of mediocrity." The film explores the fine line between genius/madness, the seductive and sycophantic nature of celebrity, and how the quest for fame and monetary riches can destroy us all. Each of these themes is cynically—and appropriately—reviewed by Salieri, whose own dreams of fame were limited by his talent.

 ROCK ME, AMADEUS—FALCO (1986)

Falco's campy blend of classical music and synth pop topped both the American and British charts in the wake of *Amadeus*' cinematic success. Though the film tells the twisted tale of prerock composer/genius Wolfgang Amadeus Mozart, director Milos Forman depicts Mozart as a precursor to the rock 'n' roll era, his lifestyle and behavior as excessive and drug-induced as Elvis Presley or Jim Morrison. The resulting faux rap dance confection caught the ear of rock fans everywhere and gave Falco his only hit. The video is an excellent example of the growing connection between pop/rock music and movies during the 1980s, here taking the subject of a popular film and turning it into a pop culture video phenomenon.

Amadeus is both a yuppie fable about fear of failure and disillusionment and a treatise on rock stardom. When Mozart cannot decide which of three powdered wigs to wear to an upcoming gala, he bursts out in self-deprecating mockery, "Oh, I wish I had three heads so I could wear them all." Part fop, part genius, part social misfit, Mozart becomes the prototype for today's rock 'n' roll stars. His excessive drinking and partying, his inability to handle money, his carefree, if crude flirtations—all fit with notions about the lifestyles of rock stars.

To complete the success of *Amadeus* as a pre–rock 'n' roll tale is the film's sound track. A two-disc collection of Mozart's finest music conducted by Neville Mariner and the St. Martin of the Fields orchestra, the sound track scored on *Billboard*'s charts, spawned a second volume, and showed that a classical composer with a rock idol persona could still connect with a contemporary audience.

The 1980s boasted other stories about rock stardom. The cult classic *Eddie and the Cruisers* (1983) maintained the perfect rock idol premise: the disappearance of a popular rock singer just before the release of a most critically acclaimed album. With nods to Elvis, Buddy Holly, and Jim Morrison, the quest to find out what happened to the Cruisers—and possibly resurrect rock legend Eddie Wilson—drives an otherwise unimaginative script. A vibrant performance by Michael Paré as the elusive, dissatisfied poet-rocker Eddie and a memorable sound track by John Cafferty gave the film a large enough fan base to produce a sequel, *Eddie and the Cruisers II: Eddie Lives* (1989), which failed at the box office and at music stores.

Women Rock: *Fame, Flashdance*, and *Dirty Dancing*

The notion that women in rock 'n' roll have been—and, to some extent, still are—second-class citizens is represented in a variety of ways on film during the 1980s. *Fame*, which kicks off the decade in 1980, is not only about women aspiring for a career in music, dance, or theater. It is more of an ensemble piece about a group of high school students at New York's High School for the Performing Arts who dream about breaking down social and economic barriers as a way of realizing their goals. In a film where most of the stories were forgettable (and many loose ends left on the cutting-room floor), *Fame* is still most identified with Irene Cara's passionate vocals on the title song. Whatever other insights the film may have intended to offer, gender-based and otherwise, the film is more of a segue into subsequent energy-charged, dance-fused sound tracks that usually focused on a sexy woman as part of the marketing package.

Flashdance (1983) is such an example. The film's unlikely setting (in a Pittsburgh industrial district), and unassuming star (the waifish Jennifer Beals), is yet another Cinderella story for the post–high school crowd. Welder by day, sexy dancer at night, courted by her boss (Michael Nouri as Nick), and mentored by an aging ballerina, Alex (Beals) longs to join a real dance company. Driven by a sound track that is composed mostly of women artists—Irene Cara singing

 TAKE MY BREATH AWAY—BERLIN (1986)

One of the 1980s most influential and important film composers was Giorgio Moroder (born 1940 in Italy), whose new wave techno-pop style influenced bands like Blondie and created sexy, almost ethereal backdrops to films like *American Gigolo*. In 1987, Moroder won "Best Original Song" for "Take My Breath Away," the love song included in 1986's box-office blockbuster *Top Gun*. The song's video, like many other film singles released since the 1980s, is really a commercial for the movie. Using film clips against Berlin's romantic ballad, the video has less to do with the song's theme and more to do with selling tickets. It did, however, set a standard for the marketing of film music, in this case, as substitute trailer for the movie and as promotional tool for both the movie and its accompanying CD.

Something happens when she hears the music…
It's her freedom. It's her fire. It's her life.

Flashdance

What a feeling.

Take your passion and make it happen!

Flashdance tried to capitalize on the dance craze and soundtrack popularity of 1977's classic *Saturday Night Fever*. Courtesy of Photofest.

the title song, "Imagination" (Laura Branigan), "Romeo" (Donna Summer), "Manhunt" (Karen Kamon), and "I'll Be Here Where the Heart Is" (Kim Carnes), *Flashdance* is a good example of capitalizing on the MTV market early. It turns a rock video (i.e., Beals's sexy dance audition to Michael Sembello's "Maniac") into a feature-length film. Giorgio Moroder's energy-charged sound track is a plus here (Moroder also scored other '80s hit sound tracks like *American Gigolo* [1980] and *Top Gun* [1986]) in an otherwise undistinguished story that probably would not generate the same audience interest today, given a market already saturated with MTV variations and confections. Yet, for its time, and in spite of its superficial attempt to give an edgier feminist theme to a rock-based story, *Flashdance* works.

Less a rock idol fable and more the story of a teen rite of passage using dance as her liberation is 1987's hit *Dirty Dancing*. A combination of nostalgia (the film takes place in the pre-Kennedy assassination '60s) and the rebelliousness of youth (portrayed in both Jennifer Grey's adult-in-waiting Baby and Patrick Swayze's irreverent dance instructor Johnny), *Dirty Dancing*, like *Flashdance*, proved to be a winner at the box office and on the charts.[30] An important distinction here is that, with its story set in the early 1960s, the film uses a unique blend of mostly '60s R&B and Motown that has an '80s sound: The Ronettes' "Be My Baby," Frank Valli and the Four Seasons' "Big Girls Don't Cry," Otis Redding's "Love Man" and "These Arms of Mine," and The Shirelles' Carole King cover "Will You Still Love Me Tomorrow" are complemented by similar-sounding new songs by Eric Carmen's "Hungry Eyes" and the hit single "Time of My Life" sung by Bill Medley and Jennifer Warnes. The result is a surprisingly effective musical link between the two decades, one that gives the film's otherwise tired and predictable story a renewed energy.

In both *Flashdance* and *Dirty Dancing*, the female leads are dependent on men. Both Alex and Baby understand their personal desires and professional potential only after discovering love. Any notions about feminist insights here, despite any marketing strategies to the contrary, are lost in what are really two old-fashioned fairy tales about women finding themselves through men. The fact that both films opened up career doors for male leads Michael Nouri and Patrick Swayze, while Jennifer Beals's and Jennifer Grey's turns on the dance floor can be likened to "one-hit wonders" is not really surprising, given that it was the music video–styled scenes and complementary sound tracks that were really responsible for the films' respective successes. Representations of women in films about rock idol stardom paralleled music videos in the early to mid-1980s where women were often marketed more for their image than their music.

A previously overlooked component of moviemaking, save for critics and scholars who took notice of innovative and effective scoring, movie sound tracks enjoyed a commercial renaissance during the 1980s and, in doing so, intrinsically changed the way movies are made and viewed. Today, directors are as careful in their selection (or nonselection) of pop/rock songs as they are cognizant of camera angles and special effects. Whether it is John Williams composing majestic sci-fi scores, the Alan Parsons Project adding a theater-rock foundation to medieval fairy tales like *Ladyhawke*, or Sting composing the title song for a film, the importance of using catchy pop/rock melodies and themes in films cannot be ignored. During the 1980s, movie sound tracks broadened their appeal to reach teen and adult audiences and, in the process, impacted the total movie experience significantly.

The concept of movie soundtracks as ersatz pop/rock compilations was not new in the 1980s, but the popularity of such anthologies in the wake of *Easy Rider*'s and, especially, *Saturday Night Fever*'s phenomenal success increased as the decade progressed. Overall, the key component found in 80s soundtracks was the dominance of rock 'n' roll music. No longer underscored by vapid or forgettable mood music, rock 'n' roll took center stage as the art form most likely to stay in the audience's aural and visual memory. It should not be surprising that Simple Minds' insipid "Don't You

 WICKED GAME—CHRIS ISAAK (1987; VIDEO 1991)

Even though the video did not appear until 1991, *Wicked Game* had a long history that reinforces the growing link between popular music and film. Chris Isaak (born 1956 in Stockton, California), a retro rockabilly artist who sounded like a mix of Elvis Presley and Roy Orbison, originally released "Wicked Game" on his critically acclaimed 1987 *Heart Shaped World* album. Enter avant-garde director David Lynch, who plucked the song from relative obscurity and included it in his 1990 film *Wild at Heart*. Film fans were intrigued by the song's hauntingly erotic sound, so that, by 1991, Isaak had made an appropriately sexy video, directed by famed photographer Herb Ritts and co-starring exotic model Helena Christensen. The video's provocatively lyrical scenario, showing Isaak and Christensen on a deserted beach, remains one of the most erotic music videos ever made, with its distinctive black-and-white photography underscoring the song's minimalist musical accompaniment and desperately melancholy lyrics.

(Forget About Me)" became *The Breakfast Club*'s fans' anthem, or that Tom Cruise's adolescent sexuality is forever connected to Bob Seger's jubilant "Old Time Rock and Roll." Connecting popular music with favorite films—or other significant life events and experiences—became the post-modern equivalent of saving love letters or souvenirs. Directly tied to its newest foray into MTV's video generation, rock 'n' roll infiltrated the big screen as well, changing the way we hear and remember films and keeping the light of every rock 'n' roll genre—from heavy metal to jazz rock—alive and well in our eyes, heads and hearts.

NOTES

1. Dennis Hopper, director, *Easy Rider* (Production Company, 1969), starring Dennis Hopper, Peter Fonda, and Jack Nicholson; Hopper discussed his use of a rock compilation sound track on *Inside the Actors Studio*, hosted by James Lipton (Bravo, 1996).

2. Martin Scorsese, director, *Mean Streets* (Production Company, 1973), starring Robert De Niro and Harvey Keitel; Scorsese discussed his use of music from his childhood to underscore themes of street violence on *Inside the Actors Studio*, hosted by James Lipton (Bravo, 2001).

3. John Badham, director, *Saturday Night Fever* (Paramount Pictures, 1977); and Robert Stigwood, producer, *The Original Movie Sound Track: Saturday Night Fever* (Rhino Records, 1977); *Billboard* magazine reported record-setting sales of $28 million in 1978.

4. Nicholas Ray, director, *Rebel without a Cause* (Production Company, 1955), starring James Dean, Natalie Wood, and Sal Mineo; also see Robert Sklar, *Movie-Made America* (New York: Random House, 1994).

5. Amy Heckerling, director, *Fast Times at Ridgemont High* (Production Company, 1982), starring Sean Penn, Judge Reinhold, Jennifer Jason Leigh, and Phoebe Cates.

6. Film critic Molly Haskell has commented extensively on Heckerling's feminist themes in *Fast Times at Ridgemont High*; from Molly Haskell, *From Reverence to Rape: The Treatment of Women in the Movies*, 2nd ed. (Chicago: University of Chicago Press, 1987).

7. Taken from the "Rat Pack"—a group of entertainers in the early 1960s whose liberal politics and social antics were well known, the "Brat Pack" was crowned such for their frequent pairings in film about late boomers and for their apolitical views.

8. Chris Barsanti, Review of *The Breakfast Club*, 1999, at http://www.filmcritic.com.

9. Ibid.

10. Christopher Null, Review of *Pretty in Pink*, 2002, at http://www.filmcritic.com.

11. Various film critics, including Christopher Null, Roger Ebert, and Leonard Maltin, have praised *Some Kind of Wonderful* as more poignant than *Pretty in Pink* but almost too understated to generate box-office appeal. See http://www.filmcritic.com; also Leonard Maltin, ed., 2000, *Movie & Video Guide* (New York: Penguin, 2000), 1286.

12. Tim Hunter, director, *River's Edge* (Production Company, 1986), starring Crispin Glover, Keanu Reeves, and Dennis Hopper; the film recounts the true story of Reagan-era

teens who refuse to turn in one of their friends who has killed his girlfriend and left her body at the river's edge.

13. Christopher Null, Review of *Bill & Ted's Excellent Adventure*, 2001, at http://www.filmcritic.com.

14. Maltin, *Movie & Video Guide*, 587.

15. Veronica was the sexy but duplicitous girlfriend of comic-strip teen Archie; Wynona Ryder's character in *Heathers* suggests a darker, anti-Veronica interpretation.

16. Allan Moyle, director, *Pump Up the Volume* (Production Company, 1990), starring Christian Slater and Samantha Mathis; the film offers a darkly satiric look at teenage angst and pushes the envelope when teen suicide becomes the result of Slater's careless pop-psychology response to a troubled friend.

17. Greil Marcus, *Mystery Train: Images of America in Rock 'N' Roll Music* (New York: Plume Paperbacks, 1997), preface.

18. William J. Palmer, *The Films of the Eighties: A Social History* (Carbondale: Southern Illinois University Press, 1993), 299.

19. Ibid., xiii.

20. Ibid., 280.

21. Ibid.

22. Barry Levinson, director, *Diner* (Studio, 1982), starring Steve Guttenberg, Mickey Rourke, Kevin Bacon, and Daniel Stern.

23. David Abrams, Review of *Diner*, 2001, at http://www.ecritic.com.

24. Ibid.

25. "Power of Love" ranked among *Billboard*'s best-selling singles of the 1980s.

26. Abrams, *Diner*.

27. Lawrence Kasdan, director, *The Big Chill* (Columbia Pictures, 1983), starring Kevin Kline, Glenn Close, Tom Berenger, Mary Kay Place, William Hurt, and Jeff Goldblum; Kasdan's juxtaposition of his son (as Kline and Close's toddler) singing "Joy to the World" at the beginning of the film followed by Three Dog Night's recording at the end frames his themes about generation change and coming of age musically and memorably.

28. Maltin, *Movie & Video Guide*, 1116.

29. Ibid., 577; also see other reviewers, for example, Roger Ebert at http://www.rogerebert.com.

30. Both sound tracks ranked among the Top 50 best-sellers of the 1980s, with *Dirty Dancing* among the Top 25.

A-TO-Z OF ROCK, 1981–1990

Alternative Rock. A phrase coined in the early 1980s to describe music that did not fit into a traditional rock mainstream genre. Sometimes derived from the raw, elemental sound of late 1960s garage bands, the alternative style is most closely tied to the **punk** sound of the late 1970s and influenced by folk, reggae, and jazz. Notable alternative rock bands include **R.E.M.**, **Sonic Youth**, the **Replacements**, and Talking Heads. Alternative rock experienced peak popularity during the 1990s with such groups as the Smashing Pumpkins, Pearl Jam, and the Dave Matthews Band.

***Amadeus* (1984).** Director Milos Forman's MTV-inspired interpretation of the life and works of Wolfgang Amadeus Mozart. Using dazzling visuals, quick cuts, and an energized sound track of Mozart's compositions, Forman suggests that long before Elvis Presley or the Beatles Austria's eighteenth-century musical wunderkind was really the first rock star. Living a life of excessive drinking, partying, dating, and drug use, Amadeus set the standard for contemporary rock idols. The best-selling sound track also introduced the MTV generation to classical music, while Austrian rock singer Falco (1957–1998) scored with a 1986 techno-rap hit, "Rock Me, Amadeus."

***American Fool* (1982).** The album that established **John (Cougar) Mellencamp** as an artist in the blues-folk-rock tradition and made him a superstar, *American Fool* included the hits "Hurts So Good" and "Jack and Diane." "Hurts So Good," which raised some ire from feminists who objected to its misogynist tone, was also paired with other, more richly lyrical tracks like the homespun "Jack and Diane." The album sold over 9 million records, making it one of the best-selling albums of the decade. Its success also spurred Mellencamp to drop the "Cougar" stage name imposed on him as an apparent marketing ploy by then–MCA producer Tony De Fries.

Anthrax. This quintet of "nice Jewish boys" from Queens, New York, formed in mid-1981 and became one of the most popular **thrash/speed metal** bands of the 1980s, competing with megagroups **Metallica** and **Megadeth**. Anthrax's original members included lead singer Neil Turbin, lead guitarist Dan Spitz, rhythm guitarist Scott "Not" Ian, bassist Dan Lilker, and drummer Charlie Benante. After their first album release *Fistful of Metal* (1984), bassist Frank Bello replaced Lilker and vocalist Joey Belladonna, who helped the band become a leader in the speed metal movement.

***Appetite for Destruction* (1987).** Considered one of the strongest debut albums released by a **hair**-metal band, *Appetite for Destruction* was released during **Guns N' Roses'** first European tour. The album rose to No. 1 and stayed there five weeks. In addition, the album produced three Top 10 singles, including the No. 1 hit "Sweet Child o' Mine."

***Bad Reputation* (1981).** Debut album of **Joan Jett** and the Blackhearts, *Bad Reputation* was originally released in the United States as a self-titled independent effort (by producer Kenny Laguna, who helped finance the project). *Bad Reputation* was an in-your-face fusion of "post-glitter ranch-pop," floating easily on a healthy dose of **punk** potency.

Band Aid. The name for a British and Irish charity supergroup founded by **Bob Geldof** and Midge Ure in 1984 to raise money for famine relief in Ethiopia. The name was chosen because it had a double meaning: On one hand, it means a band of musicians getting together to offer aid and assistance to a needy cause; on the other, it suggests the notion that sticking a Band-Aid on a gaping wound will not heal it, as the problem of world famine was something that demanded more than a "bandage" approach. Band Aid's seminal project was the release of a holiday single titled **"Do They Know It's Christmas?"** The single raised over $3 million in the United States and approximately £8 million worldwide.

The Bangles. Formed in 1981, a group called the Bangs led by lead singer/bassist Susanna Hoffs, who had responded to an ad placed by Peterson sisters Debbie and Vicki became the Bangles in 1982. The trio added—briefly—bassist Annette Zilinskas, who was replaced by ex-Runaways bassist Michael Steele. The group's post-**punk** garage pop sound generated hits like "Manic Monday" and the megahit "Walk Like an Egyptian," before breaking up due to personal differences in 1989.

B-boys. Also b-girls. A term associated with the early **rap** and **hip-hop** movements, b-boys referred to break dancers who, along with the MC, DJ, and Graffiti artist, rounded out the artist quartet that defined hip-hop culture.

The Beastie Boys. Organized in Greenwich Village, New York, in 1981 by "MCA" Adam Yauch and "Mike D" Mike Diamond, the Beastie Boys were initially a quartet. After drummer Kate Schellenbach and guitarist John Berry's quick departure, Yauch and Diamond recruited Adam Horovitz as their replacement. After two **indie** single releases, the trio was signed to **Def Jam** records, with friend and co–Def Jam founder **Rick Rubin** taking a spin as the group's DJ/scratcher. After several single and extended-play albums, the Beastie Boys became **rap** celebrities with the release of their 1986 debut album, *Licensed to Ill*, which included the teenage mantra "Fight for Your Right (To Party)."

"Beat It" (1982). From **Michael Jackson's (b. 1958)** 1982 *Thriller* album, "Beat It" was released as a single in February 1983. On March 31, MTV debuted a video of the hit single. Combining the edgy guitar riffs of Eddie Van Halen with *West Side Story*–inspired choreography to simulate a kind of faux urban gang confrontation, the video remains a classic among MTV's archives and a favorite to fans spanning several generations.

Belafonte, Harry (b. 1927). Singer who had promoted the concept of a benefit concert for Africans by African American artists, Belafonte's idea eventually became **USA for Africa** and produced the multimillion-selling single **"We Are the World"** in 1985.

Benatar, Pat (b. 1953). An early MTV star affecting a "tough chick" image, Benatar took her operatic training, paired it with future husband Neil Geraldo's guitar wizardry, and became one of the most successful pop/rock recording artists of the 1980s. **Miss Sweet Petite**, as Benatar became known, soon shed her shoulder pads and tights for a softer image but ultimately failed to sustain the initial interest generated by her feminist-induced songs. Though critics generally concluded Benatar's bluster masked nothing more than mainstream pop/rock, she did prove to be an arena draw with hits that included "Treat Me Right," "You Better Run," and "Hit Me With Your Best Shot," all from her platinum selling 1980 sophomore effort *Crimes of Passion*.

The Big Chill (1983). Popular baby-boomer film directed by Lawrence Kasdan about a group of former college friends who reunite for the funeral of one of their friends. The film featured an all-star cast, including Kevin Kline, Glenn Close, and William Hurt, and boasted a best-selling sound track (plus a follow-up release with more music) that renewed interest in songs from the 1960s.

"Billie Jean" (1982). Michael Jackson's first MTV hit, a video of "Billie Jean" (which premiered in March 1983), like **"Beat It"** (1982), became an instant video classic and demonstrated how powerful a medium **music video** could be. The song's moody, R&B-funk sound coupled with the video's effective nod to film noir turned another track from 1982's *Thriller* into a hit for the "King of Pop." It was during Jackson's performance of this hit during television's *25th Anniversary of Motown* (1983) special that he introduced his now-famous **moonwalk**.

Black Flag. California-based **indie** band formed in 1977 that included founding guitarist Greg Ginn, bassist Chuck Dukowski, drummer Brian Migdol, and lead singer Keith Morris. Morris was later replaced by the now-legendary Henry Rollins. When MCA-Unicorn Records found their musical style too outrageous, Greg Ginn and Steve "Mugger" Corbin helped found **SST Records**, which went on to produce a series of brilliant musical efforts by indie bands like **Hüsker Dü**, **the Minutemen**, and Meat Puppets.

Bon Jovi. New Jersey–based **hair**-metal band formed in 1983 and fronted by lead singer Jon that also included power guitarist Richie Sambora, keyboardist David Bryan, drummer Tico Torres, and bassist Alec John Such. The band, known for popularizing the now-staple "power ballad," became one of the best-selling metal bands of the 1980s, with their monster-selling 1986 album *Slippery When Wet* establishing their now-iconic status among metallers who crossed over into the pop/rock mainstream.

Born in the U.S.A. (1984). The album that turned Bruce Springsteen into a superstar. *Born in the U.S.A.* produced several hit singles, including "Dancing in the Dark" (a popular concert video featured a young Courtney Cox as the girl Springsteen pulls from the crowd to dance with), "Cover Me," "Glory Days," and "I'm on Fire." *Born in the U.S.A.* went on to become the biggest-selling rock album of the 1980s.

Break Dancing. Form of solo dancing that involves rapid acrobatic moves in which different parts of the body touch the ground; normally performed to the rhythm of **rap** music.

Brown Sound. The nickname given to the combination of Eddie Van Halen's own relaxed style of guitar playing coupled with his experimentation in guitar tweaking and effects processing that produced a distinctive tone many other musicians tried to emulate.

Child, Desmond (b. 1953). Enjoying an early career as both singer and songwriter, Child went on to compose songs for Cher, Aerosmith, Michael Bolton, and Ricky Martin. His collaborations with **Bon Jovi** produced the hits "You Give Love a Bad Name" and "Livin' on a Prayer."

***Chimes of Freedom* (1988).** Extended-play album released by Bruce Springsteen from his Amnesty International Tour, with proceeds going to that cause.

***Club MTV* (1987).** MTV's first venture beyond the **music video** format, *Club* MTV became the network's first daily show. The program featured members of its viewing audience enjoying a dance club setting in which DJs and popular artists performed.

Conspiracy of Hope (1986). Produced by Amnesty International to mark its twenty-fifth anniversary, the Conspiracy of Hope tour hopscotched across America using a 707 jet that included passenger/performers **U2**, plus Sting and Canadian rocker Bryan Adams, along with assorted one-night stand-ins that included Bob Dylan and **Bob Geldof**. The tour was the idea of ex-Franciscan monk John Healey, who became a Peace Corps worker heading the American office of Amnesty that searched to bring left- and right-wing oppressors to justice. Healey won the 1977 Nobel Peace Prize but remains little known in the United States.

***Daydream Nation* (1988).** In 1988, **Sonic Youth** was poised and ready for its breakthrough effort and came through with this masterpiece double-album released by Enigma Records. Hailed as a tour de force, *Daydream Nation* yielded the college radio hit "Teen Age Riot" and elicited high praise from both mainstream and **indie** critics.

Dead Kennedys. Independent **alternative** band formed in San Francisco early in 1978, Dead Kennedys included founder vocalist Jello Biafra, who recruited guitarist East Bay Ray and bassist Klaus Flouride through a magazine ad. Drummer Bruce Slesinger (Ted) joined soon after, and the band began playing locally throughout the Bay Area, occasionally venturing outside their local neighborhoods. Dead Kennedys were known for their scathing satire about American politics and culture.

Def Jam. Cutting-edge recording label founded in 1984 by entrepreneurs **Russell Simmons** and **Rick Rubin**. Def Jam is responsible for popularizing many of the pre–gangsta **rap** artists, including **Run-D.M.C.** (co-founded by Simmons's brother Joseph).

Def Leppard. In the minds of many critics and fans, Def Leppard, formed in 1977, is the most definitive hard rock band of the 1980s. Really a fusion of the glam-rock and metal movements from earlier in that decade, including a curious combination of Queen's energized musical theatrics and Led Zeppelin's heavy guitar sound. Within a year of its initial formation in 1977 as Atomic Mass, Def Leppard expanded beyond original members Rick Savage, Pete Willis, and Tony Kenning to include singer Joe Elliot. Soon after, the band changed its name to Deaf Leopard, altering its spelling to the more rock 'n' roll sounding Def Leppard. The group added guitarist, Steve Clark in time for its first real gig and replaced Kenning with drummer Frank Noon prior to its first recording and single release (January 1979). Later that year, Rick Allen established himself as the band's permanent drummer, while Noon went on to play with Lionheart and Waysted.

Dis. A musical response, in **rap/hip-hop**, to a previously released song.

"Do They Know It's Christmas?" (1984). A single released in 1984 by **Band Aid**, a group of British rock stars who used proceeds from the song to benefit world hunger. The straight-to-No. 1 single in England earned over £8 million worldwide.

***Double Nickels on the Dime* (1984).** Indie band **the Minutemen**'s takeoff on Pink Floyd's 1969 double-album *Ummagumma, Double Nickels* is considered one of the most influential **alternative** albums of the 1980s.

***Dr. Feelgood* (1989).** Glam-metal bad boys **Mötley Crüe**'s most celebrated album, *Dr. Feelgood* produced several hit singles, including "Kickstart My Heart," "Don't Go Away Mad (Just Go Away)," "Without You," and the No. 1 title track.

Duran Duran. British rock teen idol video stars included founding members Nick Rhodes and John Taylor, who solicited fellow classmates Simon Colley (bass) and Stephen Duffy (vocals) in 1978. Duran Duran's first two years were unstable, plagued by musicians who came and went very quickly. Colley and Duffy exited the group within a year, replaced by drummer Roger Taylor and vocalist Andrew Wickett, whose stay with the band only last a few months. When former punker **Simon Le Bon** joined the post-**punk new romantics**–styled group, their popularity soared, later aided by their poster-boy good looks and **music video**. Known as much for their photogenic qualities as their music, Duran Duran dominated MTV in its early years, with its 1981 hit **"Girls on Film"** among its most controversial hits and 1982's "Hungry Like the Wolf," its most popular.

Emcee. A **rap/hip-hop** term that evolved from party shouts like, "Grand M is in the house and he'll walk right out without a doubt," and refers to the individual who creates such rhymes.

E Street Band. Bruce Springsteen's famous backup group, formed in 1973, led by drummer Max Weinberg, guitarist Steve Van Zandt, and saxophonist Clarence Clemens, who helped "The Boss" establish his famous New Jersey–based rock sound. Their first album was *The Wild, the Innocent and the E-Street Shuffle* (1973).

Etheridge, Melissa (b. 1961). Hailing from Leavenworth, Kansas, Etheridge was a budding singer/songwriter by the time she reached her teens and traveled east to study at the Berklee College of Music in Boston. Her blues-rock vocals, reminiscent of Janis Joplin, helped establish this acoustic guitar–playing rocker as one of the 1980s most important musical discoveries, although her commercial breakthrough did not occur until the early 1990s. Her self-titled debut album was released in May 1988.

***Faith* (1987).** George Michael's solo debut album came fully loaded with six Top 5 hits, four of which—"Faith," "Father Figure," "One More Try," and

"Monkey"—went to No. 1. The album was No. 1 for twelve weeks and won the 1988 Grammy Award for Album of the Year.

Farm Aid (1985). Within two months of **Live Aid**'s international success, another charitable venture emerged to help American farmers; on September 22, 1985, musical artists including Bob Dylan, **Tom Petty**, Billy Joel, **Van Halen**, **Bon Jovi**, and Foreigner performed at the first Farm Aid concert in Champaign, Illinois. Some 80,000 people packed the outdoor stadium in spite of inclement weather. The concert event raised over $7 million for America's family farmers.

***Full Moon Fever* (1989).** **Tom Petty**'s breakthrough album as a solo artist, *Full Moon Fever* was both a critical and commercial success, making it one of the most influential and celebrated albums of the 1980s.

Geldof, Bob (b. 1951). Lead singer of the Boomtown Rats, whose charitable work organizing the **Live Aid** concert for world hunger in 1985 is as important as his musical accomplishments.

"Girls Just Want to Have Fun" (1984). Post–**new wave** artist **Cyndi Lauper**'s campy feminist manifesto about young women became an early favorite on MTV. It was released on her 1984 debut album, *She's So Unusual*. Unfortunately, Lauper created an image so kooky that it became difficult for her to venture into new musical areas.

"Girls on Film" (1981). **Duran Duran**'s controversial peep show raised some angry voices among feminists and set an early standard for issues involving the objectification of women on MTV.

The Go-Go's. Original band members included vocalist Belinda Carlisle, lead guitarist Charlotte Caffey, rhythm guitarist Jane Wiedlin, bassist Margot Olaverra, and drummer Elissa Bello, who started as the "Misfits" in 1978. Before the group's first single release, Gina Schock replaced Bello, and shortly after their first UK concert tour in 1980, Kathy Valentine replaced Olaverra. Though they would later cultivate a more wholesome image for MTV audiences, the Go-Go's initially lived the hard-partying, drug-taking life associated with most rock bands, with one of their 1979 shows ending in a much-publicized riot. Their effervescent sound became synonymous with the Valley Girl stereotype and was epitomized in hits like "Our Lips Are Sealed" and "We Got the Beat." The group disbanded in 1985 due to internal tensions.

Grandmaster Flash (b. 1958). One of **rap/hip-hop**'s greatest innovators, Flash was born Joseph Saddler and spent his early years in Barbados before moving to the Bronx. He is credited as being one of the seminal artists of rap, developing a series of groundbreaking techniques—including cutting (moving between tracks exactly on the beat), back-spinning (manually turning records to repeat brief snippets of sound), and phasing (manipulating turntable speeds)—thus creating the basic vocabulary that DJs continue to follow today.

Guns N' Roses. The original lineup of **heavy metal**'s ultimate bad boys included Axl Rose, Izzy Stradlin, Traci Guns, Ole Beich, and Rob Gardner, formed early in 1985. By June 6, 1985, the lineup had changed: Axl and Izzy remained but were joined by Duff McKagan, Slash, and Steven Adler. Becoming a fan favorite among serious glam-metal fans, Guns N' Roses released its most popular (and critically acclaimed) album *Appetite for Destruction* in 1987.

Hair Bands. A sometimes derogatory term used to describe 1980s **heavy-metal** bands whose image was as (if not more) important as their music. Bands like **Van Halen, Bon Jovi, Poison,** and **Mötley Crüe** were often targeted for their good looks, excessive "big" hair, and muscular appearance. These groups generally produced more melodic, mainstream-style power rock as opposed to some of the edgier, more eclectic sound of **speed-** or **thrash-metal** bands.

Hammersmith Odeon. London's "rock mecca" and the place frequented by artists from **U2** to AC/DC to the **Police**. Best known from Motörhead's 1981 live album *No Sleep 'Til Hammersmith*, the Hammersmith has been a rock venue for decades. Located in West London in the heart of a bustling commercial and transport center, the theater has boasted concerts by countless rock legends including the Who, AC/DC, Black Sabbath and David Bowie, who performed his last concert as Ziggy Stardust there in 1973.

Hardcore Rock. See **Punk Rock; Underground Rock.**

Hayden, Jackie. CBS Records impresario who discovered **U2** in 1978.

Headbangers' Ball **(1986).** MTV acknowledged its **heavy-metal** fans by creating this popular annual event that invited fans to dress up and party as their favorite metal bands performed.

The Heartbreakers. Tom Petty's backup band that included himself, guitarist Mike Campbell, and keyboardist Benmont Tench. Initially known as Mudcrutch. By 1976, the group expanded to include L.A. musicians Ron Blair (bass) and Stan Lynch (drums) and changed its name to the Heartbreakers. Their style of folk/blues-based rock 'n' roll is a staple among traditional rock musicians. In 2004, the band was inducted into the Rock and Roll Hall of Fame and Museum in Cleveland, Ohio.

Heavy Metal. The term derived from Steppenwolf's "Born to Be Wild" lyrics, which mention "heavy metal thunder," a phrase that describes a musical genre where blues-rock guitar riffs and power chords mix to create a "heavy," sometimes harsh sound. Metal music is usually characterized by an aggressive, driving beat and highly amplified, often distorted guitars. Themes explored in heavy metal lyrics are often described as dark, depressing, or angry.

Hib-Tone Records. Independent record label responsible for producing many **indie/alternative** bands. Most impressively, Hib-Tone helped launch the career of **R.E.M.** with its 1981 release of "Radio Free Europe."

Hip-hop. The cultural expansion of **rap** music, hip-hop integrates "rapping" with music and extends beyond the music to include an urban style of dress, speech, and art. Hip-hop originated in the South Bronx section of New York City in the mid-1970s.

House of Style **(1989).** Another of MTV's innovative series, *House of Style* featured supermodel host Cindy Crawford exploring various aspects of popular culture, from fashion to food to music.

Hughes, John (b. 1950). Film director responsible for a quintet of teen flicks in the 1980s, Hughes is credited with examining the adolescent experience from the perspective of the teenager. His use of popular and rock music helped the multi-artist sound track become a staple companion to films.

Hüsker Dü. Hailing from the Minneapolis/St. Paul area, Hüsker Dü formed late in 1978 and consisted of vocalist/guitarist/keyboard-percussionist Bob Mould, guitarist/bassist Greg Norton, and drummer Grant Hart. They remained one of the most popular **underground** bands of the 1980s but never crossed over to mainstream celebrity.

Hysteria **(1987). Def Leppard**'s blockbuster *Hysteria* signaled many things for the band and metal fans, including another world tour, this one beginning in the United Kingdom. Seven of the album's twelve songs were released as singles, and *Hysteria* wound up selling 16 million copies worldwide; 12 million were sold in the United States alone.

Indie Rock. Another name for **alternative rock**, indie—short for "independent"—rock is associated with the rise of little-known bands who, early in the 1980s, recorded for smaller, unknown record labels. **R.E.M.**, often considered the first indie band to cross over to mainstream success, first recorded for a small record label called **Hib-Tone**. Other indie groups, including **Hüsker Dü** and **Mission of Burma**, established limited but loyal audiences recording for independent record labels. Most indie groups never achieved a wide audience or commercial success but often won critical acclaim for their innovative contributions to popular music.

Iovine, Jimmy (b. 1953). Recording master who began his career as a sound engineer, Iovine went on to produce hits for artists as varied as **Tom Petty**, Stevie Nicks, and Patti Smith. He is considered one of the most successful and influential producers of the 1980s.

It Takes a Nation of Millions to Hold Us Back **(1988). Public Enemy**'s masterpiece, *It Takes a Nation of Millions to Hold Us Back* has been described as a brilliantly chaotic mix that relied as much on found sounds and avant-garde noise as it did on old school. Hailed by both **rap** and rock critics as a **hip-hop** tour de force, the album helped established hip-hop as an active agent for social change, crediting Public Enemy as an innovative force in the push to make rap more politically charged and controversial, and raising substantive political topics ranging from structural racism to corporate control and police brutality.

"I Want My MTV." Phrase that became a marketing mantra for MTV audiences, one that helped the cable network's subscribers grow by leaps and bounds. Appropriately, Dire Straits incorporated the line into one of their songs, "Money for Nothing."

Jackson, Michael (b. 1958). The self-proclaimed "King of Pop," Michael Jackson turned a solo career into solid gold with his impressive **music videos**. Helping define the MTV generation, Jackson's album *Thriller* (1982) became the largest-selling album of all time, selling 60 million copies worldwide; the video for the title track raised the bar for music video standards, and the singles **"Beat It"** and **"Billie Jean"** remain pop/rock classics.

"Jessie's Girl" (1981). Megahit for pop/rocker **Rick Springfield**, "Jessie's Girl" was an early entry with the MTV crowd. The song itself, which has been hailed as an "almost perfect" pop/rock composition, jump-started Springfield's stalled career and revealed a new age of the teen idol.

Jett, Joan (b. 1960). An early role model for the tough, independent, post-**punk** female rocker. Jett's music harkened back to an earlier, simpler musical era. Her rock paean anthem "I Love Rock 'n' Roll" (1981) became an instant classic, while her debut album with the Blackhearts, *Bad Reputation* (1981), remains among the decade's most influential.

Jones, Quincy (b. 1933). Record producer extraordinaire who is responsible for **Michael Jackson's** artistic renaissance in the early 1980s, Jones is credited with *Thriller's* success and recognized as an innovator in the recording industry. Jones was also one of the founders of USA for Africa in 1985.

***The Joshua Tree* (1987).** U2's album masterpiece, *The Joshua Tree* is often listed as the best and most influential album of the 1980s. With its hauntingly ethereal Irish folk sound fused with post–**new wave punk**, the album included such hits as "With or Without You," "Where the Streets Have No Name," and the drivingly wistful "I Still Haven't Found What I'm Looking For."

Kraftwerk. German synth-tech band often viewed as a quirky band of nerds propounding the values of a mechanized state through systematic electronic pop music. Kraftwerk has influenced countless genres and musicians, especially the rumbling **hip-hop** of Afrika Bambaataa and the politically rhythmic sync of **Public Enemy**. Kraftwerk's original band members (from the Organisation) included Ralf Hütter (b. 1946, Krefeld, Germany), electric organ and strings; Florian Schneider-Esleben (b. 1947, Düsseldorf), on flute, echo unit, and strings; Butch Hauf on bass and percussion; Fred Monicks, drums; and Basil Hammond, vocals.

Landis, John (b. 1950). A native Chicagoan, Landis originally worked in the 20th Century Fox mailroom and as a stuntman before becoming a director. He is responsible for **Michael Jackson's** *Thriller* (1982), which forever changed the face and artistic possibilities of **music video**.

Lauper, Cyndi (b. 1953). With a voice that did not mask her Queens upbringing, Cyndi Lauper remains one of the biggest—and most important feminist—stars of the early MTV era. A purveyor of the post-**punk new wave** sound of the early 1980s, Lauper's hit single/video **"Girls Just Want to Have Fun"** remains a video classic, although its 1984 release was done primarily to promote Lauper's album *She's So Unusual.*

***Learning to Crawl* (1984).** Although reviews were mixed, *Learning to Crawl* remains the **Pretenders'** signature album. The album performed well in the United States, peaking at No. 5, and was only slightly less successful in the United Kingdom, cresting at No. 11. The now-classic single "Back on the Chain Gang" was one of the album's—and the group's—stellar achievements.

Le Bon, Simon (b. 1958). A drama student at Birmingham University and former member of the **punk** band Dog Days, Le Bon joined **Duran Duran** as lead singer early in 1980. His naturally good looks and model-perfect image helped put Duran Duran at the top of the MTV and teen idol charts during the early 1980s.

Lennox, Annie (b. 1954). Born in Aberdeen, Scotland, Lennox began playing music as a child, mastering both piano and flute before winning a scholarship to London's Royal Academy of Music in her late teens. Her pairing with Dave Stewart to form the Eurythmics opened the door to new musical venues, but it was Lennox's searing androgyny that captured the eye of MTV audiences and propelled her to rock stardom.

***Let It Be* (1984).** Breakthrough album for garage **punk** band the **Replacements** in 1984, *Let It Be* holds a niche as one of the most influential albums of the 1980s.

***Licensed to Ill* (1986).** Released in November 1986 to international acclaim, *Licensed to Ill* become the fasting-selling debut in Columbia Records' history and turned the **Beastie Boys** into the first successful white **rap** group.

***Like a Virgin* (1984).** The album (and single) that made **Madonna (b. 1958)** a star, *Like a Virgin* broke new grounds as a crossover between post–**new wave** disco and pop. Madonna's subsequent faux masturbation dance while performing the song at the MTV Awards raised additional controversy that only added to the song—and star's—unique persona.

Live Aid (1985). Landmark concert held on July 13 simultaneously in London and Philadelphia and simulcast globally. The concert was the brain-child of Boomtown Rats' lead singer **Bob Geldof**. Networks estimated that 95 percent of all television sets in the world—and a projected audience of over 2 billion people—were tuned in to the concert. It has further been estimated that more people watched Live Aid than Neil Armstrong's first step on the moon in 1969. The Live Aid concert benefited famine victims in Ethopia and other African nations, and included performances by Sting, Phil Collins, **Rick Springfield**, **U2**, John Baez, **Run-D.M.C.**, the Four Tops, Stevie Wonder, and Paul McCartney.

Madonna (b. 1958). The quintessential pop star of the 1980s who has rein-vented herself more times than **Michael Jackson** has changed gloves, Madonna was one of the first—and only—artists to capture successfully the **music video** medium. Not only did she use MTV to advance her own career, but in doing so, she broke new and often controversial ground for the format and content of music video as a medium. Her successful *Like a Virgin* (1984) album release was followed by many other critical and commercial efforts, including 1986's *True Blue* and the controversial *Like a Prayer* (1989).

Mann, Aimee (b. 1960). A graduate of the prestigious Berklee College of Music, Mann began her professional career working with future industrial-metal rocker Al Jourgensen. She later went on to form her own group, **'Til Tuesday**, before launching a solo career in 1993.

***Master of Puppets* (1986).** Metallica's **heavy-metal** masterpiece, *Master of Puppets* features the virtuosity of bass player Cliff Burton (1962–1986) and enough hooks and power chords to satisfy headbangers and rockers alike.

Megadeth. Co-founded by vocalist/lead guitarist Dave Mustaine and bassist David Ellefson in 1983, Megadeth originally included guitarist Chris Poland and drummer Gar Samuelson. By 1987, both Poland and Samuelson had been replaced with Jeff Young and Chuck Behler, respectively. Taking a cue from **Metallica**'s tendency toward aural assault (Mustaine had briefly been a mem-ber), Megadeth took on an even more intense, speed-driven variation of **heavy metal** and became one of its darkest musical proponents. Megadeth disbanded in 2002 only to reunite in 2004.

Mellencamp, John (Cougar) (b. 1951). A rocker from America's heart-land, Mellencamp established himself as an artist in the tradition of Bob Dylan and Bruce Springsteen with his 1982 album *American Fool*. By the end of the 1980s, he had experimented with a variety of musical sounds and had been one of the forces behind the **Farm Aid** concerts. Mellencamp remains one of the most important rock artists of the decade.

Metallica. Formed in the summer of 1981 by drummer (and British **new wave heavy-metal** fanatic) Lars Ulrich, the original California-based trio also included lead singer/bass guitarist James Hetfield and recruited lead guitarist Lloyd Grant, who had done mostly studio work. Although a series of tragedies and replacements make the band's history uneven, Metallica is credited with redefining the boundaries of heavy metal and pushing the genre to new and innovative musical heights.

The Minutemen. Formed in San Pedro, California, in 1979 as the Reactionaries, singer/songwriter D Boon and bassist Mike Watt used music to promote their own revolutionary left-wing politics. Joining Boon and Watt were drummer George Hurley and front man/vocalist Martin Tamburovich. Though their politics were clearly what drove their compositions, the Minutemen's musical signature became its brief (less than a minute) tracks. Their 1984 magnum opus **Double Nickels on the Dime** still ranks among the most influential albums of the 1980s.

Mission of Burma. Forming in 1979 when two Boston-based groups, Moving Parts and the Molls, merged, guitarist Roger Miller and bassist Clint Conley joined Peter Prescott to form Mission of Burma, adding Martin Swope to coordinate tape loops and live sound. Capturing an early '80s sound that is typical of its vintage post-**punk** era, Mission of Burma's sound included jittery rhythms, odd shifts in time, declamatory vocals, and a welcome aural assault on the listener. The group broke up in 1983.

Miss Sweet Petite. Nickname for the tough but diminutive **Pat Benatar (b.1953)**.

Monsters of Rock. A series of marathon **heavy-metal** concerts held during the 1980s at Castle Donnington, England, Monsters of Rock headlined such acts as **Bon Jovi**, **Metallica**, **Megadeth**, and **Ozzy Osborne**. The heavy-metal concert marathons continued into the 1990s.

Moonwalk. The iconic backward dance step created by **Michael Jackson** first performed on the *25th Anniversary of Motown* television special in 1983.

Moroder, Giorgio (b. 1940). Celebrated composer/arranger responsible for many of the popular techno-pop sound tracks and original film scores of the 1980s, including *American Gigolo* and *Top Gun*.

Mötley Crüe. Glam-metal party band that was one of the first formed in the 1980s, Mötley Crüe is considered second only to **Guns N' Roses** for its gritty reputation and bad-boy antics. The band's mischievous roots can be traced to 1981 when bassist Nikki Sixx and drummer Tommy Lee left their respective bands to start a new project that would include guitarist Mick Mars and vocalist Vince Neil. The group peaked in 1989 with the commercial success of *Dr. Feelgood*.

***MTV Unplugged* (1990).** With first guests Squeeze, Syd Straw, and Elliot Easton of the Cars, MTV revealed yet another programming innovation with this popular award-winning series that asked artists to strip down the electronics and play from the heart. Guests have included Eric Clapton, Rod Stewart, **Bon Jovi**, and others.

***Murmur* (1983).** The momentous album debut of **R.E.M.**, *Murmur* has been praised for its stunning contribution to **underground rock**, sharpening the band's previously uneven hooks, honing the guitar sound, and generally engendering a compelling air of mystique. It remains one of the most influential albums of the decade.

Music Videos. See **Videos, Music**.

NME. *NME* (New Musical Express), established in 1996, is considered to be the most authoritative weekly music magazine on the market. Published in the United Kingdom, *NME* includes a mix of news, features, and opinionated reviews and keeps readers up to date with what everyone is talking about in music each week.

Nesmith, Mike (b. 1942). Former Monkee Nesmith gained even more significant pop culture fame when he initiated a **music video** concept that evolved into MTV. Nesmith developed a series called *Popclips* that featured video jockeys (**VJs**) playing visual versions of popular songs that was later sold to cable as MTV.

New Romantics. A musical term associated with the early 1980s UK music scene, where a direct backlash emerged against the **punk** movement. To many fans, the term became synonymous for quite disparate bands working within the pop world and thus works better as a description of a specific time rather than a sound or a style. Where punk railed against life on England's council estates, the new romantics celebrated glamour, ostentatious clothes, and hedonism. Examples of the new romantics include Spandau Ballet and **Duran Duran**.

New Wave. A phrase referring to the post-**punk** music that became popular in the early 1980s, the new wave concept was characterized by a synthesized sound and a repetitive beat. This emotionally detached subgenre of rock 'n' roll was highly influenced by simple 1950s-style rock 'n' roll and emerged as a rejection of the complexities of art rock and **heavy metal**. An example of 1980s new wave was the group Blondie, fronted by popular lead singer Deborah Harry.

***1984* (1984).** **Van Halen**'s Orwellian-inspired album initiated parallel groundbreaking for Eddie Van Halen's guitar genius and the electric keyboard, heretofore unheard of as a **heavy-metal**/hard-rock instrument. Hit tracks include "Jump," "Panama," and "Hot for Teacher."

Osbourne, Ozzy (b. 1948). Born John Michael in Aston (a suburb of Birmingham), England, Osbourne first gained notoriety as the lead singer of

Black Sabbath (1968–1979). His post-Sabbath solo career included hit albums *Blizzard of Ozz* (1980) and *Diary of a Madman* (1981), while his personal struggle with drugs and onstage antics (including the infamous biting of a bat's head) brought as much celebrity as his music.

Osbourne, Sharon (b. 1952). Record promoter and wife of famed metaller **Ozzy Osbourne**, Sharon Osborne has been credited with both saving his life and restarting his career after Black Sabbath unceremoniously dismissed him in 1979.

Petty, Tom (b. 1950). The press may have called Petty's early work "power pop," but fans came to know him as a rocker in the finest American tradition. The 1980s saw Petty teaming up with Fleetwood Mac vocalist Stevie Nicks for the hit "Stop Draggin' My Heart Around" and formed the **Traveling Wilburys** with Jeff Lynne, George Harrison, Bob Dylan, and Roy Orbison. His debut solo effort, *Full Moon Fever* (1989), ranks among the most popular and most critically acclaimed albums of the decade.

Poison. Formerly known as Paris, the Harrisburg, Pennsylvania–based band was formed in 1984 by singer Bret Michaels, bassist Bobby Dall, and drummer Rikki Rockett. Guitarist C. C. DeVille was added to the group after they traveled from Pennsylvania to Los Angeles. Poison's meteoric rise to metal stardom upon release of the 1986 album *Look What the Cat Dragged In* coupled with their commercial popularity was equaled only by its rapid decline from the charts and fan loyalty. Poison vanished almost as soon as it arrived but still managed to leave a huge dent in the metal scene during its time in the spotlight. The group more or less disbanded by 1996, but returned in the new millenium with two albums: *Crack A Smile . . . and More* and *Power to the People* (2000), both cobbled together from previously recorded sessions and outtakes from live concerts.

The Police. One of the most influential bands of the late 1970s and early 1980s, the British trio, formed in 1977, consisted of drummer Stewart Copeland, vocalist/bassist Sting, and guitarist Andy Summers. The band's short but celebrated life span included the jazz-infused eclecticism of another time and the of-the-minute post-**punk** sound of the early 1980s. Among The Police's many musical highlights were the albums *Regatta de Blanc* (1979), *Zenyatta Mondatta* (1980), and the classic *Synchronicity* (1983). Conflicts between Sting and Copeland led to the group's demise after the *Synchronicity* tour (1983). The group tried unsuccessfully to reunite in 1984.

***Popclips* (1980).** Precursor of MTV that ran on the Nickelodeon network and was the brainchild of former Monkee **Mike Nesmith (b. 1942)**. The show featured video jockeys (**VJs**) hosting visual interpretations of popular songs.

The Pretenders. Led by singer/guitarist Chrissie Hynde (b. 1951), the Pretenders, formed in 1978, included guitarist James Honeyman-Scott, bassist

Pete Farndon, and drummer Martin Chambers. Hynde's sultry vocals and aggressive postfeminist style took the band to critical and commercial success, with 1984's **Learning to Crawl** among their greatest musical accomplishments. The Pretenders were among rock's all-star **Live Aid** (1985) line up.

Prince (b. 1958). Named after his father's jazz band, Prince Rogers Nelson became one of the most important and influential artist of the 1980s, combining pop, funk, folk, and rock in new and aurally intriguing ways. His 1984 film and soundtrack **Purple Rain** established him as a new creative force in pop/rock music. Like **Madonna**, he has undergone numerous reincarnations, but the heart of his significance remains with the uniquely innovative fusion that remains his musical signature.

Public Enemy. Formed in New York City in 1982 when Chuck D, then a graphic design student (and side DJ) at Adelphi University on Long Island, met Spectrum City's main DJ Hank Shocklee (who would become Public Enemy's co-producer). The two subsequently paired up for Bill Stephney's **rap** show on WBAU radio. Their imaginative collaborations piqued the interest of Flavor Flav, one of the show's most enthusiastic listeners and notable DJ in his own right. Flavor Flav eventually joined the show as a co-host, setting the stage for what would become Public Enemy. The group would change the face and nature of rap in the mid to late 1980s, focusing on more politically charged lyrics and initially what would later be known as "gangsta" rap. Their 1988 album **It Takes a Nation of Millions to Hold Us Back** became a statement of political purpose and social initiative as well as a music-altering force.

Punk Rock. Sometimes called "hardcore rock" or "**underground rock**," the punk scene began in London in the late 1970s before emerging in New York City early in the 1980s. During the 1980s, the punk scene was often described as not being beautiful but honest, a description tied to punk artists' aversion to mainstream popularity. Eschewing contracts with major record labels or music that had wide mainstream appeal, punk rock fought to retain its rebellious, antiestablishmentarian, anticorporate image in the face of rising rock commercialism, with artists ranging from **Michael Jackson** to Bruce Springsteen. Led by the Sex Pistols in England and the Ramones in the United States, the punk movement appealed to countless disaffected youth in the post–Vietnam/Watergate era. Punk music was most often characterized by aggressive performances of three-chord songs played rapidly in a three-minute format.

Purple Rain (1984). Prince's autobiographical film might not be the stuff Oscars are made of, but his accompanying sound track is the stuff associated with rock legends. The critically and commercially acclaimed album went on to become one of the 1980s top sellers, and Prince retained a niche among the decade's most creative and influential artists. The album remained No. 1 on the U.S. charts for twenty-four weeks.

***Pyromania* (1983).** **Def Leppard**'s third—and most critically acclaimed—album, *Pyromania*, which included mega-single "Photograph," was released to huge sales. In the United States alone, *Pyromania* sold 100,000 a week for most of the year and ended up selling over 7 million copies.

Queen Latifah (b. 1970). Born Dana Owens and hailing from Newark, New Jersey, the reinvented Queen Latifah might not have been the first female rapper, but she certainly claims the title of first female **rap** star. Her 1989 debut album *All Hail the Queen* received favorable reviews from the critics, with her third album, 1993's *Black Reign*, going gold, making her the first female rap artist to achieve that success.

Quiet Riot. Originally founded in 1975 by singer Kevin DuBrow, Quiet Riot featured guitar impresario **Randy Rhoads**, bassist Kelli Garni, and drummer Drew Forsyth. After failing to break out of the LA metal scene with a recording contract, as **Van Halen** had done, Quiet Riot ultimately landed a deal with Columbia Records in Japan. Two album releases, *Quiet Riot* (1978) and *Quiet Riot II* (1979) failed to score with critics or audiences, and Rhoads left to help **Ozzy Osborne**, launch his solo career.

Rap. Musical form in which rhyming lyrics are chanted to a musical accompaniment. Developed in the South Bronx in the mid-1970s, rap has evolved to embrace the broader **hip-hop** culture and has perhaps rivaled only rock 'n' roll as the single most important musical and culture phenomenon of the postmodern age.

"Rapture" (1981). Blondie hit that became the first "**rap**" sound to crack the Top 20 and the first one performed by a white artist that was accepted with the urban rap community.

***Rattle and Hum* (1988).** Brilliant documentary of **U2**, directed by Phil Joanou, that chronicles the band's world tour after the release of their iconic *The Joshua Tree*. The film is as dazzling in its visual cuts and editing as it is in its presentation of U2's intensely haunting music.

R.E.M. In 1980 bass player Mike Mills and drummer Bill Berry met shy record store clerk and fledgling guitarist Peter Buck and army brat singer/lyricist Michael Stipe. First known as the Twisted Kites, the quartet eventually adopted the name R.E.M. and became the darlings of the **indie/underground** movement early in the '80s. Their crossover to mainstream superstardom was as phenomenal as the searingly emotional lament of their music. Their 1983 debut album **Murmur** holds a deserved and respected slot among the decade's most influential creations.

The Replacements. Originally formed in 1979 in Minneapolis, Minnesota, when vocalist/songwriter Paul Westerberg joined a garage **punk** band led by guitarist brothers Bob and Tommy Stinson and drummer Chris Mars, the

Impediments became The Replacements after being banned from a local club for disorderly behavior. The group went on to enjoy considerable **underground** success, with their 1984 album release *Let It Be* a critical success.

Rhoads, Randy (1956–1982). One of rock's greatest guitarists and saddest stories, Rhoads gained early success with **Quiet Riot** before joining **Ozzy Osborne's** band in 1981. Rhoads's brilliant guitar playing can be heard on both groups' albums, and he ranks with Jimi Hendrix and Eddie Van Halen as one of rock's guitar-playing geniuses. On the verge of returning to college to pursue a Ph.D. in the classical music he always loved, Rhoads's life ended tragically in a plane crash in March 1982.

Roth, David Lee (b. 1954). Van Halen's first and, arguably, best lead singer, Roth joined the band in 1977 and he brought the insanity of rock 'n' roll to his own self-absorbed testosterone-driven performances. After his stint with **Van Halen** ended in 1985, Roth embarked on a solo career but never quite achieved the celebrity (or success) of his vocal rendition of hits like "Jump" and "Hot for Teacher" or "The Cradle Will Rock." His cover of the Beach Boys' "California Girls" became an easy MTV hit, and Roth's backstage antics remain a legend.

Rubin, Rick (b. 1963). Entertainment entrepreneur who formed **Def Jam** records with **Russell Simmons** in early 1984.

Run-D.M.C. First forming in 1982 out of middle-class Hollis (Queens), New York, **rap** group Run-D.M.C. consisted of childhood friends Run, DMC, and DJ Jam Master Jay. The group became as popular for its style—their Addidas shoes and funky attire—as their crossover success, recording a cover of Aerosmith's "Walk This Way" with the famous metal band. The rapid rise of groups like **Public Enemy** coupled with personal issues among band members made Run-D.M.C.'s stint as hip-hop innovators shortlived. By 2002, the release of a greatest hits album prompted a tour with Aerosmith. Tragically, Jam Master Jay was senselessly murdered only two weeks after the tour ended, signalling an end to an important era in hip-hop.

Salt-N-Pepa. Rap's first all-female crew, formed in 1985, Salt-N-Pepa members included Cheryl "Salt" James and Sandy "Pepa" Denton. Late in 1987, Salt-N-Pepa original DJ Pamela Green with rapper/DJ Spinderella (Deidre "Dee Dee" Roper). The group's entry into rap/**hip-hop** culture was no small feat for the previously male-dominated genre, and they quickly became one of the most popular rap acts of the 1980s.

Scratching. The process of using turntables to create the rhythms for **rap** and **hip-hop** artists, scratching is often credited to artist Kool Herc, who introduced the Jamaican style of "breaking" in the South Bronx when he used two turntables to create a rhythmic backdrop to rap poetry.

Simmons, Russell (b. 1957). Co-founder (with **Rick Rubin**) of the groundbreaking **Def Jam** record label in 1984. Simmons, sometimes called the "Berry Gordy of his time," established rap as one of the most influential forms of Black music. Growing up in New York City's middle-class borough of Queens, and at one time a street-gang member, Simmons went on to study sociology at the Harlem branch of the City College of New York, focusing on **rap**'s connection to inner-city youth.

Slippery When Wet (1986). To prepare for 1986's *Slippery When Wet*, **Bon Jovi** hired songwriter **Desmond Child** as a collaborator. The result was a megahit for the group, establishing them among the best purveyors of the "power ballad" and spawning hits like "Livin' on a Prayer" and "You Give Love a Bad Name." The album remains among the all-time best-sellers of the era and earned critical praise from many skeptics who dissed the musical quality of many glam-rock metal bands.

Some Kind of Monster (2004). A critically acclaimed documentary co-directed by Joe Berlinger and Bruce Sinofsky, *Some King of Monster* follows the recent career of **heavy-metal** band **Metallica**, offering insights into both the band's personal struggles and professional triumphs.

Sonic Youth. Considered one of the most unlikely success stories of American **underground rock** during the 1980s, Sonic Youth first formed when guitarists Thurston Moore and Lee Ranaldo united with bassist Kim Gordon in New York City early in 1981. Becoming one of the underground's most innovative groups, Sonic Youth scored with critics upon the release of 1988's ***Daydream Nation***, with Gordon becoming an unlikely (and uneasy) model for a new generation of women in rock.

Speed Metal. Also known as **"thrash" metal**, speed metal borrowed much of the style associated with the classically influenced structures of neoclassical progressive **heavy metal** from the 1970s and merged them with the harshly muted, yet choppy strum of violent British hardcore, infused with lightning speed and a driving tempo. An example of the first influence can be found in the violent **indie** sounds of **Black Flag**. The fast guitar playing was often paired with slower drums and vocals, creating an ambient music sound with a disorientation of pace and thus of activity. Classic speed metal bands included **Metallica**, **Megadeth**, and **Anthrax**, but other, less commercial speed and thrash bands existed concurrently throughout the 1980s.

Springfield, Rick (b. 1949). The Sydney, Australia, native found a renewed career in the 1980s (he had previously scored a modest hit, "Speak to the Sky," in the early 1970s) with the megahit single **"Jessie's Girl"** (1981), which was released during his simultaneous stint on the daytime drama *General Hospital*. Springfield's good looks proved fatal to his attempt to achieve rock stardom, even though subsequent releases indicate that he is really a traditional rock 'n' roller at heart.

SST Records. Formed in the early 1980s, SST Records became the mecca for independent record artists, including **Black Flag**, **Mission of Burma**, and **Sonic Youth**.

Synchronicity (1983). One of the **Police's** best efforts, *Synchronicity* featured three hit singles, the eerily erotic "Every Breath You Take," the intense "King of Pain," and the lively jazz funk composition "Wrapped Around Your Finger." *Synchronicity* was a commercial and critical success, although fans lamented when the band broke up shortly after its release.

Tapping. Guitar technique created by Eddie Van Halen. Both right and left hands are used on the guitar neck.

This Is Spinal Tap (1984). Director Rob Reiner's brilliant mockumentary about a fictitious rock band called "Spinal Tap." The film gained a cult following and served as a prototype for a new cinematic genre.

Thrash (Speed) Metal. Form of **heavy metal** attributed to groups like **Metallica** and **Megadeth**, thrash—or speed—metal helped some metal bands gain mainstream popularity generally traced to the late 1970s, early 1980s. These variations on the heavy-metal genre generally included blistering drum beats and a sensibility that suggested **punk rock** played loud and hard, almost like growling into the pathological. Unlike speed metal bands, thrash metal was considered crossover music based more in hardcore, which added heavier metal riff stylings to hardcore song forms.

Thriller (1982). **Michael Jackson's** landmark album and video, *Thriller*, which MTV debuted on December 2, 1983, moved the artistic possibilities of **music video** up several notches with its fourteen-minute movie-within-a-movie format and groundbreaking special effects.

'Til Tuesday. Founded by **Aimee Mann** in 1983, 'Til Tuesday's **new wave**, pop/rock sound included guitarist and backup singer Robert Holmes, keyboardist Joey Pesce, and drummer Michael Hausman. The group disbanded in 1990 when Mann left to start a solo career.

The Traveling Wilburys. The brainchild of former Electric Light Orchestra (ELO) member Jeff Lynne, the Wilburys were the faux name for real musicians Lynne, **Tom Petty**, George Harrison, Bob Dylan, and Roy Orbison. The real supergroup recorded a hit first album, *Traveling Wilburys, Vol. 1*, followed by two others, but ultimately disbanded in the wake of Orbison's unexpected death in December 1988.

Underground Rock. Tied to the **punk, indie,** and hardcore movements, underground rock is considered a 1980s derivative of progressive rock from a decade earlier. In general, underground rock refers to nonmainstream artists whose musical style emphasizes rebelliousness, antisocial themes, and eclectic, often dissonant chords and rhythms.

USA for Africa. An effort to raise awareness about famine in Ethiopia, USA for Africa was the result of an idea suggested by singer **Harry Belafonte** and shaped by producer **Quincy Jones** and singer Lionel Richie. The effort resulted in a single recording, **"We Are the World,"** recorded on January 28, 1985. Artists from Bob Dylan to Ray Charles to Bruce Springsteen to Stevie Wonder and **Michael Jackson** contributed to the record's success and USA for Africa's charitable objectives. The single became the fastest selling in music history and helped USA for Africa raise over $62 million.

U2. Called the greatest rock 'n' roll band of the 1980s (or any other decade), U2's post-**punk**, Irish folk sound was born when lead singer Bono, guitarist/keyboardist "The Edge", drummer Larry Mullen, Dik Evans, and bassist Adam Clayton joined and made rock history. Of their many critical and commercial successes, 1987's *The Joshua Tree* shines brightly above many other stellar recordings.

Van Halen. In 1967 the Van Halen family, including brothers Alex and Eddie, emigrated from the Netherlands, where both brothers had received early training in classical piano, to California. Original band members included bassist Michael Anthony and lead singer **David Lee Roth**. Van Halen's musical virtuosity was integrated rock/metal sounds to create one of the most popular crossover bands in the 1980s.

Video Hits I (VH1) (1985). A spin-off of MTV, VH1 became the sole network devoted entirely to music when MTV ventured into other, broader types of (not exclusively music-based) programming.

"Video Killed the Radio Star" (1979). Catchy hit by British band the Buggles, "Video Killed the Radio Star" was the first song played on MTV when it began broadcasting on August 1, 1981.

Videos, Music. A revolutionary concept in how rock music is visualized and heard, music videos are often attributed as the brainchild of former Monkee **Michael Nesmith**, who created minimovies of popular songs for a 1980 Nickelodeon show called *Popclips*. Some rock historians reach farther back in time for music videos' inception, citing Richard Lester's 1964 film *A Hard Day's Night* as a precursor to music videos; others point to Elvis Presley's self-designed choreography to "Jailhouse Rock" in the 1957 movie of the same name as the first music video. In 1981, a cable network called MTV became the first to broadcast music videos, forever changing the face of rock 'n' roll.

VJ. Video jockey. As created for MTV, VJs served as on-air hosts to **music videos**. Original VJs included Nina Blackwood, Alan Hunter, J. J. Jackson,

Mark Goodman, and Martha Quinn, when the network premiered in August 1981.

Warrant. Another 1980s metal band whose life in the spotlight was brief but shining was Warrant. Formed in Los Angeles in 1984, the group featured guitarists Joey Allen and Erik Turner, bassist Jerry Dixon, drummer Steven Sweet, and lead singer Jani Lane. Like **Poison**, Warrant's pop metal sound could not sustain itself commercially, but while they were together, the band produced two double platinum albums. Warrant continued to record and tour throughout the 1990s, last performed as a group in 2001.

"We Are the World" (1985). USA for Africa recording released on Tuesday, March 7, 1985. The single sold 800,000 during its first weekend in release. The recording, penned by **Michael Jackson** and Lionel Richie, was part of an artistic effort to raise global awareness about famine in Ethopia.

World Music. A term that became synonymous with global or internationally influenced rock sounds during the 1980s. In the aftermath of **USA for Africa** and **Live Aid**, artists often integrated Asian, African, or Latin American instruments and rhythms into contemporary mainstream music. A classic example of this is Paul Simon's 1986 album *Graceland*, which successfully combined the sounds of African group Ladysmith Black Mambazo with his own folk rock roots.

***Yo! MTV Raps* (1988).** MTV's first foray into **rap/hip-hop** arrived after the musical genre had gained mainstream viability but helped ease racist accusations against the network. The show aired from 1988 to 1995.

***Zenyatta Mondatta* (1980).** The album that broke the **Police** into mainstream success, *Zenyatta Mondatta* contained hits "Don't Stand So Close to Me" and the **rap**/sync-ed "De Do Do Do, De Da Da Da." The album's commercial accessibility moved the band toward greater commercial and artistic successes with follow-up releases *Ghost in the Machine* (1981) and *Synchronicity* (1983).

APPENDICES

List of Best-Selling Singles, 1981–1990

Singles in order by release date. Release date refers to the date the song was released as a *single*. Each song's inclusion on an album may have occurred prior to or following its release as a single.

Blondie
"Rapture"
January 1981

Rick Springfield
"Jessie's Girl"
June 1981

Stevie Nicks with Tom Petty
"Stop Draggin' My Heart Around"
July 1981

Foreigner
"Waiting for a Girl Like You"
October 1981

Human League
"Don't You Want Me?"
November 1981

J. Geils Band
"Centerfold"
November 1981

Joan Jett & the Blackhearts
"I Love Rock and Roll"
January 1982

John (Cougar) Mellencamp
"Hurts So Good"
May 1982

John (Cougar) Mellencamp
"Jack and Diane"
January 1983

Michael Jackson
"Beat It"
March 1983

David Bowie
"Let's Dance"
March 1983

The Police
"Every Breath You Take"
May 1983

Men at Work
"Down Under"
July 1983

Billy Joel
"Uptown Girl"
October 1983

Van Halen
"Jump"
January 1984

Madonna
"Like a Virgin"
November 1984

Huey Lewis & the News
"The Power of Love"
August 1985

Starship
"We Built This City"
October 1985

The Bangles
"Walk Like an Egyptian"
September 1986

Bon Jovi
"Livin' on a Prayer"
October 1986

U2
"With or Without You"
March 1987

U2
"I Still Haven't Found What I'm
   Looking For"
May 1987

Whitesnake
"Here I Go Again"
July 1987

Bob Seger
"Shakedown"
August 1987

Guns N' Roses
"Sweet Child o' Mine"
August 1988

Source: Fred Benson, ed., *Billboard's Hottest Hot 100 Hits*, 3rd ed. (New York: Billboard Books),
   2003.

List of Best-Selling Albums, 1981–1990

Albums in order by release date. All albums released between 1981 and 1990; peak sales occurred during that time.

The Rolling Stones
Tatoo You
September 1981

John (Cougar) Mellencamp
American Fool
November 1982

Michael Jackson
Thriller
December 1982

The Police
Synchronicity
June 1983

Huey Lewis & the News
Sports
September 1983

Van Halen
1984
January 1984

Bruce Springsteen
Born in the U.S.A.
June 1984

Prince
Purple Rain
July 1984

Madonna
Like a Virgin
November 1984

John Fogerty
Centerfield
February 1985

Dire Straits
Brothers in Arms
May 1985

Heart
Heart
October 1985

Van Halen
5150
April 1986

Madonna
True Blue
July 1986

Bon Jovi
Slippery When Wet
September 1986

The Beastie Boys
Licensed to Ill
November 1986

Bruce Springsteen & the E Street Band
E Street Band Live, 1976–1985
December 1986

U2
The Joshua Tree
March 1987

Guns N' Roses
Appetite for Destruction
August 1987

Def Leppard
Hysteria
August 1987

Bruce Springsteen
Tunnel of Love
October 1987

Bon Jovi
New Jersey
September 1988

U2
Rattle and Hum
October 1988

Metallica
And Justice for All
October 1988

Mötley Crüe
Dr. Feelgood
September 1989

Sources: Peter Dodd, Dan Auty, Justin Cawthorne, and Chris Barrett, Best Selling Albums of The 80s (New York: Barnes and Noble Books), 2004; and http://www.80sxchange.com; http://www.riaa.com.

List of Most Influential Albums, 1981–1990

In alphabetical order by year of release.

Joan Jett
Bad Reputation
1981

Black Flag
Damaged
1981

Elvis Costello
Imperial Bedroom
1982

Mission of Burma
Vs.
1982

Madonna
Madonna
1983

Talking Heads
Speaking in Tongues
1983

The Police
Synchronicity
1983

Violent Femmes
Violent Femmes
1983

Bruce Springsteen
Born in the U.S.A.
1984

The Minutemen
Double Nickels on the Dime
1984

The Pretenders
Learning to Crawl
1984

The Replacements
Let It Be
1984

Van Halen
1984
1984

Prince
Purple Rain
1984

Run-D.M.C.
Run-D.M.C.
1984

Tom Waits
Rain Dogs
1985

The Beastie Boys
Licensed to Ill
1986

Bon Jovi
Slippery When Wet
1986

Guns N' Roses
Appetite for Destruction
1987

U2
The Joshua Tree
1987

Sonic Youth
Daydream Nation
1988

Public Enemy
*It Takes a Nation of Millions to
    Hold Us Back*
1988

Tom Petty
Full Moon Fever
1989

REFERENCE GUIDE

PRINTED SOURCES

Alan, Carter. *Outside Is America: U2 in the U.S.* Boston: Faber and Faber, 1992.

Andersen, Christopher P. *Madonna, Unauthorized.* New York: Island Books, 1992.

Azerrad, Michael. *Our Band Could Be Your Life: Scenes from the American Indie Underground 1981–1991.* Boston: Little, Brown, 2001.

Bank, Jack. "MTV and the Globalization of Popular Culture." *Gazette* 59.1 (February 1997): 43–60.

Bashe, Philip. *Heavy Metal Thunder: The Music, Its History, Its Heroes.* Garden City, NY: Doubleday, 1985.

Benson, Carol, and Allan Metz. *The Madonna Companion: Two Decades of Commentary.* New York: Schirmer Books, 1999.

Berger, Arion. *Hardcore Rap: A Fusion of Metal, Rock, and Hip-Hop.* New York: Universe Publications, 2001.

Berman, Eric. "The Godfathers of Rap: The Rise and Fall of the First Heroes of Hip-Hop." *Rolling Stone* 672.3 (December 23, 1993): 137–142.

Bird, Elizabeth. "'Is That Me, Baby?' Image, Authenticity, and the Career of Bruce Springsteen." *American Studies* 35.2 (Fall 1994): 39–57.

Blake, Andrew. "Making Noise: Notes from the 1980s." *Popular Music and Society* 21.3 (Fall 1997): 19–34.

Bogdanov, Vladimir. *All Music Guide to Hip-Hop: The Definitive Guide to Rap and Hip-Hop.* San Francisco, CA; Berkeley, CA; Milwaukee, WI: Hal Leonard, 2003.

Bordowitz, Hank, comp. and ed. *The U2 Reader: A Quarter Century of Commentary, Criticism, and Reviews.* Milwaukee, WI: Hal Leonard, 2003.

Boyd, Todd. *Young Black, Rich and Famous: The Rise of the NBA, the Hip Hop Invasion, and the Transformation of American Culture.* New York: Doubleday, 2003.

Brown, Rodger Lyle. *Party Out of Bounds: The B-52's, R.E.M., and the Kids Who Rocked Athens, Georgia*. New York: Plus, 1991.

Burgoyne, Patrick. "Is MTV Killing Music Video?" *Creative Review* 22.12 (December 2002): 40–43.

Burns, Gary. "How Music Video Has Changed, and How It Has Not Changed: 1991 vs. 1985." *Popular Music and Society* 18.3 (Fall 1994): 67–79.

Cavicchi, Daniel. *Tramps Like Us: Music & Meaning among Springsteen Fans*. New York: Oxford University Press, 1998.

Chang, Jeff. *Can't Stop Won't Stop: A History of the Hip-Hop Culture*. New York: St. Martin's Press, 2005.

Connelly, Christopher. "Madonna Goes All the Way." *Rolling Stone* (November 22, 1984): 14–20.

Cooper, B. Lee. *Rock Music in American Popular Culture III: More Rock 'n' Roll Resources*. New York: Haworth Press, 1999.

Crampton, Luke, and Rees Dafydd. *Rock & Roll Year by Year*. First American ed. New York: DK Publishers, 2003.

Cross, Charles R. *Backstreets: Springsteen, the Man and His Music*. New York: Harmony Books, 1989.

Cullen, Jim. *Born in the U.S.A.: Bruce Springsteen and the American Tradition*. New York: HarperCollins, 1997.

———. "Bruce Springsteen's Ambiguous Musical Politics in the Reagan Era." *Popular Music and Society* 16.2 (Summer 1992): 1–23.

DeCurtis, Anthony, Sheila Rogers, and David Handelman. "80s. The Gimme Decade." *Rolling Stone* 591 (November 15, 1990): 59–64.

———. "Music's Mean Season." *Rolling Stone* 567568 (December 14, 1989): 15–16.

———. "The Year in Music." *Rolling Stone* 541542 (December 15, 1988): 13–14.

Dee, Johnny. "From U2 to the White Stripes." *Q Special Edition 50 Years of Rock 'n' Roll* (2004).

DeRogatis, Jim, and Carmél Carrillo. *Kill Your Idols*. Fort Lee, NJ: Barricade Books, 2004.

Duffy, John W. *Bruce Springsteen: In His Own Words*. London: Omnibus, 1993.

Dunphy, Eamon. *Unforgettable Fire: The Story of U2*. New York: Viking, 1987.

Eddy, Chuck. *Stairway to Hell: The 500 Best Heavy Metal Albums in the Universe*. New York: Harmony Books, 1991.

Eleveld, Mark, ed. *The Spoken Word Revolution: Slam, Hip-Hop & the Poetry of a New Generation*. Narrated by Marc Kelly Smith. Naperville, IL: Sourcebooks MediaFusion, 2003.

———. *Bruce Springsteen, An Underground Album Discography: The Bootlegs 1975–1984*. [S.I.]: Jolly Roger Books, 1984.

Ernhart, Peter Maxon. *Can Bono, Bruce Springsteen and Peter Gabriel Change the World?: The Role of Celebrities in the Promotion of Domestic and International Human Rights*. 2003.

———. *The Famous Guide to Bon Jovi*. London: Famous Publishing, 1996.

Fletcher, Tony. *Remarks: The Story of R.E.M.* London: Omnibus, 1993.

Fricke, David. "R.E.M. (Peter Buck Talks about the 1980s and His Athens, Georgia Band)." *Rolling Stone* 591 (November 15, 1990): 124–130.

Fricke, Jim, and Charlie Ahearn. *Yes Yes Y'all: The Experience Music Project Oral History of Hip-Hop's First Decade*. Cambridge, MA: Da Capo Press, 2002.

Friend, Tad. "The Rocker in Repose." *New York* 28.15 (April 10, 1995): 64.

———. "The Secret Sorrow of Jon Bon Jovi." *New York* 28.15 (April 10, 1995): 64–68.

Gaar, Gillian G. *She's a Rebel: The History of Women in Rock & Roll.* Exp. 2nd ed. New York: Seal Press, 2002.

Gaugler, Audra. "Madonna, an American Pop Icon of Feminism and Counter Hegemony Blurring the Boundries of Race, Gender, and Sexuality." M.A. thesis, Lehigh University, 2001.

George, Nelson. *Hip Hop America.* New York: Penguin Books, 1998.

———. *Hip Hop America.* New York: Viking, 1998.

Goodman, Sam. *U2: Burning Desire: The Complete U2 Story.* Chessington, Surrey, UK: Castle Communications, 1993.

Goshert, John Charles. "Punk after the Pistols: American Music, Economics and Politics in the 1980s and 1990s." *Popular Culture and Society* 21.1 (Winter 2000): 85–106.

Gray, Marcus. *An R.E.M. Companion: It Crawled from the South.* Enfield, UK: Guiness, 1992.

Greer, Jim. *R.E.M.: Behind the Mask.* London: Sidgwick & Jackson, 1993, 1992.

Guilbert, Georges-Claude. *Madonna as Postmodern Myth: How One Star's Self-Construction Rewrites Sex, Gender, Hollywood and the American Dream.* Jefferson, NC: McFarland, 2002.

Hahn, Alex. *Possessed: The Rise and Fall of Prince.* New York: Billboard Books, 2003.

Hallstein, Lynn O'Brien. *The Materialism of Madonna's Postmodernism.* Babson Park, MA: Babson College, 1996.

Handelman, David. "Bon Jovi Makes Good with 'A Bad Name.'" *Rolling Stone* 48.7 (November 20, 1986): 35.

Heatley, Michael. *Bon Jovi.* London: Omnibus Press, 1997.

Hill, Dave. *Hip-Hop Divas.* New York: Three Rivers Press, 2001.

———. *Prince: A Pop Life.* London: Faber, 1989.

Hogan, Peter K. *The Complete Guide to the Music of R.E.M.* London: Omnibus Press, 1995.

Holden, Stephen. "Waking Up from the California Dream." *New York Times,* August 6, 1989, H28.

Iglesias, Carlos. "The Madonna Phenomenon: A Sociological Perspective." M.A. thesis, University of Houston, 1992.

Ingham, Chris, and Tommy Udo. *Metallica: Nothing Else Matters: The Stories behind the Biggest Songs.* New York: Thunder's Mouth Press, 2003.

Jackson, Laura. *Bono: His Life, Music, and Passions.* New York: Citadel Press, 2003.

———. *Jon Bon Jovi.* New York: Citadel Press, 2004.

Jackson, Robert, and James Williams. *The Last Black Mecca, Hip Hop: A Black Cultural Awareness Phenomena and Its Impact on the African American Community.* Chicago, IL: Research Associates, 1994.

Johnson, Fred. "U2, Mythology, and Mass-Mediated Survival." *Popular Music and Society* 27.1 (February 2004): 79–99.

Konow, David. *Bang Your Head: The Rise and Fall of Heavy Metal.* New York: Three Rivers Press, 2002.

Lacayo, Richard. "The '80s: When Springsteen and Jackson Ruled the Charts, and Madonna Took Care of Business." *Life,* December 1, 1992, 94–99.

Layport, Jill E. " 'The Grind': MTV and Female Body Image." M.A.I.S. thesis, Oregon State University, 1997.

Lewis, Lisa A. *Gender Politics and MTV: Voicing the Difference*. Philadelphia, PA: Temple University Press, 1990.

———. *MTV*. Iowa City: Iowa Center for Communication Study, 1986.

———. *MTV: Uncensored*. London: Simon & Schuster, 2001.

Mackey-Kallis, Susan, and Ian McDermott. "Bruce Springsteen, Ronald Reagan and the American Dream." *Popular Music and Society* 16.4 (Winter 1992): 1–9.

———. "Madonna." *Current Biography* 47 (May 1986): 320–332.

———. *Madonna: The Rolling Stone Files: The Ultimate Compendium of Interviews, Articles, Facts, and Opinions from the Files of Rolling Stone*. New York: Hyperion, 1997.

Marsh, Dave. *Born to Run*. New York: Thunder's Mouth Press, 1996.

———. *Bruce Springsteen: Two Hearts: The Definitive Biography, 1972–2003*. New York: Routledge, 2004.

———. *Glory Days: Bruce Springsteen in the 1980s*. New York: Pantheon Books, 1987.

———. *Glory Days: Bruce Springsteen in the 1980s*. New York: Dell, 1991.

McGrath, Tom. *MTV: The Making of a Revolution*. Philadelphia, PA: Running Press, 1996.

Mills, Nicolaus. "Culture in an Age of Money: The Legacy of the 1980s." *Dissent* 37.1 (Winter 1990): 11–17.

Mitchell, Tony. *Global Noise: Rap and Hip-Hop outside the USA*. Middletown, CT: Wesleyan University Press, 2001.

Morton, Andrew. *Madonna*. New York: St. Martin's Press, 2001.

Newberry, Searlett. "1989 Yearbook: A Rock & Roll Medley." *Rolling Stone* 567568 (December 14, 1989): 45.

———. "Rock Tours: '87 Was Banner Year." *Rolling Stone* 520 (February 25, 1988): 18.

Orlean, S. "Rock Musicians." *Rolling Stone* 500 (May 21, 1987): 34.

Pareles, Jon. "Rock's Own Generation Gap, from Paula Abdul to The Who." *New York Times*, December 24, 1989, 29; at http://web.lexis-nexis.com.

Pettegrew, John. "The Pick of 1988: Top Entertainments in a Bountiful Year." *Maclean's* 102.1 (January 2, 1989): 60–62.

———. "A Post-Modernist Movement: 1980s Commercial Culture & the Founding of MTV." *Journal of American Culture* 15.4 (Winter 1992): 57–65.

Platt, John A. *Murmur: R.E.M.* New York: Schirmer Books, 1999.

Popoff, Martin. *The Top 500 Heavy Metal Songs of All Times*. Toronto: ECW Press, 2003.

Potter, Russell A. *Spectacular Vernaculars: Hip-Hop and the Politics of Postmodernism*. Albany: State University of New York Press, 1995.

Puterbaugh, Parke. *Bruce Springsteen: The Rolling Stone Files: The Ultimate Compendium of Interviews, Articles, Facts, and Opinions from the Files of Rolling Stone*. London: Pan, 1998.

———. *R.E.M.: The Rolling Stone Files: The Ultimate Compendium of Interviews, Articles, Facts, and Opinions from the Files of Rolling Stone*. New York: Hyperion, 1995.

Reynolds, Simon, and Joy Press. *The Sex Revolts: Gender, Rebellion, and Rock 'n' Roll*. Cambridge, MA: Harvard University Press, 1995.

Ro, Ronin. *Bad Boy: The Influence of Sean "Puffy" Combs on the Music Industry*. New York: Pocket Books, 2001.

————. *Gangsta: Merchandizing the Rhymes of Violence.* New York: St. Martin's Press, 1996.

Roberts, Robin. *Ladies First: Women in Music Videos.* Jackson: University Press of Mississippi, 1996.

Rodak, Thomas J. "Meanings and Measures Taken in Concert Observations of Bruce Springsteen, September 28, 1992, Los Angeles." 1996.

Rogers, Sheila. "Jon Bon Jovi." *Rolling Stone* 531 (June 28, 1990): 9–12.

Rolling Stone. *Bruce Springsteen: The Rolling Stone Files: The Ultimate Compendium of Interviews, Articles, Facts, and Opinions from the Files of Rolling Stone.* New York: Hyperion, 1996.

Rooksby, Rikky, and Chris Charlesworth. *The Complete Guide to the Music of Madonna.* London: Omnibus Press, 1998.

Ross, Andrew. "Princes among Thieves: Sampling the '80s." *Artforum International* 417 (March 2003): 249(5).

Sawyers, June Skinner, ed. *Racing in the Street: The Bruce Springsteen Reader.* New York: Penguin Books, 2004.

Stokes, Niall, and Liam Mackey. *U2: In the Name of Love: A History from Ireland's Hot Press Magazine.* New York: Harmony Books, 1986.

————. *U2: Three Chords and the Truth.* New York: Harmony Books, 1988.

Stuessy, Joe, and Scott Lipscomb. *Rock and Roll: Its History and Stylistic Development.* 4th ed. Upper Saddle River, NJ: Prentice Hall, 2003.

Sullivan, Denise. *Talk about the Passion: R.E.M.: An Oral History.* London: Pavillion, 1995.

Taraborrelli, J. Randy. *Madonna: An Intimate Biography.* New York: Simon & Schuster, 2001.

Turner, Kay. *I Dream of Madonna: Women's Dreams of the Goddess of Pop.* San Francisco: Collins Publishers San Francisco, 1993.

Vandenberg, Victoria C. *Bodies, Gender, and Rock 'N' Roll: Making Music Dance on MTV.* N.p., 1992.

Van Elteren, Mel. "Populist Rock in Postmodern Society: John Cougar Mellencamp in Perspective." *Journal of Popular Culture* 28.3 (Winter 1994): 95.

Victor, Barbara. *Goddess.* New York: Cliff Street Books, 2001.

————. *U2: The Rolling Stone Files: The Ultimate Compendium of Interviews, Articles, Facts, and Opinions from the Files of Rolling Stone.* New York: Hyperion, 1994.

Walker, Greg B., and Melinda Bender. "Is It More Than Rock and Roll? Considering Music Video as Argument." *Argumentation and Advocacy: The Journal of the American Forensic Association* 31.2 (Fall 1994): 399.

Wall, Mick. *Guns n' Roses: The Most Dangerous Band in the World.* New York: Hyperion, 1992.

————. *Iron Maiden: Run to the Hills: The Official Biography.* London: Sanctuary, 1998.

Walser, Robert. *Running with the Devil: Power, Gender, and Madness in Heavy Metal Music.* Hanover, NH: University Press of New England, 1993.

Waters, John. *Race of Angels: The Genesis of U2.* London: Fourth Estate, 1994.

Watkins, S. Craig. *Representing: Hip Hop Culture and the Production of Black Cinema.* Chicago: University of Chicago Press, 1998.

Watson, Albert, and David Fricke. "Michael Stipe: The Rolling Stone Interview." *Rolling Stone* 625 (March 5, 1992): 45(6).

Weinstein, Deena. *Heavy Metal: A Cultural Sociology.* New York: Lexington Books, M.A. thesis, Florida State University, 1991.

———. *Heavy Metal: The Music and Its Culture.* New York: Da Capo Press, 2000.

Well, Charles W. "Like a Thesis: Postmodern Readings of Madonna Music Videos." M.A. Thesis, Florida State University, 1991.

Westbrook, Alonzo. *Hip Hoptionary: The Dictionary of Hip-Hop Terminology.* New York: Harlem Moon, 2002.

———. *Who's Who in Rock Video: A Guide to Video Music Artists.* Long Beach, CA: Quill, 1983–1984.

Williams, Peter, and Steve Turner. *U2: Rattle and Hum: The Official Book of the U2 Movie: A Journey into the Heartland of Two Americas.* New York: Harmony Books, 1988.

Zimmerman, Kevin. "Rock 'n' Roll in the '80s: High Tech, Low Excitement: Era Brought Us MTV, Pricey Label Mergers and a Paucity of Musical Innovation." *Variety* 338.3 (January 14, 1990): 171–172.

WEB SITES

http://www.mtv.com

The cable network's Web site contains comprehensive artist biographies and discographies as well as a historical timeline of its landmark moments and current tour and album release information.

http://www.vh1.com

Similar in format and organization to its sister cable MTV Web site, VH1 includes many of the same artist biographies from the *All Music Guide* as well as program information, *Behind the Music* series summaries, and concert tour updates.

http://www.80sxchange.com

A thorough, if incomplete, survey of popular culture during the 1980s. Links to music trends, artists, and albums make this Web site a must-visit for individuals interested in a topical look at the decade.

http://www.rollingstone.com

Rolling Stone's Web site is a combination of archived articles, album and film reviews, and artist biographies since its inception in 1972. Not always easy to navigate, this Web site also promotes product sales and artist memorabilia of some of the 1980s most popular artists.

http://www.billboard.com

For statisticians and collectors, this Web site offers exhaustive lists of the magazine's best-selling singles and albums from the prerock era to the present day. Those interested in comparing record sales dollars to copies, especially in light of the corporate takeover of the rock industry during the 1980s, will find the information helpful and the data accurate.

http://www.madonnaweb.com

The Material Girl's Web site offers the artist's biography, discography, and current personal and professional information. Visitors can share their thoughts and experiences with the artist and purchase various merchandise.

http://mlvc.org

This Web site offers provocative and intriguing commentary on Madonna's artistry, music, and videos.

http://www.launch.com

A general Web site for encyclopediclike information on rock 'n' roll artists from Elvis Presley to Maroon 5. The launch Web site includes artist discographies as well as album ratings and reviews.

http://www.heavy-metalinks.com

Devoted to heavy-metal artists from the 1980s on, this Web site provides musical and artist information about heavy metal as art form, social commentary, and musical movement. Links connect visitors to specific artist Web sites and chat rooms.

http://www.threechords.com

One of the best artist Web sites, ThreeChords takes the punk notion as literally as it applies to post-punk icons U2. The Web site includes the group's biography, key recording moments during the 1980s, and recent concert information.

http://home.theboots.net/theboots/default.html

A newly designed and comprehensive Web site dedicated to the life and artistry of Bruce Springsteen. Visitors can read his biography, interact with other fans about "The Boss," and receive updates on current recordings.

http://forum.interference.com/index.php

Perhaps the most sophisticated among '80s artists' Web sites, Interference offers multiple opportunities for interaction among U2 fans. Upon registering, visitors can surf various topics, read articles and interviews, and engage in chat with other fans.

http://www.furious.com/perfect/sst1.html

For indie fans, the "Furious" Web site focuses on the inception and evolution of SST Records, one of the most important catalysts for the underground rock movement of the 1980s. Musical discussions and information about various SST artists from Black Flag to Mission of Burma are comprehensive and detailed.

http://www.sundin.net/denim

The home page for all 1980s heavy metal and hard rock, "sundin" includes artist biographies, discographies, and interactive discussions on the musical impact of metal bands like Metallica and Megadeth.

http://www.mjsite.com

A comprehensive fan site for Michael Jackson admirers, MJSite contains the star's biography and discography as well as song lyrics and links to current information.

http://www.thepolicefile.com

The ultimate Police Web site, "the Police file" includes individual artist and group biographies, discographies, and photos and opportunities for visitors to share ideas and stories via chat rooms and message boards. Current information on band members rounds out a comprehensive and thoughtful Web site.

VIDEOS

Fast Times at Ridgemont High (1982). Directed by Amy Heckerling; starring Sean Penn, Judge Reinhold, Jennifer Jason Leigh, and Phoebe Cates.

A cutting-edge teen flick that helped popularize the multiple-artist sound track. *Fast Times at Ridgemont High* also used music to underscore themes, issues, and relationships depicted through the film's characters.

The Big Chill (1983). Directed by Lawrence Kasdan; starring Kevin Kline, Glenn Close, William Hurt, Mary Kay Place, Tom Berenger, and Jeff Goldblum.

A 1980s film in tone and temperament, *The Big Chill* is notable for repopularizing music from the late 1980s, including songs by Smokey Robinson and the Miracles, Creedence Clearwater Revival, and Three Dog Night.

Amadeus (1984). Directed by Milos Forman; starring F. Murray Abraham and Tom Hulce.

An audacious film biography of Wolfgang Amadeus Mozart, *Amadeus* contains no music from the 1980s but defiantly asserts the notion that the eighteenth-century composer may, in fact, have been the first real "rock" star in terms of his excessive behavior, flamboyant style, and drug-induced adventures.

Purple Rain (1984). Directed by Albert Magnoli; starring Prince, Clarence Williams III, and Apollonia Kotero.

Prince's tour de force sound track saves an otherwise banal rags-to-riches story about a Minnesota musician longing for celebrity.

This Is Spinal Tap (1984). Directed by Rob Reiner; starring Michael McKean and Christopher Guest.

The quintessential "mockumentary," Reiner's film follows the fictitious rock band Spinal Tap on a faux concert tour, keenly observing the excesses and idiosyncracies of rock superstardom on the way.

Rattle and Hum (1988). Directed by Phil Joanou; starring U2.

Perhaps the definitive rock documentary, *Rattle and Hum* artistically combines concert footage of U2 with backstage banter and gritty interviews and comments from band members.

Pump Up the Volume (1990). Directed by Allan Moyle; starring Christian Slater and Samantha Mathis.

An example of an underground iconoclast, *Pump Up the Volume* boasted a contemporary cutting-edge sound track and themes about 1980s teenage isolation and alienation.

Truth or Dare (1991). Directed by Alek Keshishian; starring Madonna.

A provocative and revealing look at the "Material Girl" on tour, *Truth or Dare* combines performance with candid backstage interviews and Madonna's own inimitable view of the world, music, sex, and relationships.

Rock and Roll: A Film by Ken Burns: The History of Rock and Roll in Five Episodes. (1995).

A multiseries documentary that traces the development of rock 'n' roll from its post–World War II origins to the present day. The segment on the 1980s is more pop than rock but identifies critical themes from the punk, metal, and underground movements.

Some Kind of Monster (2004). Directed by Joe Berlinger and Bruce Sinofsky; starring Metallica.

A recent, critically acclaimed (and Oscar-nominated) documentary about the personal and musical evolution of metal group Metallica.

INDEX

About the Author

MARYANN JANOSIK was recently named Dean of Ohio University's Lancaster campus. She was Director of Education at the Rock and Roll Hall of Fame and Museum in Cleveland, Ohio, and has previously been an associate professor of history and dean of a division of Oakton Community College. Dr. Janosik continues to teach courses and design professional development workshops in the areas of rock music, American film and popular culture.